THE COMPOSITE NOVEL

THE SHORT STORY CYCLE
IN TRANSITION

STUDIES IN LITERARY THEMES AND GENRES

Ronald Gottesman, Editor

University of Southern California

THE COMPOSITE NOVEL

THE SHORT STORY CYCLE IN TRANSITION

MAGGIE DUNN

and

ANN MORRIS

Twayne Publishers
New York

Maxwell Macmillan Canada
Toronto

Maxwel Macmillan International
New York Oxford Singapore Sydney

The Composite Novel: The Short Story Cycle in Transition
Maggie Dunn and Ann Morris

Studies in Literary Themes and Genres No. 6

Twayne Publishers
Macmillan Publishing Company
866 Third Avenue
New York, New York 10022

Maxwell Macmillan Canada, Inc.
1200 Eglinton Avenue East
Suite 200
Don Mills, Ontario M3C 3N1

Library of Congress Cataloging-in-Publication Data

Dunn, Maggie.
    The composite novel : the short story cycle in transition / by
Maggie Dunn and Ann Morris.
        p. cm.—(Studies in literary themes and genres ; no. 6)
    Includes bibliographical references and index.
    ISBN 0-8057-0966-5
    1. American fiction—History and criticism—Theory, etc.
2. English fiction—History and criticism—Theory, etc. 3. Short
stories, American—History and criticism. 4. Short stories,
English—History and criticism. 5. Cycles (Literature) 6. Fiction—
Technique. 7. Short Story. I. Morris, Ann R. II. Title.
III. Series.
PS374.S5D86   1995
813.009—dc20   94—34996
                                                        CIP

10 9 8 7 6 5 4 3 2 1 (hc)

Printed in the United States of America

For our children—
Wes, Kelley, Christine, and Julie
Jan and Lee

General Editor's Statement

Genre studies have been a central concern of Anglo-American and European literary theory for at least the past quarter century, and the academic interest has been reflected, for example, in new college courses in slave narratives, autobiography, biography, nature writing, and the literature of travel as well as in the rapid expansion of genre theory itself. Genre has also become an indispensable term for trade publishers and the vast readership they serve. Indeed, few general bookstores do not have sections devoted to science fiction, romance, and mystery fiction. Still, genre is among the slipperiest of literary terms, as any examination of genre theories and their histories will suggest.

In conceiving this series we have tried, on the one hand, to avoid the comically pedantic spirit that informs Polonius' recitation of kinds of drama and, on the other hand, the equally unhelpful insistence that every literary production is a unique expression that must not be forced into any system of classification. We have instead developed our list of genres, which range from ancient comedy to the Western, with the conviction that by common consent kinds of literature do exist—not as fixed categories but as fluid ones that change over time as the result of complex interplay of authors, audiences, and literary and cultural institutions. As individual titles in the series demonstrate, the idea of genre offers us provocative ways to study both the continuities and adaptability of literature as a familiar and inexhaustible source of human imagination.

Recognition of the fluid boundaries both within and among genres will provide, we believe, a useful array of perspectives from which to study literature's complex development. Genres, as traditional but open ways of understanding the world, contribute to our capacity to respond to narrative and expressive forms and offer means to discern moral significances embodied in these forms. Genres, in short, serve ethical as well as aesthetic purposes, and the volumes in this series attempt to demonstrate how this double benefit has been achieved as these genres have been transformed over the years. Each title in the series should be measured against this large ambition.

Ron Gottesman

Contents

When you coin a term, it ought to mark a
real species, and a specific difference.
Aristotle, The Rhetoric

Preface

In this book we define, discuss, and trace the 200-year history of a literary genre that has hitherto existed and evolved without a name, except in the discussions of a few critics, most of whom have settled for the term *short story cycle*. In contrast, we choose the term *composite novel*—or reasons that are explained in detail in chapter 1, in which we also propose and defend the following definition:

> *The composite novel is a literary work composed of shorter texts that— though individually complete and autonomous—are interrelated in a coherent whole according to one or more organizing principles.*

What we are dealing with, then, is a structural aesthetic through which autonomous text-pieces, most often "short stories," are interrelated in a coherent whole text. The best-known twentieth-century example of such a literary text is probably Sherwood Anderson's *Winesburg, Ohio* (1919), but other well-known works in this genre include Sarah Orne Jewett's *The Country of the Pointed Firs* (1896), Gertrude Stein's *Three Lives* (1909), James Joyce's *Dubliners* (1914), Ernest Hemingway's *In Our Time* (1919), Jean Toomer's *Cane* (1923), William Faulkner's *Go Down, Moses* (1942), Eudora Welty's *The Golden Apples* (1947), Albert Camus's *Exile and the Kingdom* (1957), Italo Calvino's *Cosmicomics* (1965), John Barth's *Lost in the Funhouse* (1968),

Maxine Hong Kingston's *The Woman Warrior* (1976), Louise Erdrich's *Love Medicine* (1984), and Whitney Otto's *How to Make an American Quilt* (1991). We focus specifically on these significant works, among others, in various chapters.

After an introduction in chapter 1, during which we discuss terminology and explain in detail the parameters of our genre definition, we move in chapter 2 to a historical overview of composite novels and precursors produced during the nineteenth century in America, the British Isles, and Europe. In this chapter we discuss "village sketch" composite novels, many of which will be familiar to most readers, as will the concept of the village sketch itself. In contrast, we also define and discuss "patchwork" composite novels, encompassing both a concept and a number of literary works that some readers will perhaps be encountering for the first time.

In each of the next five chapters we discuss specific twentieth-century composite novels in terms of an "organizing principle": a common setting in chapter 3; a single protagonist in chapter 4; a collective protagonist in chapter 5; recurrent patterns in chapter 6; and the process of fiction making in chapter 7.

We explore in chapter 8 the wide spectrum of experimentation and genre blending in twentieth-century composite novels, then focus on specific works that exemplify variations on the "organizing principles" discussed in the previous five chapters. Finally, in chapter 9, we discuss the possibilities inherent in the composite novel's aesthetic—an aesthetic that we find "user-friendly" because it reflects the complexity of contemporary life.

In addition to a bibliographic essay, this book contains two "lists" of composite novels. The first, entitled "Chronology: Composite Novels and Precursors," precedes chapter 1 and is organized from early (1820) to late (1993). Giving only title, author, and year of first publication, this lengthy yet hardly exhaustive list helps support our contention that an individual composite novel such as *Winesburg, Ohio* is not sui generis but is, rather, just one representative text in a long-developing genre.

The second list, entitled "An Annotated List of Selected Composite Novels," follows the bibliographic essay. This annotated list is intended to assist students, teachers, and other interested readers in choosing composite novels that suit their classes, research projects, and general reading. Thus we have tried to include a preponderance of works that are easily available through bookstores (still in print and in inexpensive editions) and libraries (well known enough to be on the shelves). For the same reason, we have tried to make this list broadly representative in terms of themes, topics, national literatures, and so on.

We do not include in either list (or in chapter discussions) composite novels that have not been translated into English. Also, we list and discuss only composite novels that we have personally read and examined—although more than a few nineteenth-century works were available for "reading" only on microfiche or microfilm.

For ease in reading, so that the reader need not be distracted by excessive notes or parenthetical citations, we have followed this plan of documentation: (1) All twentieth-century composite novels mentioned in the text are fully cited in the annotated list; (2) all nineteenth-century composite novels and precursors are fully cited, at first mention, in a note; (3) all secondary works are fully cited, at first mention, in a note; and (4) all subsequent citations to a given work appear parenthetically in the text.

Acknowledgments

Our research on the composite novel developed on a number of different fronts that are reflected in conference papers presented and in articles published, singly and collaboratively, over the past 12 years, as well as in courses each of us has taught at Stetson University, the University of Central Florida at Daytona Beach, and Rollins College. We were assisted in pulling all of this together by numerous colleagues, students, and friends who responded to and commented upon our work in its various piecemeal manifestations. To these people we must simply say, "Thank you—you know who you are," because to mention one is to omit—inadvertently—another.

We are grateful to Stetson University for three summer grants and two sabbaticals, to Indiana University for a dissertation grant, and to Rollins College for Ashforth and Critchfield awards—all of which supported aspects of our research and writing.

We are grateful to the library faculty and staff at Indiana University–Bloomington for their unflagging cooperation while we were finding and photocopying mountains of information. Certainly we owe an immense debt of gratitude to the faculty and staff of the DuPont-Ball Library at Stetson University in DeLand, Florida, for their cheerful assistance while we inundated them with innumerable requests for searches. We are especially grateful to Jane Bradford, Susan Connell, Judi Shaeffer,

Bob Ervin, Library Director Sims Kline, Betty Johnson, and Anne Hurst, now retired but most emphatically not forgotten.

Our personal thanks go to Professor Ron Gottesman in Los Angeles, Series Editor, for sound advice, instant accessibility, enthusiastic encouragement, and a wonderful sense of humor. We also thank Lewis DeSimone in San Francisco, for superb editing and advice regarding the final draft of this manuscript, and Sylvia Miller in New York, for being so responsive and willing to help us meet the final countdown.

Finally, our personal thanks go to Catherine Lane for unwavering, unquestioning support.

Chronology: Composite Novels and Precursors

Books are listed by *first* date of publication. All titles are in English, even if the first publication was in another language. (Foreign-language composite novels are included only if they have been translated into English.)

This list is representative, not exhaustive.

1820   *Melmoth the Wanderer,* by Charles Maturin. *The Sketch Book,* by Washington Irving.

1821   *Annals of the Parish,* by John Galt.

1824   *Our Village,* by Mary Russell Mitford.

1829   *Sketches of American Character,* by Sarah Josepha Hale.

1831   *The Tales of Ivan Belkin* (in Russian), by Alexander Pushkin. *Evenings near the Village of Dikanka* (in Russian), by Nikolai Gogol.

1835   *Georgia Scenes,* by Augustus Baldwin Longstreet.

1837   *Three Experiments of Living,* by Hannah Farnham Sawyer Lee.

1838   *Sketches of a New England Village, in the Last Century,* by Eliza Buckminster Lee.

1839 *A New Home—Who'll Follow? or, Glimpses of Western Life*, by Caroline Kirkland.

1840 *A Hero of Our Time* (in Russian), by Mikhail Lermontov.

1844 *The Belle, the Blue, and the Bigot; or, Three Fields for Woman's Influence*, by Louisa Caroline Tuthill. *Girlhood and Womanhood; or, Sketches of My Schoolmates*, by Mrs. A.J. Graves.

1846 *Aunt Patty's Scrap-Bag*, by Caroline Lee Hentz. *Reveries of a Bachelor; or, A Book of the Heart*, by Donald George Mitchell.

1851 *Clovernook; or, Recollections of Our Neighborhood in the West*, by Alice Cary. "Legends of the Province House" (in *Twice-Told Tales*), by Nathaniel Hawthorne.

1853 *Cranford*, by Elizabeth Gaskell. *Fern Leaves from Fanny's Portfolio*, by Fanny Fern [Sarah Willis Parton].

1854 *Atherton*, by Mary Russell Mitford.

1855 *A Sportsman's Sketches*, by Ivan Turgenev.

1856 *Mimic Life; or, Before and behind the Curtain: A Series of Narratives*, by Anna Cora Mowatt Ritchie. *The Piazza Tales*, by Herman Melville.

1858 *Scenes of Clerical Life*, by George Eliot.

1861 *Incidents in the Life of a Slave Girl, Written by Herself*, by Harriet A. Jacobs.

1863 *Hospital Sketches*, by Louisa May Alcott.

1865 *Husbands and Homes*, by Marion Harland. *Tales of a Traveler*, by Washington Irving.

1870 *Letters from My Mill* (in French), by Alphonse Daudet.

1871 *Sam Lawson's Oldtown Fireside Stories*, by Harriet Beecher Stowe.

1872 *Aunt Jo's Scrap Bag*, by Louisa May Alcott (first volume of four). *Sketches of Southern Life*, by Frances E. W. Harper.

1875   *Castle Nowhere: Lake Country Sketches,* by
        Constance Fenimore Woolson.

1879   *Old Creole Days,* by George Washington Cable.

1880   *Rodman the Keeper: Southern Sketches,* by
        Constance Fenimore Woolson. *Three Tales* (in
        French), by Gustave Flaubert.

1884   *In the Tennessee Mountains,* by Mary Noailles
        Murfree.

1889   *Chita: A Memory of Last Island,* by Lafcadio Hearn.

1891   *Dreams,* by Olive Schreiner. *A Group of Noble
        Dames,* by Thomas Hardy. *Main-Travelled Roads,*
        by Hamlin Garland.

1892   *Balcony Stories,* by Grace King. *Silhouettes of
        American Life,* by Rebecca Harding Davis.

1893   *Irish Idylls,* by Jane Barlow.

1894   *Bayou Folk,* by Kate Chopin. *Vignettes of
        Manhattan,* by Brander Matthews. *The Story of
        Gösta Berling* (in Swedish), by Selma
        Lagerlof.

1895   *Tenement Tales of New York,* by James William
        Sullivan.

1896   *The Country of the Pointed Firs,* by Sarah Orne
        Jewett.

1897   *A Night in Acadie,* by Kate Chopin.

1898   *Old Chester Tales,* by Margaret Deland. *Patchwork,*
        by Maley Bainbridge Crist. *The People of Our
        Neighborhood,* by Mary E. Wilkins Freeman.

1899   *The Conjure Woman,* by Charles Chesnutt. *The
        Goodness of St. Rocque and Other Stories,* by Alice
        Dunbar-Nelson.

1901   *Understudies,* by Mary E. Wilkins Freeman.
        Whilomville Stories, by Stephen Crane.

1902   *Reminiscences of My Life: A Black Woman's Civil
        War Memoirs,* by Susie King Taylor.

1903   *The Land of Little Rain,* by Mary Austin. *The Pool in
        the Desert,* by Sara Jeannette Duncan. *Six Trees,*

by Mary E. Wilkins Freeman. *The Souls of Black Folk*, by W. E. B. DuBois. *The Untilled Field*, by George Moore.

1905   *Tales of the Fish Patrol*, by Jack London. *The Troll Garden*, by Willa Cather.

1906   *The Mirror of the Sea*, by Joseph Conrad.

1908   *Friendship Village*, by Zona Gale.

1909   *Memories of Childhood's Slavery Days*, by Annie L. Burton. *Three Lives*, by Gertrude Stein. *The Whole Family: A Novel by Twelve Authors*, by William Dean Howells, Mary E. Wilkins Freeman, Henry James, Elizabeth Stuart Phelps, Elizabeth Jordan, et al.

1910   *The Finer Grain*, by Henry James.

1912   *Mrs. Spring Fragrance*, by Sui Sin Far [Edith Eaton].

1913   *O Pioneers!*, by Willa Cather.

1914   *Dubliners*, by James Joyce. *Tender Buttons: Objects, Food, Rooms—Studies in Description*, by Gertrude Stein.

1917   *The Sturdy Oak: A Composite Novel of American Politics by Fourteen American Authors*, edited by Elizabeth Jordan.

1918   *Edgewater People*, by Mary E. Wilkins Freeman. *My Ántonia*, by Willa Cather.

1919   *Winesburg, Ohio*, by Sherwood Anderson.

1920   *Hungry Hearts*, by Anzia Yezierska.

1921   *American Indian Stories*, by Gertrude Bonnin [Zitkala-Sa].

1922   *City Block*, by Waldo Frank.

1923   *Cane*, by Jean Toomer. *Children of Loneliness: Stories of Immigrant Life in America*, by Anzia Yezierska. *Roman Pictures*, by Percy Lubbock.

1924   *A Hunger Artist* (in German), by Franz Kafka.

1938 *Tropisms* (in French), by Nathalie Sarraute. *Two by Two*, by Martha Gellhorn. *Uncle Tom's Children*, by Richard Wright. *The Unvanquished*, by William Faulkner.

1939 *The Wild Palms*, by William Faulkner. *Wind, Sand and Stars* (in French and English), by Antoine de Saint-Exupéry.

1940 *The Hamlet*, by William Faulkner. *My Name is Aram*, by William Saroyan. *Portrait of the Artist as a Young Dog*, by Dylan Thomas.

1942 *The Company She Keeps*, by Mary McCarthy. *Go Down, Moses*, by William Faulkner.

1943 *Georgia Boy*, by Erskine Caldwell.

1944 *Golden Harvest* (in Spanish), by Jorge Amado.

1945 *The Folded Leaf*, by William Maxwell. *The Friendly Persuasion*, by Jessamyn West. *Mexican Village*, by Josefina Niggli. *The Red Pony* (first complete four-story edition), by John Steinbeck.

1946 *Memoirs of Hecate County*, by Edmund Wilson.

1947 *The Golden Apples*, by Eudora Welty. *Smoke over Birkenau* (in Italian), by Liana Millu. *Tales of the South Pacific*, by James A. Michener

1949 *The Kingdom of This World* (in Spanish), by Alejo Carpentier. *Knight's Gambit*, by William Faulkner.

1950 *I, Robot*, by Isaac Asimov. *The Martian Chronicles*, by Ray Bradbury.

1951 *Between Fantoine and Agapa* (in French), by Robert Pinget. *The Smoking Mountain: Stories of Postwar Germany*, by Kay Boyle.

1952 *City*, by Clifford Simak. *The Petrified Planet*, by John D. Clark et al. *Pictures from an Institution: A Comedy*, by Randall Jarrell.

1954 *The Romantic Egoists: A Reflection in Eight Mirrors*, by Louis Auchincloss. *The Widows of Thornton*, by Peter Taylor.

1956   *A Scarcity of Love*, by Anna Kavan.

1957   *Exile and the Kingdom* (in French), by Albert
       Camus. *Last Exit to Brooklyn*, by Hubert Selby, Jr.
       A Maine Hamlet, by Lura Beam. *Memories of a
       Catholic Girlhood*, by Mary McCarthy. *Pnin*, by
       Vladimir Nabokov. *The Star Diaries* (in Polish), by
       Stanislaw Lem.

1958   *Stories and Texts for Nothing* (in French), by
       Samuel Beckett.

1959   *Brown Girl, Brownstones*, by Paule Marshall. *A
       Canticle for Leibowitz*, by Walter M. Miller, Jr.
       Cider with Rosie, by Laurie Lee. *Mrs. Bridge*, by
       Evan S. Connell, Jr. *Naked Lunch*, by William S.
       Burroughs.

1960   *Our Ancestors* (in Italian), by Italo Calvino.

1961   *Franny and Zooey*, by J. D. Salinger. *Soul Clap
       Hands and Sing*, by Paule Marshall.

1962   *Mobile: Study for a Representation of the United
       States* (in French), by Michel Butor. *Pale Fire*, by
       Vladimir Nabokov. *Spillway*, by Djuna Barnes.

1963   *Marcovaldo, or The Seasons in the City* (in Italian),
       by Italo Calvino. *Up the Junction*, by Nell Dunn.

1964   *Olinger Stories: A Selection*, by John Updike. *Save
       Every Lamb*, by Jesse Stuart. *Sister Age*, by M. F. K.
       Fisher.

1965   *Bech: A Book*, by John Updike. *Cosmicomics* (in
       Italian), by Italo Calvino. *Everything That Rises
       Must Converge*, by Flannery O'Connor. *Genoa*, by
       Paul Metcalf. *Going to Meet the Man*, by James
       Baldwin. *Pretty Tales for Tired People*, by Martha
       Gellhorn.

1966   *The Road Past Altamont* (in French), by Gabrielle
       Roy.

1967   *Change of Skin* (in Spanish), by Carlos Fuentes.
       The Cyberiad: Fables for the Cybernetic Age (in
       Polish), by Stanislaw Lem. *Tales of Manhattan*, by

Louis Auchincloss. *Time and the Hunter* (in Italian, as *t-Zero*), by Italo Calvino. *The Woman Destroyed* (in French), by Simone de Beauvoir.

1968 *Bloodline,* by Ernest Gaines. *The Cancer Ward,* by Alexander Solzhenitsyn. *In the Heart of the Heart of the Country,* by William Gass. *Land without Thunder,* by Grace Ogot. *Lost in the Funhouse: Fiction for Print, Tape, Live Voice,* by John Barth.

1969 *An Apprenticeship, or The Book of Delights* (in Portuguese), by Clarice Lispector. *The Chosen Place, The Timeless People,* by Paule Marshall. *Futility and Other Animals,* by Frank Moorhouse. *The Gift* (posthumously), by H. D. [Hilda Doolittle]. *The Inner World of the Outer World of the Inner World* by Peter Handke. *Mr. Bridge,* by Evan S. Connell, Jr. *Pictures of Fidelman: An Exhibition,* by Bernard Malamud. *Pricksongs and Descants: Fictions,* by Robert Coover. *The Way to Rainy Mountain,* by N. Scott Momaday.

1970 *A Bird in the House,* by Margaret Laurence. *City Life,* by Donald Barthelme. *Lunar Landscapes,* by John Hawkes. *The Wheel of Love,* by Joyce Carol Oates.

1971 . . . *And the Earth Did Not Part,* by Tomas Rivera. *Lives of Girls and Women,* by Alice Munro. *McAfee County: A Chronicle,* by Mark Steadman. *The Night Country,* by Loren Eiseley. *A Perfect Vacuum,* by Stanislaw Lem.

1972 *The Americans, Baby: A Discontinuous Narrative of Stories and Fragments,* by Frank Moorhouse. *Chimera,* by John Barth. *Mumbo Jumbo,* by Ishmael Reed. *Sadness,* by Donald Barthelme.

1973 *The Basil and Josephine Stories* (posthumously), by F. Scott Fitzgerald. *The Castle of Crossed Destinies* (in Italian), by Italo Calvino. *The Pegnitz Junction: A Novella and Five Short Stories,* by Mavis Gallant. *Rembrandt's Hat,* by Bernard Malamud. *Spirits in the Street,* by Alexis DeVeaux. *Stradbroke*

Dreamtime, by Kath Walker [Oodgeroo Noonuccal].

1974 *The Ebony Tower,* by John Fowles. *The Goddess and Other Women,* by Joyce Carol Oates.

1975 *Bech Is Back,* by John Updike. *Her Mothers,* by E. M. Broner. *The Periodic Table* (in Italian), by Primo Levi. *Searching for Survivors,* by Russell Banks. *Three Solid Stones,* by Martha Mvungi.

1976 *Alyx,* by Joanna Russ. *The Butterfly Ward,* by Margaret Gibson [Gilboord]. *Crossing the Border: Fifteen Tales,* by Joyce Carol Oates. *Orsinian Tales,* by Ursula K. LeGuin. *Speedboat,* by Renata Adler. *The Winthrop Covenant,* by Louis Auchincloss. *The Woman Warrior: Memoirs of a Childhood among Ghosts,* by Maxine Hong Kingston.

1977 *The Collector of Treasures,* by Bessie Head. *White Rat,* by Gayl Jones.

1978 *The Actes and Monuments,* by John William Corrington. *The Beggar Maid: Stories of Flo and Rose,* by Alice Munro. *Blue in Chicago,* by Bette Howland. *The Legacy,* by Shashi Deshpande. *The Monkey's Wrench* (in Italian), by Primo Levi. *Moose Meat & Wild Rice,* by Basil Johnston. *Tales of the City,* by Armistead Maupin. *The Weather in Africa,* by Martha Gellhorn. *A Weave of Women,* by E. M. Broner.

1979 *A Certain Lucas* (in Spanish), by Julio Cortázar. *All the Good People I've Left Behind,* by Joyce Carol Oates. *The Bloody Chamber,* by Angela Carter. *Emergency Exit,* by Clarence Major. *Rounds,* by Frederick Busch. *Too Far to Go: The Maples Stories,* by John Updike. *The Wanderground: Stories of the Hill Women,* by Sally Miller Gearhart.

1980 *China Men,* by Maxine Hong Kingston. *Claiming an Identity They Taught Me to Despise,* by Michelle Cliff. *The Danzig Trilogy* (in German), by Gunter Grass. *Kolyma Tales* (posthumously), by Varlam Shalamov.

Morales. *Iron and Silk*, by Mark Salzman. *The Last of the Menu Girls*, by Denise Chavez. *The Mixquiahuala Letters*, by Ana Castillo. *Monkeys*, by Susan Minot. *Only the Little Bone*, by David Huddle. *Resident Alien*, by Clark Blaise. *Slaves of New York*, by Tama Janowitz. *When in Florence: A Cycle of Stories*, by Richard Cortez Day.

1987   *Borderlands/La Frontera: The New Mestiza*, by Gloria Anzaldua. *Breaking Bread*, by Joyce Reiser Kornblatt. *It's Raining in Mango: Pictures from a Family Album*, by Thea Astley. *Luisa in Realityland: A Novel*, by Claribel Alegría. *A Night at the Movies: or, You Must Remember This*, by Robert Coover. *Postcards from the Edge*, by Carrie Fisher. *The Tidewater Tales: A Novel*, by John Barth. *A Yellow Raft in Blue Water*, by Michael Dorris. *You Can't Get Lost in Cape Town*, by Zoe Wicomb.

1988   *Indecent Dreams*, by Arnost Lustig. *In Nueva York*, by Nicolasa Mohr. *Kitchen* (in Japanese), by Banana Yoshimoto. *The Last English Plantation*, by Jan Shinebourne. *Limestone and Lemon Wine*, by Thomas Shapcott. *Love in Beijing and Other Stories*, by William Goede. *The Middleman and Other Stories*, by Bharati Mukherjee. *Tracks*, by Louise Erdrich. *Wapping Tales: A Kiwi in the East End*, by Norma Ashworth.

1989   *Cartographies*, by Maya Sonenberg. *Constancia and Other Stories for Virgins* (in Spanish), by Carlos Fuentes. *The House on Mango Street*, by Sandra Cisneros. *A History of the World in 10 1/2 Chapters*, by Julian Barnes. *The Joy Luck Club*, by Amy Tan. *Like Water for Chocolate: A Novel in Monthly Installments with Recipes, Romances and Home Remedies* (in Spanish), by Laura Esquivel. *Obabakoak* (in Spanish), by Bernardo Atxaga [Joseba Irazu Garmendia]. *Tales from Margaritaville: Fictional Facts and Factual Fictions*, by Jimmy Buffett.

1990   *The Bluebird Cafe: A Novel,* by Carmel Bird. *Closing the Sea* (in Hebrew), by Yehudit Katzir. *Intaglio: A Novel in Six Stories,* by Roberta Fernández. *Killing Mister Watson,* by Peter Matthiessen. *The Kneeling Bus,* by Beverly Coyle. *The Laws* (in Dutch), by Connie Palmen. *Lucy,* by Jamaica Kincaid. *Silent Dancing: A Partial Remembrance of a Puerto Rican Childhood,* by Judith Ortiz Cofer. *The Things They Carried,* by Tim O'Brien.

1991   *African Visas: A Novella and Stories* (posthumously), by Maria Thomas [Roberta Worrick]. *Agassiz: A Novel in Stories,* by Sandra Birdsell. *Almanac of the Dead,* by Leslie Marmon Silko. *Drinking Dry Clouds: Stories from Wyoming,* by Gretel Ehrlich. *Heat and Other Stories,* by Joyce Carol Oates. *How the Garcia Girls Lost Their Accents,* by Julia Alvarez. *How to Make an American Quilt,* by Whitney Otto. *Now You See it,* by Cornelia Nixon. *Searoad: Chronicles of Klatsand,* by Ursula K. LeGuin. *The Stories of Eva Luna,* by Isabel Allende. *Street Games: A Neighborhood,* by Rosellen Brown. *Typical American,* by Gish Jen. *Under the Shadow,* by Gilbert Sorrentino. *Without Extremeties,* by Dayo Okunlola.

1992   *Bailey's Cafe,* by Gloria Naylor. *Dreaming in Cuban,* by Christina Garcia. *A Good Man to Know: A Semi-Documentary Fictional Memoir,* by Barry Gifford. *A Good Scent from a Strange Mountain,* by Robert Olen Butler. *High House and Radio,* by Rooplall Monar. *Let the Dead Bury Their Dead: And Other Stories,* by Randall Kenan. *Maqroll: Three Novellas* (in Spanish and English), by Alvaro Mutis. *Murasaki: A Novel in Six Parts,* by Poul Anderson et al. *Night People,* by Barry Gifford. *The Secret of Cartwheels,* by Patricia Henley. *Skating in the Dark,* by David Michael Kaplan. *Strange Business,* by Rilla Askew. *Vanishing Points,* by Thea Astley. *Veils,* by Nahid Rachlin. *The Wedding Dress: Stories from the*

Dakota Plains, by Carrie Young. *Whistling in the Dark: True Stories and Other Fables,* by George Garrett.

1993   *Angels & Insects,* by A.S. Byatt. *The Bingo Palace,* by Louise Erdrich. *The Celibacy of Felix Greenspan: A Novel in Seventeen Stories,* by Lionel Abrahams. *Cuervo Tales,* by Robert Roper. *Grasslands,* by Jonathan Gillman. *In the Sparrow Hills: Stories,* by Emile Capouya. *Jesus' Son: Stories,* by Denis Johnson. *Little Kingdoms: Three Novellas,* by Steven Millhauser. *A Plague of Dreamers: Three Novellas,* by Steve Stern. *The Rest of Life: Three Novellas,* by Mary Gordon. *A River Sutra,* by Gita Mehta. *Tahuri,* by Ngahuia Te Awekotuku. *A Tidewater Morning: Three Tales from Youth,* by William Styron. *Van Gogh's Room at Arles: Three Novellas,* by Stanley Elkin. *Working Men,* by Michael Dorris.

Chapter 1

The Composite Novel

Naming and Defining a
Developing Genre

The composite novel is a literary form that combines the complexities of a miscellany with the integrative qualities of a novel. In other words, it is a grouping of autonomous pieces that together achieve whole-text coherence. Although the composite novel as a literary genre has predecessors in early composite texts and in the loosely connected framed tales of the medieval and Renaissance periods, its closely traceable development did not begin until the nineteenth century. Only in the twentieth century did the composite novel become a mature genre. Literary critics have long been unsure what to call such important twentieth century texts as *The Country of the Pointed Firs* (1896), *Dubliners* (1914), *Winesburg, Ohio* (1919), *In Our Time* (1925), *Go Down, Moses* (1942), *The Golden Apples* (1947), *Lost in the Funhouse* (1968), and *The Woman Warrior* (1976). Are they "novels"? Are they "mere collections"? Or are they something else? In the 1970s the term *short story cycle* was proposed and, to some extent, it caught on. But as a generic label for these works, the term has inherent limitations. We propose, instead, *composite novel*—which more closely fits the literary form whose definition, based on our observation of its development as a genre, we propose as follows:

> *The composite novel is a literary work composed of shorter texts that—though individually complete and autonomous—are interrelated in a coherent whole according to one or more organizing principles.*

In this introductory chapter we will discuss each element of this definition, beginning with the term *composite novel*.

"The composite novel . . ."

Although the composite novel as we are defining it here has been in existence for almost two centuries, *composite novel* is a term that one seldom sees. To those few people who are familiar with it, *composite novel* traditionally means a collaborative work—a novel written by a number of authors, each of whom contributes a chapter or individual section. Several such collaborative works were produced during the years 1880–1930, especially in the United States, popularizing the concept of multiple authorship. One of these works, published in 1917, used the term *composite novel* in its subtitle: *The Sturdy Oak: A Composite Novel of American Politics by Fourteen American Authors.*[1] The connotative connection between *composite novel* and collaboration, along with the appearance of the term *composite novel* in *The Sturdy Oak*'s subtitle, apparently struck critics as appropriate. Thus one finds the term on the dust jacket of Ungar's 1986 reissue of *The Whole Family: A Novel by Twelve Authors* (a 1908 collaborative work that is better known than *The Sturdy Oak*). And in the introduction to this edition, Alfred Bendixen writes that "*The Whole Family* is the most interesting *composite novel* in American literature, but it is not the only one," and then goes on to mention several others (italics ours).[2] *The Whole Family* achieved moderate popular success in its time, but it was hardly on the tip of every critic's tongue. However, it did help wed in the critical mind the concept of collaborative authorship and the term *composite novel*. As Ungar's edition of *The Whole Family* illustrates, those generic connotations were still unquestioned in 1986.

2

But in the midseventies another critic, Eric Rabkin, had begun using the term *composite novel* in a new way. As Rabkin explained to us in a personal letter, he had "felt the need" for such a term in his own teaching and writing when discussing such books as Sherwood Anderson's *Winesburg, Ohio* and William Faulkner's *Go Down, Moses.* Rabkin's first published mention of the composite novel appeared in the context of literary science fiction, in a 1976 discussion of Isaac Asimov's *I, Robot* (1950). Subsequently, Rabkin honed his definition of *composite novel* while applying it to other science-fiction works, such as Walter M. Miller, Jr.'s *A Canticle for Leibowitz* (1959) and Ray Bradbury's *The Martian Chronicles* (1950).[3] Most important, Rabkin in these critical analyses dealt extensively with each work as if it were a novel, stressing its ultimate novelistic cohesion. That is (to paraphrase Rabkin), though these books may be composed of autonomous pieces, each book is nevertheless, in toto, a composite novel.

Certainly literary critics had for decades been analyzing disjunctive works similar in structure to those discussed by Rabkin. For many of these critics there was no middle ground between a "novel" and a "collection of stories." When they encountered *Winesburg* or *Go Down, Moses,* therefore, they expended a great deal of energy in a debate over unity versus disunity, all the while trying to avoid making a generic designation. These books were clearly not novels in the traditional sense, just as they were clearly more than collections of stories chosen at random to reside together under one cover. The dilemma seemed unsolvable for critics who admitted no middle ground, who insisted that a work such as *Winesburg* be tagged either as a novel or as a story collection.

Other critics, however, believed that such works were representatives of a separate, definable literary genre. As early as 1932, Joseph Warren Beach in *The Twentieth Century Novel* identified what he called a "composite view" exhibited by authors who "build up a set of stories into a larger whole, in which, by some compositional device, they are given a semblance of organic unity."[4] In 1949 Malcolm Cowley wrote that several of Faulkner's works, including *Go Down, Moses,* are "something more" than collections, that they belong "to a genre that Faulkner has made peculiarly his own." Subsequently, Cowley extended this judgment to *Winesburg,* when he wrote in 1960 that it "lies midway between the novel proper and the mere collection of stories."[5]

Although Cowley used the terms *cycle* and *cycle of stories* when discussing these works, he seems not to have gone so far as officially proposing a name for this generic half-breed. Many others have done so, however, suggesting and using numerous generic labels, including *story cycle, short story cycle, multi-faceted novel, story novel, paranovel, loose-leaf novel, short story composite, rovelle, composite, short story compound, integrated short story collection, anthology novel, modernist grotesque, hybrid novel, story chronicle, short story sequence, genre of return, short story volume,* and *narrative of community.* Many of these terms were proposed in unpublished dissertations and hard-to-find articles, while others have been proposed "in passing" in critical works that do not focus on genre identification as such. Thus most of the alternatively proposed terms received little or no attention, even though some proposers proffered convincing arguments against *short story cycle* as the generic term of choice.[6]

But the term *short story cycle* caught on, primarily because Forrest L. Ingram proposed and defined it in 1971 in the first published book-length study of this incipient genre, *Representative Short Story Cycles of the Twentieth Century: Studies in a Literary Genre.*[7] In 1977 Ian Reid gave the term further generic credentials. In *The Short Story,* Reid adopted Ingram's terminology and definitions, and, following Ingram and others, suggested that *Winesburg, Ohio* is the genre's quintessential example.[8] By 1989, when Susan Garland Mann published *The Short Story Cycle: A Genre Companion and Reference Guide,* the term "short story cycle" seemed to have been adopted over all others.[9] Mann, who gave copious credit to Ingram for his helpful and influential "terminology and incipient genre theory," referred to the short story cycle as a "distinct genre" that reflects "the concept of the unified short story collection" (x).

During all this time, other critics were discussing works that inhabit this "distinct genre," but only Eric Rabkin was using and applying the term *composite novel* rather than *short story cycle* or some other. Though terminology is hardly the most important factor in genre identification and theory, it is—especially in this case—significant. First of all, the term *composite novel* emphasizes kinship to the novel itself, the modern era's predominant literary genre. When critics were debating what to call *Winesburg* and *Go Down, Moses,* the choice was often posed, to quote the words of

Malcolm Cowley cited just a few paragraphs ago, as one between "the novel proper and the *mere* collection of stories" (italics ours). And as for readers, any publisher will confirm that readers are more likely to buy novels than story collections. Why this value judgment on the part of critics? Why this preference on the part of readers? Theories abound, many of which are encapsulated in Mikhail Bakhtin's evaluation that, compared to all other genres, the novel "is the highest incarnation of intertextual play."[10] The novel, in other words, offers infinite possibilities for both writer and reader. A common-sense explanation—one implied in Forrest Ingram's term "cyclical habit of mind" and in Claude Levi-Strauss's concept of the "symbolic function"—is simply that human beings need to seek order, to arrange, to make connections.[11] But this need to make connections is frustrated by a collection of unrelated stories because a reader must constantly begin over again, starting anew with each story, and literally becomes exhausted in the process. Although the explanation for the long-standing popularity of the novel is undoubtedly more complex than all of these factors put together, one thing remains clear: in the pigeon house of genre the novel occupies a lofty perch, and any generic label that emphasizes "story" rather than "novel" roosts at a lower level.

Second, and just as important, *composite novel* and *short story cycle* are terms diametrically opposed in their generic implications and assumptions. *Composite novel* emphasizes the integrity of the whole, while *short story cycle* emphasizes the integrity of the parts. In addition, a "cycle" in anyone's definition implies cyclical motion, a circular path, a return to the beginning, all of which preclude linear development. Thus the term *short story cycle* itself is doubly problematic: it not only implies inferior status in the generic hierarchy, but also prescribes or at least suggests generic limitations.

In contrast, *composite novel* emphasizes its affinity to "the novel proper," in Cowley's words. Although a novel is usually structured by plot, a linear narration involving causation, it can be structured alternatively, or by association—that is, by juxtaposing events, images, themes, and/or characters in some sort of coherent pattern. E. M. Forster in 1927 referred to this associative structure as "rhythm," seeing it as akin to the way a musical score develops.[12] The composite novel, too, may be structured by causation or association or both, and again the emphasis is on the whole rather than the parts. Continuing his analogy between music and literature, Forster speaks of both "simple rhythm" and "complex rhythm," and though he intended both terms to apply to the traditional novel's aesthetic, his concept of complex rhythm describes precisely the composite novel's aesthetic:

> Is there any effect in novels comparable to the effect of the Fifth Symphony as a whole, where, when the orchestra stops, we hear something that has never actually been played? The opening movement, the andante, and the trio-scherzo-trio-finale that composes the third block all enter the mind at once, and extend one another into a common entity. This common entity, this new thing, is the symphony as a whole, and it has been achieved mainly (though not entirely) by the relation between the three big blocks of sound which the orchestra has been playing. (240)

Forster's "complex rhythm," therefore, is effected not only through repetition of melodies and motifs, such as occurs in a musical line or page or score, but also through a dynamic relationship such as that which exists between the movements and the symphony, between the parts and the whole. In sum, this is the aesthetic of the composite novel: its parts are named, identifiable, memorable; their *interrelationship* creates the coherent whole text. Encompassed within this aesthetic is the inherent capability of the composite novel to reflect and extend the protean qualities of the novel itself.

". . . is a literary work composed of shorter texts . . ."

Note the use of the terms *literary work* and *text* rather than *fiction* or *prose.* As it happens, most composite novels are clearly works of prose fiction, but others are less easy to classify because they appear to cross over, at least in part, into folktale, history, or autobiography. Leslie Marmon Silko's *Storyteller* (1981), for example, and Gloria Anzaldua's *Borderlands* (1987) contain folktales and historical sketches, and both books are undeniably autobiographical. Mary McCarthy's *The Company She Keeps* (1942) was fiercely attacked by critics in the 1940s for trying to pass autobiography off as fiction, yet four decades later, Maxine Hong Kingston's *The Woman Warrior* (1976) garnered high praise for its "innovative" blend of fiction and reminiscence. Some critics might judge that works born of holocaust, such as Liana Millu's *Smoke over Birkenau* (1947) and Varlam Shalamov's *Kolyma Tales* (1980), are so thoroughly grounded in historical reality as to be outside the realm of fiction. And others may believe that there is little if any fiction contained in Antoine de Saint-Exupéry's *Wind, Sand, and Stars* (1939) or Loren Eiseley's *The Night Country* (1971). Whether any or all of these works are sufficiently "fictional" may well be a matter of personal judgment and critical leaning, though it does seem that the current critical stance is aptly encapsulated by George Levine: "In the last fifteen years . . . the boundaries between non-fiction and fiction have been all but obliterated." Levine, writing in 1992, further asserts that "the generic separation of nonfiction and fiction, which seemed twenty-five years ago an important aesthetic problem, seems now . . . largely beside the point."[13] The test that we apply is this: If a writer begins with memories of observed reality, or with stories heard from others, or with historical accounts—and then stirs in imagined detail—such an imaginative re-creation lies squarely within the literary realm of "fiction."

Consider also that neither *story* nor *short story* appears anywhere in our definition. Again it so happens that most composite novels are composed entirely of shorter texts that are immediately identifiable as short stories (or "sketches" or "vignettes"). But this need not always be the case. Jean Toomer's *Cane* (1923), for example, contains, among its text-pieces, poems and a one-act play; E. M. Broner's *A Weave of Women* (1978) includes rituals and ceremonies; Ntozake Shange's *Sassafrass, Cypress & Indigo* (1982) contains recipes; and Ursula K. LeGuin's *Always Coming Home* (1985) includes plays, song lyrics, and collections of aphorisms. This is not to say, of course, that a book composed entirely or even largely of poems or plays or recipes is generically a composite novel. The point is that the composite novel's structural aesthetic permits the inclusion of text-pieces that *short story cycle* might reject, text-pieces that have not traditionally been thought of as "stories" or even "fiction" or "prose."

There is one caveat, however. Throughout the twentieth century, boundaries between various types of prose (fiction, auto/biography, reportage, memoir, and so on) have become more and more permeable. But the boundary between "prose" and "verse," even though the difference between the two is sometimes difficult to describe and define, is still theoretically impermeable. In regard to the composite novel, this means that such works as Walt Whitman's *Leaves of Grass* and Edgar Lee Masters' *Spoon River Anthology*—that is, composite works composed entirely in verse—should not be designated as composite novels, any more than Chaucer's *Troilus and Criseyde* (an integrated narrative composed entirely in verse) should be called a novel.

Regarding the text-pieces of composite novels, there is also a related question of length. Susan Mann deals with this issue by defining "short" stories as "shorter than novels and generally longer than a few pages" (6). Other critics, such as Ian Reid and Forrest Ingram, use similarly nebulous parameters. Since the text-pieces of the composite novel may not all be stories, however, acceptable length as determined by some minimum and maximum number of "pages" appears inappropriate. Certainly the poems, rituals, recipes, lyrics, and so on mentioned above are not length-specific. But what of a five-line paragraph that has a title and is clearly meant to be self-contained? Julio Cortázar's *A Certain Lucas* (1984) includes this text-piece. Even more extreme, what of a seven-word sentence that has a title and is, like all of its companion text-pieces, clearly meant to be autonomous? Gertrude Stein's *Tender Buttons* (1914) includes several such pieces. At the other end of the spectrum, composite novels such as John Barth's *Chimera* (1972) and Leslie Epstein's *Goldkorn Tales* (1985) are composed entirely of novella-length pieces. Many critics working in this genre (whether they call it "short story cycle" or something else) might balk at accepting Stein's seven-word sentence as a viable text-piece, but few have any difficulty accepting a novella as a text-piece simply because of its length. Again, we propose that if a work meets other genre criteria of the composite novel, then it is not precluded from consideration simply because it includes unusually brief or extended or otherwise generically "peculiar" text-pieces.

"... [are] individually complete and autonomous ..."

An important point, stated clearly in our definition, is that the text-pieces of the composite novel are individually complete and autonomous. This means, in most cases, that individual text-pieces are titled. Such a work as Anaïs Nin's *Collages* (1964) illustrates this point. Structurally, the book adheres to the composite novel's aesthetic of autonomy and interconnection. As Sharon Spencer describes it, *Collages* is composed of 19 "short, self-sustaining episodes or vignettes" that as a whole text exhibit a "particular design" in which the "fixative . . . is always a self in relationship."[14] The text-pieces, then, combine into a unified collagelike text (Nin chose her title quite deliberately, aware of its nuances as well as its technical definition and its history as an art form). But the text-pieces of Nin's book have no titles whatsoever, and this makes it virtually impossible to excerpt and/or refer to any particular one. They are not individually identifiable, in other words, because they are not named. Like untitled bars of music, they are parts of a whole, but not autonomous parts.

The question of autonomy can be tricky in other ways. Some literary works consist of text-pieces that are grouped into numbered "parts," "books," or "sections" that may or may not have titles of their own. One also finds, particularly in nineteenth- and early twentieth-century works, text-pieces that carry chapter numbers as well as titles. And then one comes upon the curious case of John Steinbeck's *The Pastures of Heaven* (1932), which many critics want to call a "short story composite" or "short story cycle." Steinbeck himself considered it "made up of stories each one complete in itself, having its rise, climax and ending."[15] Yet the so-called stories that comprise the book do not and never did have titles, only numbers (roman numerals). Referring to sections of the book, then, means speaking of "Number Four" or "Roman Numeral Seven." To say the least, this is awkward; in addition, it weakens the argument that the book contains "stories" rather than "chapters," self-contained though these text-pieces may be in terms of structure and closure.

Further, some composite novels contain frame-pieces or interleaving that, while they might be titled, are not really able to stand on their own. Prologues and epilogues, forewords, framing vignettes, interchapters, artwork, drawings of various kinds, even photographs—any of these or some combination may be included in a composite novel. Some of the shorter texts that comprise a composite novel may be more excerptable, more independent of context, than others. The reasonable approach here seems to be to accept that all text-pieces need not be equally autonomous for a work to meet the genre criteria of the composite novel. Generally speaking, then, and realizing that there will always be those exceptions that prove the rule, the text-pieces that make up a composite novel must be named, must have titles. Only then can they achieve the autonomy necessary to function dynamically within the whole text.

It would be helpful in many cases to know an author's intention (were the text-pieces planned as self-contained shorter texts?) or the publication history (were any text-pieces published separately, either before or after the publication of the whole text?) or both, but determining these can be difficult. It would also be helpful in some cases to know how much control an author had over the stages of production. Jamaica Kincaid's *Annie John* (1983), for example, is composed of self-contained stories, some of which had first been published individually in the *New Yorker*. In *Annie John*'s table of contents the stories are listed only by title, yet in the text of the book, the titled stories are also designated as numbered "chapters." One has to wonder whether an editor's intervention during the final stages of printing was responsible for the "chapters" in *Annie John*. Did Kincaid intend the book to be a novel or a series of linked stories? It's difficult to know.

We have to ask, too, whether authorial intention and/or editorial intervention matter at all. Forrest Ingram and Susan Mann believe that they do. Ingram, in fact, proposes three classifications that attempt to quantify authorial intention. The most unified story cycle, writes Ingram, is the "composed" cycle (one that was planned from the beginning); a less unified story cycle is the "completed" cycle (one that was conceived of as a whole text somewhere in the process of producing the individual stories); and the least unified story cycle is the "arranged" cycle (one that was put together as a whole text after all the individual stories had been completed) (17). Editorial intervention figures in this scale, also, in that an editor is usually not at all involved in a "composed" cycle but may be highly involved in or even totally responsible for the production of an "arranged" cycle.

Putting his concern for intention and intervention in context, Ingram invokes both factors in arguing for the whole-text unity of Franz Kafka's *A Hunger Artist* (1924): "[Kafka] consciously selected these particular [four] stories for inclusion in a single volume. He worked feverishly to correct the proofs on his death-bed, insisted on the present order of the stories, and became angry with his publishers for not carrying out certain details of his instructions exactly" (46). To Ingram, obviously, these factors are crucial, and Mann argues in much the same way for the whole-text coherence of Flannery O'Connor's *Everything That Rises Must Converge* (1965), saying that O'Connor (who was working on the collection when she died) "wished to include all of the nine stories in *Everything That Rises* and that she controlled the basic order in which they appear" (155).

In some cases, like Kafka's, when a living author comments upon a text, or in other cases, like O'Connor's, when a deceased author has left letters and instructions, intention may be a factor worth considering. But in many cases, it may be impossible to know or to find out. What then? The O'Connor text just mentioned is relevant here, in fact, because there is still a lingering doubt as to whether her publisher and literary executor disregarded her wishes concerning the inclusion of two stories.[16] Once again the reasonable approach, when considering whole-text coherence, seems to be that one should carefully weigh all the factors available. If an author says, in so many words, "This is a novel in stories," then that stated intention is important.

To summarize so far, the parts of the composite novel are likely to be immediately identifiable as short stories—each one titled and self-contained, able to be experienced independently by a reader, perhaps published separately before or after publication of the whole text, perhaps becoming well-known in its own right as it is anthologized in other collections. Certainly this has been the case with such renowned text-pieces as "Hands," from Anderson's *Winesburg, Ohio*; "The Bear," from Faulkner's *Go Down, Moses*; "Night-Sea Journey," from Barth's *Lost in the Funhouse*; and "No Name Woman," from Kingston's *The Woman Warrior*. Yet some composite novels contain unusual text-pieces not normally considered within the purview of "fiction" or "short story." Similarly, while the parts of the composite novel must be self-contained and autonomous, able to stand on their own as individual entities, some composite novels include framing and/or unifying text-pieces that are entirely context-dependent. Generally, text-pieces designated by "chapter" or "number" alone do not qualify. Yet some composite novels feature text-pieces that combine a title and a number, or a title and a "chapter so-and-so" designation. It would be helpful in some cases to know what an author intended or whether an editor intervened during the production process, but such information may not be available. In sum, if one were to make a judgment concerning generic designation on the basis of those criteria discussed so far, the decision would be straightforward in many cases but not in others.

". . . are interrelated in a coherent whole . . ."

The parts that make up a composite novel, as the term itself implies and as our definition states, are interrelated in a coherent whole. The emphasis, then, is not upon the parts but rather upon a whole text rendered coherent through a dynamic interaction with and among its parts. Analogically, the composite novel is a gestalt, an "organised whole," a "configuration of elements [and/or] themes" whose sum is more than its parts.[17]

The best place to begin, when determining whether a composite work functions as a coherent whole text, is with its title's generic implications. Any book whose title simply appropriates the title of one of its component stories and then adds "and Other Stories" as a subtitle appears to make no claim to be anything other than a collection (however, some books so titled have been read and interpreted as coherent whole texts).[18] In direct contrast are those works like Gloria Naylor's *The Women of Brewster Place: A Novel in Seven Stories* (1982) and Sandra Birdsell's *Agassiz: A Novel in Stories* (1991) that proclaim their composite aesthetic quite clearly. The titles of many composite novels, however, do not give clear signals. Such words as "stories," "tales," "chronicles," and the like appear in numerous titles, such as John Updike's *Olinger Stories* (1964), Latife Tekin's *Berji Kristin: Tales from the Garbage Hills* (1984), and Ursula K. LeGuin's *Searoad: Chronicles of Klatsand* (1991). All these works are composite novels, but the titles alone are ambiguous as to whether the books constitute integrated whole texts or collections. Other titles are even more problematic. Richard Cortez Day's *When in Florence: A Cycle of Stories* (1986) is also a composite novel (though the term "cycle" implies a collection rather than an integrated text), and E. L. Doctorow's *Lives of the Poets: Six Stories and a*

Novella (1984) is incontrovertibly a composite novel in intention and execution, even though the title strongly implies the contrary. Similarly, Carlos Fuentes's *Constancia and Other Stories for Virgins* (1989) and Randall Kenan's *Let the Dead Bury Their Dead and Other Stories* (1992), both composite novels, bear titles that give no hint of an integrated text.

A book's title is of course just a preliminary generic signal—perhaps a more important signal than critical practice often recognizes, but preliminary nonetheless. A more crucial factor is brought into play when one examines a work closely to determine whether and how its composite parts are interrelated. A composite novel, like any other coherent, readable text, is a tissue of fine connectives. Thus some or all of a composite novel's text-pieces may reveal repeated images or image clusters; possibly some recurring characters, shared incidents, and/or a generally common setting; probably one or more common thematic concerns; perhaps a sustained and sustaining narrative voice. But these are all subtle textual elements. Is any one, or even all of these in combination, enough to weave a textual whole cloth? Possibly, yes. But probably, no. For example, the fact that an occasional image is repeated in a few stories, creating a faint echo at best, is hardly a strong interconnective fiber. Similarly, the fact that a group of stories share a common but nebulous setting (say, in the 1960s, in a bleak but unnamed metropolitan area) is not much better in terms of textual "thread-count." And the fact that selected stories are grouped together and included under one cover simply because they share a tenuous thematic focus (all of them generally about "love" or "divorce" or "alienation" or whatever) is the whole-textual equivalent of "dropping a stitch." And so on. The issue here is one of degree. How much is enough? How much is too little? How closely woven must this textual cloth be? We can probably all agree about the whole-text coherence of a large number of works, but we will most likely agree to disagree about others.

One has to survey only a few composite novels to realize that the importance of text-piece sequencing varies widely. In a few cases, sequence matters little. John Fowles's *The Ebony Tower* (1974), for example, is composed of self-contained pieces (a novella and four stories) that arguably permit various rearrangements. In most composite novels, however, the sequence of text-pieces—at least some pieces if not all—is important, and in others the sequence permits no alteration whatsoever. There can be little or no alteration of sequence, for example, in a book such as William Faulkner's *The Unvanquished* (1938), whose seven stories follow the young Bayard Sartoris chronologically through a 10-year period covering the last half of the Civil War and the early years of Reconstruction, as he matures from a callow youth to a responsible adult. Equally sequence-specific is Bernard Malamud's *Pictures of Fidelman* (1969), which uses the history of western art as a structural analogue to the career of Fidelman, an American schlemiel in Europe. In six stories, Fidelman's artistic-cum-amorous career begins with the thirteenth-century frescoes of Giotto; schlepps through Rembrandt, Titian, Picasso, Modigliani, Kandinsky, and others in the middle stories; and careens into Jackson Pollock, Op Art, and Claes Oldenburg's *Soft Toilet* in the final story.

Occasionally an author will instruct the reader about sequence, as when Waldo Frank asserts on a prefatory page in *City Block* (1922), "The author assures the reader that *City Block* is a single organism and that its parts should be read in order . . ." (ellipsis in original). But some composite novels give few obvious signals regarding the planned sequence. In James Joyce's *Dubliners,* for example, the only common factor connecting the individual stories appears at first glance to be setting (the city of Dublin). Yet the sequence of text-pieces in *Dubliners* is crucial as, story by story, building slowly, Joyce weaves image, metaphor, and symbol into a tragic dirge for the failed glory of Ireland. Thus, though it may not be important at all in some composite novels and only moderately so in others, sequence is in some works a significant unifying element.

". . . according to one or more organizing principles"

Recognizing that interconnectedness among text-pieces is highly complex, and that most composite novels establish interconnections through a combination of unifying factors, we move now to the final element in our definition of the composite novel—that the whole text (however variously it may be comprised) is interrelated according to one or more organizing principles. In chapters 3–7, we will define five primary principles of composite-novel organization and discuss them at length by focusing on a number of works in which these principles are important elements of interconnection. Here in this introductory chapter, however, we will simply mention the five primary interconnective elements and discuss them briefly.

To begin, *setting* is a primary element of interconnection in a large number of composite novels and precursors. Nineteenth-century authors used this connective device often, especially those who wrote composite novels in the "village sketch" tradition (which we discuss in chapters 2–3), and many twentieth-century authors have followed suit.

Another primary and often-used unifying element is *a single protagonist* upon whom a work's text-pieces focus or around whom they cohere. In some cases this may be a narrator-protagonist; in others a central figure whose progress is charted in story after story, creating a bildungsroman or kunstlerroman effect; and in still others a figure who—though always the central, unifying focus—appears and reappears sporadically.

The third organizational principle, generally more complex than the single protagonist, is the *collective protagonist*, often used to forge complex interconnective links in composite novels that cut a wide swath through historical time, or in those whose focus is multigenerational or multicultural. As we define it, the collective protagonist is a "composite"—perhaps literally (a couple, a family, a club or a special interest group), or perhaps figuratively (a generation, a personality type, an archetypal embodiment).

The fourth organizing principle, *pattern*, is exemplified in part by the "patchwork" composite novels of the nineteenth century (which we discuss in chapter 2). The text-pieces of a pattern-related composite novel, like the large blocks that comprise a quilt-top, may feature identical story patterns or reflect identical, sharply etched motif patterns. In some works, then, pattern recurs exactly in each text-piece so that the same outline is visible in and interconnects them all. In other composite novels an identical pattern may structure one text-piece after another until, after having thus set a pattern precedent through repetition, a final text-piece startles (or encapsulates) through variation. Two or more patterns (story patterns and/or motif patterns) may work together, also, with one perhaps shadowing another and thus establishing counterpoint as a connective element among text-pieces.

Finally, the fifth principle of organization is *storytelling*, or the process of fiction making. Composite novels whose interconnections are established through this principle may feature a narrator who, aware of the difficulties (or joys) of telling a story, makes the telling process itself the primary focus. Such a narrator may take the reader into confidence, showing the possibilities considered in the act of storytelling. Thus in some composite novels the focus may not be on a developing protagonist, or on a developing collective protagonist, but on a developing *story*—the work's focus, in other words, is the transactional process involved in getting the story told.

These, then, are the five primary elements of interconnection that we define and discuss in detail in subsequent chapters. It is crucial to remember, though, that seldom will just one of these primary elements of interconnection work alone. More often, several will act in concert, along with less controlling devices such as cross-referencing of characters and events, repetition of image and image clusters, development of common themes, and, in many cases, the arranged sequence of text-pieces.

Some Additional Points

The genre implications of the term *composite novel* exclude two particular types of literary works that the *short story cycle* includes: multivolume works and "series hero" clustered texts. Regarding multivolume works, Susan Mann mentions as "short story cycles" John Dos Passos's three-volume *U.S.A.*, James Herriott's four-volume set beginning with *All Creatures Great and Small* and ending with *The Lord God Made Them All,* and Edith Wharton's linked 1920 tetralogy entitled *Old New York.*[19] As interesting as such works are, however, they are not composite novels—although any one volume in such a series or set may fit the genre criteria. Like the traditional novel itself, the composite novel resides under one cover.

The stories that cluster around such "series heroes" as George Washington Harris's Sut Lovingood, Sir Arthur Conan Doyle's

Sherlock Holmes, Agatha Christie's Hercule Poirot, Langston Hughes's Jesse B. Semple (the "Simple" stories), and Joel Chandler Harris's Uncle Remus may well be compiled into various single-text editions, and once again Susan Mann refers to these as "short story cycles." Indeed, these cultural icons inhabit, from story to story, a constant world with familiar and recurring characters. But, generally speaking, the stories about any particular series hero permit arrangement and rearrangement into various collections and editions, no one of which is a whole text distinguishable from any other. Surely it is pertinent in this regard that Conan Doyle could not even end his series, much less a whole-text volume, by killing off his own hero (Conan Doyle wrote Holmes's demise in a fall from a rocky cliff to a raging torrent below, but when fans were outraged, he brought Holmes back).

Although the genre designation of composite novel excludes multivolume works and series hero clustered texts, it most definitely includes collaborative works—as long as the work's autonomous text-pieces are intended as components of a coherent whole text (not just selections lumped together in an anthology). In this respect, of course, the composite novel confirms its terminological ancestral links to such early collaborative works as *The Whole Family* and *The Sturdy Oak*, both mentioned at the beginning of this chapter.

Collaborative composite novels have not been numerous since the 1920s, however, with the possible exception of what science-fiction publishing calls the "shared-world anthology." As defined by Robert Silverberg in an introduction to *Murasaki* (1992), the shared-world anthology features "new stories set within a single conceptual framework, produced jointly by a group of science-fiction writers."[20] An intriguing point here is that Silverberg's definition of the shared-world anthology could just as well describe collaborative hypertexts—those interactive texts, created on computers and existing in hyperspace, that have functioned as teaching/learning components of writing workshops and creative writing courses since the mid-1980s. Robert Coover describes collaborative hypertexts as "group fiction space" and explains that working in hyperspace—which is "nonlinear or nonsequential"—forces one to focus "on structure as much as on prose":

> The most radical element that comes to the fore in hypertext is the system of multidirectional and often labyrinthine linkages we are invited or obliged to create. . . . We are always astonished to discover how much of the reading and writing experience occurs in the interstices and trajectories *between* text fragments. That is to say, the text fragments are like stepping stones, there for our safety, but the real *current* of the narratives runs between them.[21]

As this passage indicates, Coover stresses the active role of readers who must negotiate for themselves "the interstices and trajectories." Because of this, he says, readers in hypertext "become co-learners or co-writers, as it were, fellow-travelers in the mapping and remapping of textual components" (23). In essence, the reader of a composite novel faces the same task of "mapping," that is, establishing connections between and among text-pieces. In the context of Coover's comments, in fact, the composite novel reveals itself to be future-friendly—a print-medium analogue (whether collaborative or not) of hypertext.

One final caveat: the composite novel does not include works simply because their text-pieces interact in an interesting way, because they are obviously experimental in structure, or because they self-consciously proclaim themselves to be unusual. Katherine Neville's *The Eight* (1988), for example, is an intriguing work that appears to be structured like a game of chess, divided into numerous segments and including seemingly self-contained text-pieces bearing such titles as "A Pawn Advances" and "Pawn to Queen's Fourth."[22] Neville's book is an integrated linear narrative, however—a novel, not a composite novel. Similarly intriguing, Italo Calvino's *Invisible Cities* (1972) clearly establishes for its titled text-pieces an interrelating frame (Kubla Khan talking with Marco Polo). Yet *Invisible Cities* is a novel-like oddity that has to be read as a whole text because its shorter texts—unlike the shorter texts in *Dubliners, Winesburg,* or *Go Down, Moses*—are entirely context-dependent.[23] And then there is Hilaire Belloc's *The Four Men: A Farrago* (1911), in which the author envisions four characters who walk through Sussex and talk about a disappearing way of life—the four "characters" each being one aspect of Belloc himself. Belloc's "farrago" has been likened to "a series of happy snapshots."[24] But its text-pieces are identified only by dates, and they are so interdependent that they cannot conceivably be described as self-contained. A farrago, it seems, does not a composite novel make.

As we are defining it, then, the composite novel is a single text composed of shorter texts: its aesthetic is one that insists on a coherently developed whole text, even though that whole text must, for the most part, be composed of individually autonomous pieces. Thus a dynamic tension exists between the whole and its parts. Indeed, when we refer to the "aesthetic" of the composite novel, we refer not only to the complex tension among text-pieces, but also to the dynamic tension between text-pieces and the whole text.

The possibilities inherent in this aesthetic have obviously intrigued a great number of literary artists. One of them, Joyce Carol Oates, commented on this in 1981: "I seem to want to tell a story as if it were sheer lyric, all its components present simultaneously. . . . I am fascinated too with the concept of a 'novel' shaped out of a sequence of closely related and intertwined 'short stories.'"[25] In a nutshell, Oates in this short statement defines the composite novel, whose aesthetic possibilities have sparked its development as a genre.

Chapter 2

Progenitors and Precursors

Through the
Nineteenth Century

The composite novel as we describe it had its beginnings in the
nineteenth century, but it had many earlier predecessors. It
may in fact not be wide of the mark to note the affinities between
this literary form and such composite works as the Bible, the
Koran, and the Bhagavad Gita—all of which gather stories together into sacred texts that define and embody traditions, cultures,
and peoples. Similar in this regard are the many composite texts
created from tales surrounding the legendary King Arthur: the
Welsh *Mabinogion,* the Norman *Roman de Brut,* works by Chretien
de Troyes and Wolfram von Eschenbach, Malory's *Le Morte
d'Arthur,* Tennyson's *Idylls of the King,* White's *The Once and Future
King.* In these works and many others, the Arthurian tales have
been selected, rendered, and arranged into individually config-
ured whole texts. Though individual characters and particular

story lines remain identifiable through centuries of rerendering, each whole text is a composite entity that differs from all others.

Early frame tales and their precursors in the great epic cycles are also ancestors of the composite novel. In Homer's *Odyssey*, for example, the adventures of Odysseus function as individual tales within the framework of his journey back to Ithaca after the defeat of Troy. Like the Arthurian stories, the tales of Odysseus reflect narrative patterns traceable to the folktales and legends of many lands and cultures. When these reworked early tales are given the focus of a hero, one developed consistently in character and motivation, links of continuity and coherence are forged. Thus one is always aware of the *Odyssey*'s tension between framework and tales, between whole story and story-pieces.

In works such as *The Canterbury Tales* and *The Decameron*, the frame itself is primarily an excuse for grouping together a potpourri of tales. Thus when Geoffrey Chaucer gathers at the Tabard Inn a motley group of pilgrims, a poet among them describes the travelers in a prologue and the host at the inn suggests a storytelling contest as a way to pass the time during the group's journey to and from Canterbury. Hung on a similar frame, the unrelated stories and anecdotes of Giovanni Boccaccio's *Decameron* are told by a group of young aristocrats who have fled the Black Death by escaping to the countryside, where they pass the time by telling stories. The Persian/Indian/Arabian stories gathered in *The Arabian Nights' Entertainments* are similarly framed by the storytelling of Scheherazade, who can preserve her life only by reserving the climax of each evening's tale for the following night. Chaucer proposed that his 30 pilgrims tell two stories each for a total of 60, Boccaccio's young nobles tell 10 stories each for a total of 100, and Scheherazade plans to tell stories for "a thousand and one nights." Though they differ in origin, setting, and scope, the three works are generically identical in that they are collections of disparate stories, hung on insubstantial frames.

The point here is that composite works and framed collections have been around for centuries, including and predating the age of Chaucer and Boccacio. Our purpose in this book, though, is to focus upon the composite novel as an identifiable modern form. It is far beyond our scope to attempt an extensive literary history; these few remarks are meant simply as illustrations of how the sacred composite, the epic cycle, and the framed collection constitute progenitors of the composite novels of the nineteenth and twentieth centuries. Because we believe, generally speaking, that the composite novel did not mature as a literary genre until the twentieth century, we focus almost exclusively on twentieth-century works in chapters 3 through 9. Before embarking on that discussion, however, we will focus on works produced in the nineteenth century and thus lay the historical groundwork for the remainder of the book.

The Village Sketch

Many nineteenth-century composite novels, like the early frame tales, are so tenuously unified that they are better referred to as "precursors." One such type of precursor is the village sketch composite, a group of stories linked primarily through setting. The village sketch composite was highly popular in America, yet it was pioneered by an Englishwoman, Mary Russell Mitford, in *Our Village* in 1824.[1] Mitford's book features a woman narrator who, as a longtime resident of a provincial English town, knows the inside scoop on everyone who lives there. As the narrator walks around the town she describes its various features, with some of her stories prompted by encounters with other walkers along the way. Other village sketch composites by British Isles authors include Elizabeth Gaskell's *Cranford* (1853), George Eliot's *Scenes of Clerical Life* (1858), Jane Barlow's *Irish Idylls* (1893), and George Moore's *The Untilled Field* (1903).[2] British authors were simply not writing many of these village sketch composites, however, so even though Mitford's work was highly influential, her influence was felt most strongly in America.

One of the first American writers to follow Mitford's lead was Sarah Josepha Hale, whose *Sketches of American Character* appeared in 1829.[3] Hale's book is set in New England, as are a preponderance of America's nineteenth-century village sketch composites. Other sections of the country also find representation, however. Augustus Baldwin Longstreet lovingly described his home state in *Georgia Scenes* (1835); Caroline Kirkland wrote realistically of frontier life in the American West in *A New Home—Who'll Follow?* (1839); George Washington Cable described life in Louisiana in *Old Creole Days* (1879), as did Kate Chopin in *Bayou Folk* (1894); Constance Fenimore Woolson and Hamlin Garland extended the purview of the "village" somewhat, Woolson by surveying southern life in *Rodman the Keeper* (1880) and Garland by describing the American Midwest in *Main-Travelled Roads* (1891).[4]

It goes without saying, of course, that the multitude of nineteenth-century village sketch composites varied widely in design and execution. Yet it does seem possible to generalize about their appeal, both to readers and to writers: in such works one could capture "a sense of place" in many minute particulars, including among these particulars an ethos of community that reflects a complex network of human lives. Such early composite texts, then, offered a unique opportunity for writers to convey the distinctive sense of a place through a composite picture of its people, and the village sketch tradition is justly well known among literary historians who trace the development of regional and local color writing.

The Patchwork Composite

Another tradition with equally as many pre–twentieth century practitioners is exemplified in an early eighteenth-century literary work, again by an Englishwoman: Jane Barker's *A Patch-Work Screen for the Ladies*.[5] In this book, a young girl named Galesia tells her life story while interspersing vignettes about her friends and life in general in those early times. Barker's *Patch-Work Screen*, then, reflects in its design aesthetic the principle of "piecing," and it had a number of nineteenth-century American "cousins," such as Caroline Hentz's *Aunt Patty's Scrap Bag* (1846), Louisa May Alcott's *Aunt Jo's Scrap-Bag* (1872), and Maley Bainbridge Crist's *Patchwork* (1898).[6] These works are part of a long-standing tradition in women's writing that continues to this day. Unlike the village sketch tradition, however, this one has had no name. We call it the patchwork tradition and see in it the aesthetic embodied in the pieced quilt. Like a quilt, a patchwork composite is made up of pieces; and like the cloth-pieces of a quilt, the text-pieces of a patchwork composite typically reflect an aesthetic emphasizing juxtaposition and repetition with variation.

Cloth work, of course, has been vitally important in the lives of women for centuries. Spinning, weaving, tatting, quilting,

knitting, embroidering, stitching—tasks such as these have traditionally been the stuff of women's lives, crossing boundaries of
time, place, and culture. Equally pervasive in women's lives has
been the metaphoric linkage of needle and pen. Thus it was not
unusual for a young woman to write, as Eliza Southgate did in
1801: "I pieced [my ideas] into a few patchwork opinions, . . . and
as I am about quilting a few more, I beg you will send me any
spare ideas you may chance to have."[7] In the context of this visual analogue between pieced cloth and pieced text, consider an
early patchwork composite such as Hannah Farnham Sawyer
Lee's *Three Experiments of Living* (1837).[8] In this work each of
three self-contained and titled sections describes a different period in the life of the Fultons, a married couple (they prosper, then
falter, then prosper again). Similar in overall design but more
complex in its repeated patterns is Louisa C. Tuthill's *The Belle,
the Blue, and the Bigot* (1844).[9] All three of this volume's self-contained stories feature a protagonist-antagonist contrast that
develops, in each story, along an identical narrative path (the
"bad" person fails while the "good" person is triumphant). A
similar design is developed in Marion Harland's *Husbands and
Homes* (1864),[10] a work consisting of six stories with the same pattern of action in each (a wife is abused, neglected, and dies
young).

Visualizing these works in terms of patchwork designs, one
might see Lee's worked in three-part blocks that vary from
bright to somber to bright. Tuthill's design would also be three-
part, but more complex, with a light-dark contrast in each block.
And Harland's might well be constructed on the principle of a
repeated motif. Most of us have seen a motif quilt of some sort,
one that features repeated log cabins, or five-pointed stars, or
Sunbonnet Sues. Most of us have probably also seen an album
quilt, which features a variety of motifs—each representing some
facet of a person's life, or a family's history, or a group's identity.
Album quilts are well named, in fact, considering that each quilt
tells a story much as a photo album or memorabilia album does.
Which came first, the album or the quilt? Does it matter? The
point is that both quilt-as-text and text-as-quilt tropes have been
significant for countless years in countless lives.

Two turn-of-the-century composite novels by Mary E.
Wilkins Freeman strongly suggest that they were planned as

analogues to motif quilts or perhaps album quilts. In the first, entitled *Understudies* (1901), each of 12 stories is named for a flower or an animal; in the second, entitled *Six Trees* (1903), each of six stories is named for a tree; in both works, a flower, animal, or tree symbolizes the identifying personality trait(s) of the major character.[11] In less skillful hands, such motif devices might be mere gimmicks. But through Freeman's inspired text stitchery, each composite work develops as a coherent, subtly integrated whole text.

All quilts (and quilt-texts) were not so symmetrically designed, however. Fabric-art historians point out a creative, improvisational design aesthetic in African-American cloth work generally and quilts particularly.[12] Thus it is that Frances E. Watkins Harper's *Sketches of Southern Life* (1891) and Susie King Taylor's *Reminiscences of My Life: A Black Woman's Civil War Memoirs* (1902) illustrate the text-quilt analogue in another context. Harper's book brings together a number of stories and poems that, except for one group of poems all written by a slave named "Aunt Cloe," have no obvious connections. Taylor's book consists of "random recollections" that she wrote over a 40-year period, beginning with her Civil War years as a nurse for the "33rd U.S. Colored Troops" and ending with her experience of racism in turn-of-the-century Louisiana.[13] Both works are coherent whole texts, and in this regard anticipate W. E. B. DuBois's *The Souls of Black Folk* in 1903 and Jean Toomer's *Cane* in 1923.

American Variations

Whether constructed on place frames (the village sketch composites) or design frames (the patchwork composites), these early works were exploring the possibilities and parameters of a twofold dynamic relationship: a relationship among parts of the whole *and* a relationship between the whole and its parts. Limitless variations, of course, were possible. Take, for example, *Girlhood and Womanhood* by Mrs. A. J. Graves (1844).[14] This volume, built on a substantial frame, suggests a variation on the village sketch in that its setting is one small community (a boarding school) and that a member of that community (a schoolgirl narrator) tells stories about other members. In another variation, Louisa May Alcott's *Hospital Sketches* (1869),[15] a narrator ("Nurse

Periwinkle") relates the experiences of staff and patients in one small hospital. Also derived from the village sketch tradition is Harriet Beecher Stowe's *Sam Lawson's Oldtown Fireside Stories* (1872),[16] in which Sam Lawson (the village do-nothing in Stowe's earlier novel *Oldtown Folks*) simply rambles around telling yarns to his friends. Stowe apparently intended no more whole-text coherence than the volume achieves; when she finished *Oldtown Folks* she had yarns left over, so she resurrected Sam Lawson and gave the yarns to him to tell. One could speculate on a "patchwork mandate" here, to "waste no scraps." And thus the patchwork analogue continues to make itself felt.

Women outnumbered men in writing these early composite novels for a number of reasons, including the fact that the constant interruptions in women's daily lives made it easier for them to write short self-contained pieces than longer sustained pieces. Certainly male authors were also contributing to the development of the composite novel, however, a notable example being George Mitchell, whose *Reveries of a Bachelor* was first published in 1850.[17] *Reveries* is composed of 22 titled stories contained in a tightly structured frame within a frame. It features a narrator named Ik Marvel, who moves from confirmed bachelorhood to marriage and fatherhood (several times over). In his original preface to *Reveries of a Bachelor,* Mitchell says somewhat apologetically, "If [my reveries] had been worked over with more unity of design, I dare say I might have made a respectable novel" (n.p.). Yet Mitchell's composite text went through numerous printings and editions, even though it wasn't "a respectable novel."

Intentions Confounded

In ironic contrast to Mitchell (who was apologetic about having published a composite text rather than a novel), Nathaniel Hawthorne, Thomas Hardy, and Stephen Crane labored mightily to publish composite texts that they had planned and "worked over" very carefully, but each of these authors met with limited success. Hawthorne, the least successful, was also the most ambitious in that he planned four separate composite texts. He had to give up on three, whose prospective titles were "Seven Tales of My Native Land," "Provincial Tales," and "The Story Teller." And even though the fourth, "Legends of the Province House" (consisting of four tales linked through an internal frame), was finally published by inclusion in *Twice-Told Tales* in 1837, this was hardly the same as publication under separate cover.[18]

Thomas Hardy's composite text, as Hardy himself stated, was supposed to appeal to an 1890s reading public. Briefly, *A Group of Noble Dames* centers on a group of men who gather (they're members of a "Field Club") for a two-day stint of anthropological meandering in the Wessex countryside. When they find themselves rained out (or rained in), they pass the time by telling stories (10 in all) about worthy women of the area. In the stories, Hardy characteristically broaches subjects that were not typical late-Victorian fare ("questions of childbirth" and intimate details of "relations between the sexes").[19] Hardy believed, however, that the distancing provided by the book's tales-within-a-tale structure would mitigate against publishers' and readers' disapproval. He was wrong. By the time *A Group of Noble Dames* was finally published in 1891, Hardy had had to make so many emendations and revisions that he was thoroughly disgusted, and even then the public reacted with outrage.

In still another example of intention confounded, Stephen Crane considered his "Whilomville Stories" (set in the fictional town of Whilomville) to comprise a single coherent text. Various publication snafus intervened, however, with the result that the single whole text envisioned by Crane was actually published in separate parts: a story entitled "His New Mittens" in 1898, a volume entitled *The Monster and Other Stories* in 1899, and a volume entitled *Whilomville Stories* in 1901. Textual scholars, having traced the torturous history of all this, argue for the essential cohesion of a composite text composed of "His New Mittens," *The Monster,* and *Whilomville Stories,* and these scholars refer confidently to *"Tales of Whilomville"* as the single-text entity that Crane intended.[20] Yet the fact remains that Crane's composite *Tales of Whilomville* was a desire, not a reality.

Continental Composites

America may have been the most prolific producer of composite texts throughout the nineteenth century, but Europe produced several that were highly influential on early twentieth-century writers. One such text was Ivan Turgenev's *A Sportsman's*

Sketches (1852).[21] In this sequenced series of self-contained stories, Turgenev portrays life on a feudal estate in Russia through a fictional narrator who rambles through the countryside. Some stories are told by the narrator about the characters he meets, while other stories are told to the narrator by these characters. Though Sherwood Anderson claimed that he invented a new literary form in *Winesburg,* he did write admiringly of *A Sportsman's Sketches* and admit its influence. As Frank O'Connor would later say about Turgenev's work, "Nobody, at the time it was written, knew quite how great it was, or what influence it was to have in the creation of a new art form."[22]

Another influential work was Alphonse Daudet's *Letters from My Mill* (1870), a collection of character studies, travel accounts, and anecdotal tales that celebrate the enchantment of Provence.[23] The text-pieces—framed by the author's (Daudet's) retreat to this quiet place to write—are drenched in description: of vineyards and olive trees, cobbled streets and gardens, shrines and villas. Certainly in this respect, Daudet's composite text is kin to the village sketch. But in another respect, its structural aesthetic, pulling together so many pieces in a coherent whole, Daudet's *Letters* is kin to the patchwork composite. Willa Cather was so affected by the structural possibilities suggested by Daudet's *Letters,* in fact, that she would later model her 1927 composite novel *Death Comes for the Archbishop* after it.[24]

Still another influential work was Gustave Flaubert's *Three Tales* (1877), consisting of three long stories that Flaubert conceived as a single entity (during the writing of the first story) and published as a whole text.[25] The three pattern-related stories concern, respectively, a servant woman of Normandy named Félicité, St. Julian the Hospitaller, and John the Baptist during his final day of life. The stories have no frame devices or obvious connections, and critics have not failed to note "the widest possible variety" exhibited by the three stories: in setting (modern, biblical, medieval), in time span (from 24 hours to 70 years), and in structure (from a single-strand biography to a multicharacter drama).[26] Yet *Three Tales* is a novel-in-stories, its coherence effected primarily (though not entirely) through recurrent patterns, its design aesthetic one of juxtaposition and superimposition rather than linear causation. Flaubert, unlike Turgenev, has received little credit in the matter of pioneering "a new art form."

Nevertheless, *Three Tales* would prove to be highly influential on such later writers as Gertrude Stein and Hilda Doolittle (known as H. D.).

Certainly there were other composite texts produced on the Continent in addition to these three, the most notable in terms of influence probably being Alexander Pushkin's *The Tales of Ivan Belkin* and Nikolai Gogol's *Evenings Near the Village of Dikanka*, both appearing in 1831, and Mikhail Lermontov's *A Hero of Our Time*, published in 1840.[27] And we cannot overlook Selma Lagerlof's *The Story of Gösta Berling*, published in Swedish in 1894, and surely an influential text in the body of work that would earn for Lagerlof in 1909 the Nobel Prize for Literature, making her the first woman to receive that honor.[28]

This genre that had no name, then, was developing throughout the nineteenth century, taking unto itself aspects of the novel and the short story collection while occupying a path separate from and parallel to those of the other genres. It is possible, in fact, to conceive of a three-track continuum occupied by all three genres, with the "novel proper" and the "mere collection" on either side, and the composite novel in the middle. That middle was not more than a trail at first, but it had widened perceptibly by midcentury and has continued to widen ever since. In the twentieth century, it would come into its own.

Chapter 3

The Importance of Place

Setting as "Referential Field" in the Composite Novel

"The truth is," writes Eudora Welty, "fiction depends for its life on place." Welty makes this statement in her well-known essay "Place in Fiction," and then goes on: "Place in fiction is the named, identified, concrete, exact and exacting, and therefore credible, gathering spot of all that has been felt, is about to be experienced."[1] Welty's concept of place in fiction as a "gathering spot" implies much more than the geographic location of a town or region. To read her essay, in fact, is to realize that she means "place" and "setting" to be interchangeable, so that a consideration of "where" a literary work is set may also include "when" and "for how long" and "with whom," among other factors. Thus setting, which may be highly complex and multivalent, offers numerous possibilities as an element of interconnection in the composite novel. A common setting, clearly defined, provides for the reader a necessary frame of reference; it offers, to use a term coined by Wolfgang Iser, a "referential field" upon which one can register meaning and establish connections during the act of reading (or rereading) the text.[2] Certainly the idea of a "referential field" provided by setting is highly relevant to the many composite novels that spring directly from the village sketch tradition. As discussed in the previous chapter, this tradition was pioneered by the English Mary Russell Mitford's *Our Village* in 1824. Mitford's numerous successors create works, like hers, in which setting is a primary principle of cohesion. Garrison Keillor's *Lake Wobegon Days* (1985), for example, is a direct descendant of *Our Village*. Both are firmly anchored in a small town with familiar landmarks (in Keillor's these include the Statue of the Unknown Norwegian, which graces Lake Wobegon's Main Street, and the Chatterbox Cafe, where the specialty is tuna casserole). Both books also feature inhabitants whose everyday idiosyncrasies are the stuff of local gossip (in Keillor's these include Mrs. Haley, who refuses to relinquish control of the Thanatopsis Club, and 70-year-old Myrtle Krebsbach, who drinks pink daiquiris and favors pantsuits in violent colors that cause one to squint).

Because the village *is* its people, and vice versa, variations on the traditional village sketch appear endless. In Mary E. Wilkins Freeman's *The People of Our Neighborhood* (1898), for example, the first six stories focus on individuals but the last three focus on seasonal community events such as a midsummer quilting bee, an autumn apple paring, and the annual "Christmas sing." The trajectory of the narrative, then, is from the individual to the community, reflecting the forging of communal bonds necessary for survival and growth in a village setting. Here the aesthetic of the composite novel works traditionally and effectively—story by story, against the backdrop of the village itself, and with the voice of the narrator providing an additional unifying perspective, a composite picture of "our neighborhood" emerges.

Historically, of course, "the village" became "the city," and many contemporary composite novels extend the village sketch tradition to encompass a city setting. Featuring an enormous cast of characters, Frank Moorhouse's *Futility and Other Animals* (1969) is set in Sydney, Australia, an environment that shapes what Moorhouse calls its "urban tribe" (n.p.). The characters in Hubert Selby, Jr.'s *Last Exit to Brooklyn* (1964) and Alexis

DeVeaux's *Spirits in the Street* (1973) are also members of the "urban tribe," but a tribe brutalized by living in New York City's modern urban ghetto, where, writes DeVeaux's narrator in a vivid evocation of urban decay, "the rain like vinegar is the juice for the garbage" (176). And Nell Dunn's *Up the Junction* (1963) depicts the life of Britain's working class in the byways of South London.

Some composite novels extend their grounding in "place" to encompass large regions and areas: the California desert in Mary Austin's *The Land of Little Rain* (1903); the hollows of rural Kentucky in Jesse Stuart's *Save Every Lamb* (1964); the untamed Ohio Valley in Scott R. Sanders's *Wilderness Plots* (1983); the arid flatlands of Wyoming in Gretel Ehrlich's *Drinking Dry Clouds* (1991). Again, though, setting may have numerous components. *Drinking Dry Clouds,* for example, is set in 1940s Wyoming, during and after World War II. The events of this wartime and postwar period profoundly affect Ehrlich's characters, rendering the book both time- and place-dependent.

Similarly set during World War II, James A. Michener's *Tales of the South Pacific* (1947) is another composite novel in which setting is many-faceted. As the book begins, Michener's South Pacific archipelago inhabits a referential field defined specifically as the early days of America's active involvement in the war. When the narrator, a young naval officer, begins telling the first of 19 tales, he mentions place names, such as Coral Sea and Guadalcanal, that connote the war itself. Like Gettysburg and Hiroshima, these place names evoke through synecdoche not just any war but a specific war, thereby creating an immediate field of reference. Even so, Michener's first six tales seem very loosely linked. But in the seventh tale, the narrator uncharacteristically addresses the reader, saying that D-Day in the Pacific—called "Operation Alligator"—is about to begin and that, henceforth, all lives will be affected by it. At this point the referential field is enhanced, made denser by the added element of a massive military operation. And from this point on, coherence builds, with place, time, and circumstance creating a vast interconnective framework.

Thornton Wilder's *The Bridge of San Luis Rey* (1927) construes setting in still another way, as a momentary confluence of time and place. Wilder realistically portrays the book's central event as occurring high in the mountains of Peru in 1714, when a much-traveled suspension bridge suddenly breaks loose, dropping five travelers who happen to be crossing the bridge at that particular moment into the rocky gorge below. A Franciscan monk named Brother Juniper witnesses the disaster, wonders why these particular victims were chosen by God, and decides to gather their stories into a book, which Wilder frames within a contemporary narrative. Wilder's *Bridge of San Luis Rey*, then, is a book-within-a-book. In the first of five titled stories, a contemporary narrator describes the bridge disaster and Brother Juniper's decision to investigate the victims' lives. The middle three stories are really Brother Juniper's "book," in which are presented the results of six years of investigation. And in the last story the contemporary narrator rounds out the story of Brother Juniper (the gentle monk and his book were burned for heresy) while commenting on life-connections among the victims. The "setting" here begins with a single point in time, defined by the snapping apart of the bridge: "A twanging noise filled the air, as when the string of some musical instrument snaps in a disused room, and [then Brother Juniper] saw the bridge divide and fling five gesticulating ants into the valley below" (6). The "twanging noise"— like the "plop" of a stone as it drops into a pool of water—is the inception and center of a referential field that moves outward in concentric circles, encircling centuries and lapping countless lives.

Judging from all these variations, the "village sketch" has come a long way since nineteenth-century writers grounded it in verisimilitude. One wonders, in fact, just how Miss Mitford would react if she were to encounter the far-out "villages" that center such twentieth-century composite novels as Henry Miller's *Black Spring*, Ray Bradbury's *The Martian Chronicles*, and Margaret Gibson's *The Butterfly Ward*. Each of these books, like Mitford's, uses setting as a primary element of interconnection, yet each imaginatively construes a bipolar "village."

Miller's *Black Spring* (1936) has provoked among critics a vast array of descriptive terms, many of them relating to visual art in such modes as cubism, surrealism, and dadaism. What these critics mean is that Miller's book appears fragmented, unrealistic, perhaps frenzied and hallucinatory, certainly lacking in narrative coherence. Indeed, *Black Spring*'s 10 independently titled sections are, as described by George Wickes, "a series of monologues, meditations, reminiscences, dreams, and visions, shifting back and forth from [Miller's] Paris surroundings to his early years in Brooklyn and New York."[3] In light of Wickes's description, which is accurate as well as succinct, it is not surprising that critics who discuss *Black Spring* generally avoid calling it anything. Though it is occasionally referred to as a "novel," most critics (including Wickes) sidestep the issue of genre and simply call it a "work" or a "book."[4]

Yet *Black Spring* does reflect a whole-text aesthetic. It is, in essence, a descendant of the village sketch composite, but one that features a bicontinental "village" (the open streets of Paris and New York) and a developing narrator-protagonist who encounters various inhabitants as he goes on an extended ramble (some reminiscences extend back 30-odd years). Further, Miller in *Black Spring* creates a referential field in which "ambience" is an inextricable aspect of "place." The fourteenth ward in Brooklyn is shadowed by "the grim soot-covered walls and chimneys of the tin factory" and "the ironworks where the red furnace glowed" (5). Grit, dirt, smoke, fog, rain—these define the streets of his youth, as does an aura of anti-intellectualism. But the byways of Paris and its environs are characterized by dappled light in the afternoons, gauzy light on cobblestones at night. And always the ambience of France provokes "the language prodigal and exuberant, the imagination rampant" (Wickes 123).

Mitford would likely not wax enthusiastic about *Black Spring*, which features such idiosyncratic elements as Miller's lyrical appreciation of public urinals in Paris. But she might be pleased by what "our village" has become in Ray Bradbury's *The Martian Chronicles* (1950). Bradbury's Mars, a far cry from the warlike red star of hard science fiction, is a fairyland where books sing like harps, golden fruit grows on crystal trees, and rain "mizzles" softly down, "a special elixir, tasting of spells and stars and air" (76). But Earth, too, is featured in *The Martian Chronicles*, which is really a story of two worlds, of Earth-culture's overwhelming impact on Mars-culture. Bradbury's 28 titled sections tell, chronologically, the story of a 30-year encounter during which Earth rockets bring guns, chicken pox (fatal to Martians), shantytowns, Catholic priests, and a hot dog stand to the crystal planet. This book, says one reviewer, "is not a novel but rather a series of what James Joyce called epiphanies—swift, incisive glimpses of day-to-day events, bathed in revelation."[5] Indeed, Bradbury's "revelatory" glimpses of a barbarian culture (Earth) usurping an advanced culture (Mars) are effective because the referential field created through setting (the planet Mars) is clearly meant to be fantastic. That is, since readers do not bring to the text any expectations of realism, their logical minds are free to experience "epiphanies" about the only-too-real destructiveness of twentieth-century Earth-culture.

The concept of setting as referential field gets another twist in Margaret Gibson's *The Butterfly Ward* (1976). Gibson is Canadian, and *Butterfly Ward*'s six stories appear to be set in Toronto. Certainly the physical "place" is Toronto. But the referential field in this composite novel includes, as described succinctly by one critic, "a psychic region"—"the human mind and, more specifically, the realm of the schizophrenic whose own unreality provides a kind of landscape."[6] To the schizophrenic, this inner landscape is preferable to the outside world. Thus one character says, "I crouch in the mists of my nebula where it is beautiful and everything is calm" (129). One immutable quality of this composite novel's "landscape" is its bipolarity; it is always oppositional. Through constant counterpoint, Gibson uses one pole of the referential field to question the other, opposing "sane" and "insane," "normal" and "not normal." In one story, an artist "needs" his wife's psychosis as material for his art. In another, a female schizophrenic and a gay female impersonator try to make it as a couple in the "straight" world. And in the last of the six stories, the bipolar referential field is rendered denser through metaphor. Here the "butterfly ward" is a neurological ward, part of a huge Toronto hospital designed with "new wings that gleam" (119). Inside this wing are "butterflies" (patients whose voices and hands flutter helplessly) and "pinners" (the staff with their needles and restraints). Finally the protagonist Kira undergoes a shockingly brutal medical procedure during which she is "pinned with needles like a butterfly to a board" (120), a procedure whose pain she consciously chooses to escape by going inside her head—where sanity is restored. In this unusual composite novel the "butterfly ward" is both place and metaphor, neither one more real than the other.

Thus *Black Spring, The Martian Chronicles,* and *The Butterfly Ward* offer provocative variations on "the village" and the village sketch tradition, each composite novel creating a bipolar referential field and using that field to create links among its text-pieces. Truly, then, "the village" exists in many literary manifestations. Some of these are not very different from traditional village sketch communities—places that occupy a specific geographic space and reflect a common ethos or culture. Other places are less easily defined, less concretely dependent upon physical space and more abstractly dependent upon a historical moment or period. Yet all these "villages" have one thing in common: through the referential fields that they project, the villages provide significant elements of interconnection within the composite novels that they shape. Consider now this primary element of interconnection—setting as referential field—in three well-known composite novels: Sarah Orne Jewett's *The Country of the Pointed Firs,* James Joyce's *Dubliners,* and Gloria Naylor's *The Women of Brewster Place.*

The Country of the Pointed Firs: A Writer's Site

Perhaps the quintessential example of a composite novel organized in the village sketch tradition is Sarah Orne Jewett's turn-of-the-century *The Country of the Pointed Firs* (1896).[7] The importance of place is signaled not only by the title but also by the first sentence: "There was something about the coast town of Dunnet which made it seem more attractive than other maritime villages of eastern Maine" (1). Lovingly, Jewett proceeds to describe the rocky shore, the dark woods, the steep-gabled houses of the town, and the charms of the nearby islands. As she introduces the main characters of the book, the reader begins to see how their lives are molded by their surroundings. Although the individual stories are also interrelated by the single narrator and by the repetition of characters and images, it is setting that dominates the structure throughout.

As we mentioned in chapter 1, critics have had difficulty all along in knowing what to call such books as these. Thus one can sympathize with F. O. Matthiessen's tone of uncertainty when he said in 1929 that *Pointed Firs* is a book of "loosely connected sketches" held together by "the unity of [Jewett's] vision."

Matthiessen also declared that the book is "not a novel," presenting an interesting contrast to Barbara H. Solomon, who, 50 years later, in 1979, wrote that "the book certainly is a novel."[8] Solomon goes on to maintain that *Pointed Firs'* novelistic coherence is achieved primarily through "a collective sense of place" (6). Indeed it is.

A reader's first "visit" to *The Country of the Pointed Firs* reveals a frame for the individual stories or sketches. In this frame (the first two "chapters" and the final two), a summer visitor arrives at the seacoast area called Dunnet's Landing in Maine. The summer visitor, the narrator, is seeking quiet and inspiration for her writing. Her hostess and guide (and this includes "guide" in the spiritual sense) is Almira Todd, an herbal healer and garrulous talker—one of the local eccentrics. The two introductory stories set all this up, and the final two stories (which chronicle the narrator's departure) complete the frame structure. Within this frame, Jewett places a series of four self-contained episodes— each involving a visit—which develop a thematic counterpoint between isolation and community.

In the first of these episodes (encompassing five stories), the narrator sits, trying to write, in the village schoolhouse, which is empty during the summer. In the schoolroom she seeks the quiet she has not found at Mrs. Todd's, where people are purchasing herbs and trading news at all hours. However, inspiration still eludes her. Furthermore, she feels isolated and alone, especially when she sees most of the villagers walking together in a funeral procession. Then she receives a visit from the elderly Captain Littlepage, a retired sea captain and avid admirer of the poetry of John Milton. The captain tells a strange story of a distant northern spot of land called Gaffett's Island, "a kind of waiting-place between this world an' the next," an island inhabited by "human-shaped creatures of fog and cobweb" (65–67). The captain's face as he tells this story is a study in "loneliness and misapprehension," and this, combined with the narrator's own sense of isolation, renders the first episode a bleak and haunting one that contrasts sharply with the warm sense of community in the second episode.

The next four stories, comprising the second episode, feature a very different setting: idyllic Green Island, the home of Mrs. Todd's mother and brother (86-year-old Mrs. Blackett and her son William). The time spent here, in addition to creating a peaceful "center" for the book, helps the narrator see the importance of the magic circle of humanity. She also begins to realize the complexity of Mrs. Todd, who tells the story of an unfulfilled youthful love. Mrs. Todd has transcended this sorrow by marrying another man and living a full and productive life, but glimpsing her friend's sad memories makes the narrator realize that loneliness and community exist side by side on Green Island, as elsewhere.

This theme of disappointment in love extends into the next series of four stories, episode three, and again the primary setting is an island. Shell-Heap Island, now deserted, had been the home of a recluse named Joanna who suffered an unhappy love affair, turned her back on society, and lived alone on this barren island until her death. The writer-narrator hears stories about Joanna and sails near her island. Finally she visits Shell-Heap Island herself. "In each of us," she realizes, "there is a place remote and islanded." Joanna's self-imposed hermitage was indeed highly dramatic, a visible symbol of emotional abandonment. Yet the narrator realizes, too, that "we are each the uncompanioned hermit and recluse" (111).

In the last four-story episode, the narrator accompanies Mrs. Todd and Mrs. Blackett to the Bowden family reunion. She becomes "an adopted Bowden" and feels at last, if only temporarily, part of a community. Mentions are made, however, of Captain Littlepage, Joanna, and others who remain isolated within the confines of their lives. Though these "mentions" of others help to summarize the summer's activities in the narrator's mind, they also establish the inescapable enislement of human existence.

The Bowden reunion has taken place some distance inland. In contrast, the closing frame of the book is set by the sea. The narrator's last visit—a brief one—is to a lonely, widowed fisherman who lives "along shore," where his house faces the decaying wharves and the ever-changing sea. In this penultimate story/chapter (the twentieth), Elijah Tilley's solitary life brings a reminder of Captain Littlepage and Joanna. Tilley, in effect, provides a transition for the narrator's movement from her communal involvement with the Bowdens to her islanded existence in the city.

While the entire book is grounded in the specific locale of Dunnet's Landing, then, the frame and four main episodes, in sequence, develop through place-as-metaphor a thematic counterpoint. From the loneliness of Captain Littlepage's Gaffett Island to the warmth of Green Island; again to loneliness at Shell-Heap Island and from there to warmth at the Bowden family gathering inland; again, finally, to the lonely shore—throughout her summer journey, the narrator learns that isolation and community are but opposite sides of the same coin. The "gayety and determined floweriness" (47) of the village, she realizes, is balanced by its barren farther shores, both venues reflecting the complex human beings who live there. In short, during her summer at Dunnet's Landing the narrator has come to see its people as human analogues of the pointed firs, possessing the will to flourish with the incoming tide and the strength to stand tall at its ebb. "There's sometimes a good hearty tree growin' right out of the bare rock," says Mrs. Todd, confirming through metaphor that life thereabouts is not easy. But then she continues: "Every such tree has got its own livin' spring; there's folks made to match 'em" (120). The land, the people, the sturdy trees that entitle Jewett's composite novel—all are part of the setting that provides its textual bedrock.

Dubliners: Alone in the City

Although it was first published in 1914, James Joyce had conceived of and planned *Dubliners* as a coherent whole by 1905, and by 1907 he had completed all 15 stories and arranged them in sequence.[9] Joyce did make some concessions to editorial intervention throughout this long prepublication process, but he firmly refused to omit any story or to change the sequence that he had planned. Fifteen stories, then, are the component parts of *Dubliners*, and Joyce planned them in four sequential groupings to reflect childhood (1–3), adolescence (4–7), maturity (8–11), and public life (12–15). Protagonists age gradually throughout the book, so that a Christmas dinner and dance in the last story, "The Dead," is peopled almost entirely by characters who are well past midlife. In addition, the stories' protagonists gradually become more mature, progressing from naïveté in the early stories to some degree of self-awareness in the later ones.

The interconnective effect of the factors just mentioned—protagonists who age and mature—is cumulative. The importance of setting also builds and develops, though it is also immediately evident. Thus the reality of life in Dublin is made clear on the first page of the first story, when the boy-narrator says, "I said softly to myself the word *paralysis*" (9). In this story, as in all the others, Dublin's reality is paralytic: enclosed, constricting, suffocating. Detail by detail, Joyce depicts a city of buildings that are always dark, never warm enough. The ubiquitous ashpits emit a nasty odor (especially when the weather is rainy or damp) that Dublin's residents seem to take for granted. Curtains and windowsills are always dusty. Dublin, in fact, is a place of sunlight only for its youngest inhabitants, like the narrators of the first three stories, who have not yet realized that their lives hold no hope. For all others, Dublin is a place of entrapment, an environment that renders its people weak, enervated, unable to escape. As a field of reference, then, setting is not only place but also the *effect* of place.

Indeed, the setting of *Dubliners*—as a referential field—is dense with subtleties. The aura of paralysis, for example, affects everyone. A young boy in the second story, "An Encounter," knows subliminally that the strange man who starts a conversation with him is somehow perverted. The boy wants to escape from the conversation, but nevertheless sits there, captivated. In "Eveline," the fourth story, the twenty-year-old protagonist (Eveline) has perhaps the best chance of anyone in the book to escape. Her thoughts, as she readies herself to meet her lover, Frank, reveal aspects of a life that can only get worse if she stays in Dublin—a hateful job that she is in danger of losing; a stingy, alcoholic father always teetering on the brink of violence toward her; a dingy old house that is becoming even more run-down. Yet as she stands gripping the iron railing that separates her from the steamboat that would carry her, with Frank, to a new life, Eveline is paralyzed by the thought that she should "keep the family home together." "Passive, like a helpless animal" (41), she watches Frank board the ship alone. Such examples go on and on. There is something in this place, Joyce implies, that poisons the will.

There is, to be sure, a poison here, very subtle and very slow, inherent in the traditions and institutions that Dubliners take for granted and revere. To illustrate, consider in detail the tangled ironies and barbed innuendos that lurk within "The Sisters," the first story in the book and arguably the least complex. The central event of this story is the death of an old priest, Father Flynn. The naive first-person narrator, a very young boy, simply reports what he hears and sees and thinks as a result of the old priest's dying. Father Flynn had been his friend, the boy often having taken snuff to him at the house where the priest lived with his two sisters. But the adults talk about Father Flynn's unfortunate involvement years earlier in a "peculiar case"—a situation concerning a broken chalice and an unnamed boy—and how it affected the priest's nerves. Old Cotter, a friend of the narrator's family, is overheard saying "No, I wouldn't say he was exactly . . . but there was something queer . . . there was something uncanny about him" (ellipsis in original), and Cotter then suggests that boys should steer clear of "a man like that." The young narrator, in thinking about his friend, understands fleetingly that the priest "desired to confess something," and the narrator himself feels a curious "sensation of freedom" resulting from Father Flynn's death. Even the priest's two devoted sisters realize that he was a "disappointed man" whose life was "crossed." The closer one examines the story, the more suggestive it becomes.

Whatever truth is at the root of these innuendos, it is clear that this was a failed priest. As an elderly man, which is how the young narrator knew him, he was shabby and decrepit in "ancient priestly garments" that had a "green faded look" because of the showers of snuff dispersed by his trembling hands. His nostrils were stained black from the snuff and he had "big discoloured teeth." Often when the boy would go to visit, he would find the priest muffled in an old coat, before a cold grate, in a "stupefied doze." Nevertheless, the deceased's two sisters (one of them, significantly, a deaf-mute) devoted their lives to their failed-priest brother, the three of them living together in a house that is cold, clammy, and dark. Thus these people's lives are revealed in pathetic detail. They lived without joy, the priest never questioning the institutional church and the sisters never questioning their subservience to him.

From this beginning, though there are no obvious interconnective devices such as recurring characters and cross-references, Joyce creates in fifteen stories an integrated composite picture of

Not 50

what passes for life in Dublin. The stories, for example, move progressively from midyear ("The Sisters") to end-of-year ("The Dead"), from light to less light, from summer to snow. Throughout the stories there is the ubiquitous "boose," "stout," "bitters," or simply "drink"—until one can almost see an alcoholic haze hovering over the city. Narrative point of view in the individual stories becomes more and more complex, moving from simple first-person narration to limited omniscience to omniscience. Repeated images and motifs accumulate texture and develop resonance. The interconnections go on and on. Critics have elaborated upon all this in such volume and detail that it is impossible even to summarize the criticism, the point here being simply that the aesthetic, the "method" of the composite novel is superbly illustrated in *Dubliners*. And always, setting is of paramount importance.

Even the brief mentions of other places are significant because they are linked overtly to thoughts of escape. The young boys in "An Encounter," for example, played "Wild West" games because "they opened doors of escape" (20). In "Araby," the bazaar that is redolent of faraway places and delights contrasts sharply with Dublin's drab everydayness. In "Eveline," the protagonist compares the possibility of life in Buenos Aires with her suffocating life at home; she feels "a sudden impulse of terror. Escape! She must escape!" (40) Jimmy Doyle in "After the Race," playing cards on an American's yacht, thinks "this was seeing life, at least" (47), and Little Chandler in "A Little Cloud" realizes unequivocally, "There was no doubt about it: if you wanted to succeed you had to go away. You could do nothing in Dublin" (73). And in "The Dead," after Gretta Conroy has revealed to her husband Gabriel that she has always mourned for an earlier love, Gabriel thinks, "Better [to] pass boldly into that other world, in the full glory of some passion, than fade and wither dismally with age" (241). Gabriel realizes, in other words, that the only escape open to him is death.

Dublin, then, provides a field of reference that includes attitudes and beliefs, as well as history and tradition. Certainly there are many other interconnective elements in *Dubliners* in addition to setting. Critics have argued persuasively, for example, that "the archetypal Dubliner"—a collective protagonist—is the book's focal point and center.[10] Others argue that *Dubliners* is rendered a coherent whole text through pattern, both external (the whole text is patterned after the *Odyssey* or the *Inferno*) and internal (individual stories are built on similar plot-patterns).[11] Such interpretations indicate once again the complexity of this literary work, with its multitude of interconnective elements. However one might choose to construe *Dubliners'* primary principle(s) of development, though, the work is clearly grounded in the alcoholic ennui of turn-of-the-century Dublin, the city that embodied for James Joyce the failed glory of Ireland. Robert Scholes and A. Walton Litz comment that "the real hero of the stories is not an individual but the city itself, a city whose geography and history and inhabitants are all part of a coherent vision."[12] Indeed, the vision is coherent, and the "city/hero" is tragic.

The Women of Brewster Place: Up against the Wall, Mother

Joyce's city of despair is quite different from Jewett's village of hope. Many years later, Gloria Naylor combines aspects of both in *The Women of Brewster Place* (1983), a composite novel that celebrates the forging of communal bonds in defiance of walled-off aspirations.

In a lyrical prelude and postlude entitled "Dawn" and "Dusk," Naylor tells the life story of Brewster Place and in so doing anthropomorphizes it. "Brewster Place" (actually the name of a short street as well as a four-building housing project) was conceived illegitimately, says Naylor, in a deal between two local politicians, one of whom baptized his bastard progeny with a bottle of champagne two years later. In the optimism of its youthful years, when it appeared that Brewster Place would become "part of the main artery of the town," it was peopled by the Irish. Then the inevitable disappointments of life set in, and by the time Brewster Place reached middle age, it had lost some of its luster. The Irish left. They were replaced by "Mediterraneans" who had no political connections or influence, and soon the street that runs through the project was closed at one end by a two-story brick wall, creating a dead end. By now old age was approaching, and as the Mediterraneans fled they were replaced by those "Afric" sons and daughters who "came because they had no choice" (4). Finally, decrepit and condemned, the stories of its last children told, Brewster Place quietly awaits its end.

Naylor is quite direct as to the importance of "place" in this work. Yet once again, place-as-setting involves much more than location, for place and people reflect and define each other. The stories Naylor tells focus primarily on seven women. Mattie Michael and Etta Mae Johnson have come as a last resort to Brewster Place, Mattie's house and savings having been lost by a worthless son and Etta Mae's romantic hopes for a good life dashed in a series of humiliating sexual trysts with philandering men. Arriving at Brewster in the dead of winter, Mattie first sees its forbidding dead-end wall while shadowed by a moving van that "creeps" with her meager belongings like "a huge green slug" (7). Etta Mae, also gazing upon arrival at the walled-up street, sees it "crouched there in the thin predawn light like a pulsating mouth awaiting her" (73). Two other women, Ciel Turner and Cora Lee, have had no chance to be anywhere better than Brewster. Ciel, whose husband deserted her without even attending the funeral of their two-year-old daughter, reflects in her despair "the arthritic cold" that seeps from "the worn grey bricks" of Brewster (96). Cora Lee, a first-time mother at 15, now lives with her seven children in an apartment filled with "broken furniture" and "piles of litter" (121). Another two women, a lesbian couple known as Tee and Lorraine, have fled to Brewster Place to escape homophobia. But in Brewster they find no sympathy, only a "yellow mist" of vicious gossip (161), and their hopes die irrevocably in "leaden darkness" when Lorraine is brutally gang-raped and beaten in the trash-strewn alley that lies between the last building and the brick wall. Tragically, even Brewster's young toughs, described by Naylor as "dwarfed warrior-kings" whose masculinity is threatened by the "dyke" Lorraine, are defined by the space they inhabit: "They only had that three-hundred-foot alley to serve them as stateroom, armored tank, and executioner's chamber. So Lorraine found herself, on her knees, surrounded by the most dangerous species in existence—human males with an erection to validate in a world that was only six feet wide" (169–70).

Thus are Mattie and Etta Mae, Ciel and Cora Lee, Tee and Lorraine, and a host of subsidiary characters as blocked as the dead-end street on which they live. In the words of one critic,

"No matter how diverse the women in age, talents, and experience, the wall seals them in behind barriers of racism and sexism, defines the limits of their aspirations, and shields the rest of the city from their influence."[13] Only Kiswana Browne, Naylor's seventh woman, can see beyond Brewster's wall. The product of a middle-class upbringing in nearby Linden Hills (where her name was "Melanie"), Kiswana rejects "educated blacks" who have "a terminal case of middle-class amnesia" (84–85) and chooses to live in Brewster so that she can be instrumental in civic improvement efforts. In epitomizing the hope of this place, where "practically every apartment contained a family, a Bible, and a dream" (77), Kiswana provides a counterbalance to the otherwise ubiquitous despair. And again, her vision of hope is directly place-related because she has the wherewithal to "place" herself in either world: Brewster Place or Linden Hills, whose trees she can actually "see," beyond the wall, from her dingy sixth-floor apartment.

Ultimately, hope defeats despair, for the women of Brewster Place, unlike Joyce's paralytic Dubliners, are survivors. As Barbara Christian explains, "Naylor establishes Brewster Place as a community in spite of its history of transients," a community "held together primarily by women."[14] Indeed, Naylor's women will outlive Brewster Place, even if they must go to another place like it, with roaches and rats, cracked windows and leaky pipes, street gangs and break-ins. Tragedy and pain will move with them, taking up residence again as next-door neighbors. Yet through bonds of community, through a sense of shared "herstory," as Christian puts it, they will manage to survive. And they have always managed to laugh. When Etta Mae steals a married lover's car, for example, she also steals his red monogrammed shorts so that she can retaliate if he reports the theft to the sheriff—his father-in-law. And when Cora Lee wonders how to stop having children, Mattie answers, "Same way you started, child—only in reverse" (123). Most of all, these women will celebrate life, as they do in the last story, entitled "The Block Party." It has been raining for a week since the attack on Lorraine, the waters "snaking" into "clogged gutters under sulfurous street lights like a thick dark liquid" (175). But on the day of the party, Brewster Place is "bathed in a deluge of sunlight" (188) that glints on balloons and banners. Mattie has dreamed about this party, dreamed that it will end with the women finally venting their frustration and anger by tearing down the wall, brick by brick. Clearly that will not happen, yet the party begins while storm clouds loom. Thus the symbolic "in your face" partying by the inhabitants of Brewster defies the forces that would quash them, and Naylor's "tapestry of nurturing women," again in Christian's words, have woven their kinship in the face of adversity (363).

An early reviewer of *The Women of Brewster Place* wrote that the book's protagonist is the street itself, implying that Brewster Place overpowers the women. But another reviewer emphasized the women's ability to transcend Brewster Place so that, for them, "the end of the line is not the end of life."[15] Yes, the street will die. But the "daughters of Brewster," in Naylor's final words, will "never disappear" (192), and their heroic dignity is established precisely because their drama of survival is played in stark relief against the backdrop of an inner-city dead-end street.

Place in such fiction as this, as Eudora Welty explained so eloquently, is indeed the "gathering spot of all that has been felt, is about to be experienced." Dunnet's Landing, Dublin, and Brewster Place are significant "gathering spots" in twentieth-century literature, reflecting highly disparate regions, cultures, and traditions. In much the same way, place acts as a "gathering factor" in many composite novels, providing an essential field of reference for complex interconnections.

Chapter 4

Rites of Passage

The Protagonist as Focus in the Composite Novel

Yes, we had a great-uncle who was a fish, on my paternal grandmother's side, to be precise." Thus speaks a most unusual protagonist, the protean character named Qfwfq in Italo Calvino's *Cosmicomics* (1965). Calvino's composite novel is composed of 12 stories that encompass a considerable course of events: the evolution of the universe. Tying all these stories together is Qfwfq, who talks in a chatty, comic-strip voice throughout. Qfwfq is, in fact, a protean personifier. In one story he speaks as a mollusk, in another a dinosaur, and in the story entitled "The Aquatic Uncle" (the seventh) he's an amphibian with the "great uncle who was a fish." The evolution of earth life-forms, of course, is but one short instant in the history of the universe. Qfwfq, though, has been present since "the moment when all the universe's matter was concentrated in a single point," when he and others were "packed in there like sardines" (43), and he has tales to tell about his experiences during this much longer evolutionary period. Thus he personifies in other stories such abstract concepts as a subatomic particle, the gravitational field between the earth and the moon, and a mathematical formula (the theory of relativity). Clearly, Qfwfq is a prime contender for the title of "most unusual protagonist" in all literature.

Yet *Cosmicomics* is not at all unusual in structure—not unusual, that is, as long as one thinks in terms of the composite novel, whose definition *Cosmicomics* fits as if it were tailor-made. The book's 12 component texts have individual titles and are all clearly "short stories," ranging in length from 5 to 15 pages (there are no untitled fragments or frame-pieces here). The stories are clearly autonomous (two of them were published previously in *Playboy*), each providing referential-field information, a story line, and a sense of closure. It appears, too, that most of the stories (at least the first six or seven) could be rearranged without violating any particular sequence. Thus many early reviewers of both the Italian edition (1965) and the English translation (1968) showed no hesitation in calling *Cosmicomics* just "stories."[1]

But when the stories are read sequentially, the cumulative effect is that of an integrated whole text. The stories, for example, are identically structured, each beginning with a short italicized passage about some aspect of galactic/geologic/biologic evolution, to which Qfwfq immediately replies before launching into his own version of what it was like to be there "in person." These identical story shapes unfurl one after the other like the uniform panels of a single extended comic strip (the book isn't called *Cosmicomics* for nothing). By the time a reader has completed the first two or three stories, the referential field (all space, all time, all matter) is apparent and ready to be augmented with further reading. Also quickly apparent to a reader is the fact that the evolution of the cosmos is a metaphor for the evolution of human consciousness and the evolution of each individual through one life span. The final story recapitulates all this, revealing "the essential unity of all life in the universe, from the 'first' atom and the primeval shellfish."[2]

The most important connective factor, however, is Qfwfq—whose voice personalizes the driest hypothesis. Describing the Milky Way, he explains that it "turned like an omelet in its heated pan, itself both frying pan and golden egg" (38). While playing a game with his friend Pfwfp, Qfwfq grabs the tail of a galaxy and exclaims gleefully, "[My galaxy] was the newest, the envy of the whole firmament, blazing as it was with young hydrogen and the youngest carbon and newborn beryllium. The old galaxies fled us, filled with jealousy, and we, prancing and haughty, avoided them, so antiquated and ponderous to look at" (67). Most important, Qfwfq grows. He acquires wisdom sporadically, in flashes of insight reminiscent of Joyce's "epiphanies."

The story entitled "Without Colors," for example, is set on Earth while it is evolving from a lifeless gray ball (with a molten core) into a living planet with oceans, vegetation, and atmosphere. Qfwfq in this story is a long-lived consciousness-creature who welcomes change: "I was seeking a new world beyond the pallid patina that imprisoned everything" (54); "I was in a fury to wrest unknown vibrations from things" (55). But Qfwfq is head-over-heels in love with Ayl, who does not want what he wants: "She wanted to reduce everything to the colorless beyond of their ultimate substance" (55); "Ayl was a happy inhabitant of the silence that reigns where all vibration is excluded" (54). Qfwfq, then, embraces color and sound; Ayl flees from them. This love story runs its course and the mismatched couple part. But as they do, Qfwfq realizes that "Ayl's idea of beauty" is too diametrically opposed to his own, and he experiences the "grief and fear" that accompany self-knowledge (60).

Qfwfq, then, is truly the "prototypical" composite-novel protagonist: he is the narrator and central figure in each story, and he develops throughout the book so that the "voice" one hears at the end is much fuller and wiser than it was in the beginning. Obviously the case can be made here for whole-text coherence, and this argument is buttressed by those critics and reviewers who, without any apparent agonies over what to call it, refer to *Cosmicomics* as a novel.[3]

Italo Calvino's literary fantasies are unique, as is the protean protagonist Qfwfq. But many composite novels feature, like *Cosmicomics,* a narrator-protagonist as the focus and significant element of interconnection. One thinks, for example, of Sandra Cisneros's *The House on Mango Street* (1989), whose 44 short, individually titled stories are told by and center upon Esperanza Cordero, a young girl growing up in a poor Mexican-American neighborhood in Chicago. Cisneros's multistoried *House on*

Mango Street, described by a reviewer as "a series of vignettes," is reminiscent of Mark Saltzman's *Iron and Silk* (1986), composed of 30 titled stories and described by a reviewer as "a series of episodes."[4] The two books are similar, also, in their clear focus on a developing narrator-protagonist. Saltzman's "Teacher Mark" is a recent Yale graduate who describes his experiences while spending two years teaching English and learning martial arts (wushu) in Hunan, China. By the time of the last story and Mark's impending departure for America, it is clear that he has himself learned many lessons, both in and out of the classroom. Saltzman's composite novel, like Cisneros's, is comprised of many short texts, yet each book achieves whole-text coherence through the voice of its central character.

Jamaica Kincaid's *Annie John* (1985) similarly features a narrator-protagonist (first name "Annie," surname "John") who describes in eight stories her growing-up years on the Caribbean island of Antigua. One intriguing aspect of this protagonist is her love-hate relationship with her mother, whose name is also "Annie John." The two women are always in conflict, to a greater or lesser degree, from Annie's earliest grade-school days through the time of her high-school graduation. When in the last story the 17-year-old Annie boards a ship for England, she believes that she is finally escaping. But then her mother says, "It doesn't matter what you do or where you go, I'll always be your mother and this will always be your home" (147). Annie realizes then that she will take part of her mother with her, and that she must leave part of herself behind. This protagonist named Annie John, in other words, achieves self-awareness by accepting the presence of another "Annie John" within herself.

Numerous other composite novels build whole-text coherence through a narrator-protagonist. In Beverly Coyle's *The Kneeling Bus* (1990), for example, a Methodist minister's daughter named Carrie tells her story of growing up in Florida during the 1950s, when "maypoles, nakedness, [and] graven images" (22) struck fear into the hearts of grandmothers and Baptists. David Huddle's *Only the Little Bone* (1986) features the voice of Reed Bryant as he, growing into adulthood in Virginia, negotiates the treacherous gender wars that characterize a southern family and community. Alice Munro's *Lives of Girls and Women* (1971) focuses on Del Jordan, a young Canadian woman who tells her own story as she grapples with her budding sexuality and, retrospectively in the last story, her calling as an artist. In Tomas Rivera's . . . *And the Earth Did Not Part* (1971), an unnamed boy narrator (who may also be the book's unnamed adult central character) describes life as a migrant farmworker in Texas. Laurie Lee's *Cider with Rosie* (1959) describes nostalgically but realistically in the voice of its narrator-protagonist what it was like to grow up in a rural English village (unplastered stone walls, no plumbing, no electricity) in the Cotswolds during the post–World War I era. Aram Garoghlanian, the narrator of William Saroyan's *My Name Is Aram* (1940), describes his life in an eccentric Armenian family in California in the early years of this century. And Michael Gold's *Jews without Money* (1930) features a narrator-protagonist who grows from a "little Yid" (7), living in poverty at the turn of the century in New York's infamous Bowery district, into an angry young man. All these works presented problems of classification to reviewers, some of whom called the books collections while others called them novels. However, when viewed as a group, retrospectively and in the context of the composite novel genre, these books illustrate the unifying potential of a narrator-protagonist.

The protagonist certainly need not be the narrator, though, as is the case in Willa Cather's early composite novel *My Ántonia* (1918). This work features a narrator (Jim Burden) and a central figure (Ántonia Shimerda), with Burden telling both everything he remembers about Ántonia from earlier years, when they were young together, *and* everything he has heard about her since then. Obviously this Jim-Ántonia arrangement brings complexity to the narrative—so much complexity, in fact, that critics never have been able to agree as to the identity of the protagonist in *My Ántonia*. Is Ántonia the protagonist, or Jim? Are they co-protagonists? Or are they "double protagonists" who lead "parallel lives"?[5] Fueling this ongoing discussion is *My Ántonia*'s unusual structure (a frame-introduction, followed by five titled "books" with numbered sections) and the fact that "this collection of episodes and vignettes—many of which have nothing to do with Antonia herself—somehow results in a book of 'unified emotional impact.'"[6] Indeed, *My Ántonia is* "unified." Its complexity confirms the possibilities inherent in the composite novel's aesthetic, and it presages a work that—published just one year subsequently—would come to be known as the quintessential example of this literary form that we call the composite novel.

Winesburg, Ohio: The Resisting Writer

Without much question, *Winesburg, Ohio* (1919) is the book that most people will think of when they hear the term *short story cycle* or read our definition of the composite novel. There are several reasons for this. In the first place, *Winesburg* is a well-known work often studied in schools, and it sticks in one's mind because it is clearly not a typical novel. When one of the stories—most often "Hands," "Mother," or "The Teacher"—is reprinted in an anthology, an introduction to the individual story usually describes *Winesburg* as a book of stories that is unified in several ways. Sherwood Anderson himself asserted that he saw his text as a unified whole. In his *Memoirs* he wrote, "The stories belonged together. I felt that, taken together, they made something like a novel, a complete story." But then Anderson went further: "In *Winesburg* I had made my own form. There were individual tales but all about lives in some way connected."[7]

This "Winesburg form" that Anderson apparently thought he had invented was not so different from what Edgar Lee Masters had done with poems in *Spoon River Anthology* (1915) and Gertrude Stein had done with stories in *Three Lives* (1909), both of which, according to Malcolm Cowley, Anderson read shortly before writing *Winesburg*.[8] But Anderson's book became much better known than those of Masters, Stein, or any of the nineteenth-century writers discussed in chapter 2. Joyce's *Dubliners*, of course, also preceded *Winesburg* by several years, but Anderson did not read Joyce's book until some time after completing his own. In short, Anderson thought he had indeed invented a new form, and many readers (and critics) have taken his word for it.

In many ways *Winesburg, Ohio* resembles *Dubliners*, which we discussed in chapter 3 as having the city of Dublin as its field of reference. Judging by the titles alone, one might think that both books are equally place-dependent and place-specific (though obviously both incorporate other interconnective links). To look closer, however, is to see a crucial difference between the two.

Whereas readers of *Dubliners* feel they can draw a map of the Irish city described by Joyce, readers of *Winesburg* find that Anderson's Ohio village remains indistinct. In fact, the town map included in the 1960 edition of *Winesburg* reveals that only eight specific locations are identified. Nevertheless, setting is important in *Winesburg,* playing a significant role in creating whole-text coherence—along with such other connective elements as the concept of the grotesque; the theme of alienation; certain reappearing characters, including Doctor Reefy, Elizabeth Willard, and Helen White; and repeated motifs such as hands, windows, and darkness.

But more important than any other device in pulling the Winesburg stories together is the protagonist, George Willard. In his *Memoirs* Anderson wrote that he wanted his book to give the "feeling of a boy growing into young manhood in a town" (289). Thus, unlike *Dubliners, Winesburg* is actually a bildungsroman, in which George's development results partly from his experiences with characters in the various tales. Although he does not appear at all in either "Paper Pills" or "Godliness," George does appear in 17 of the other 19 stories as protagonist, sought-out listener, or observer, and he is mentioned in the remaining two stories, "Adventure" and "The Untold Lie." Further, the centrality of George in the book's second story ("Mother") and last three ("Death," "Sophistication," and "Departure") is a significant element of interconnection.

As George appears and reappears in story after story he develops sporadically toward emotional and artistic maturity. For one thing, he chooses pen over purse. Many of the characters seem to hope that George will tell their stories for them, but at first he seems loath to commit himself to that goal. In the first story, Wing Biddlebaum chides George for being afraid to dream and for being too eager to conform to the townspeople's expectations. Like Wing, George's mother is concerned that George may be wasting his talents; she fears that her son is going to fulfill his father's desire and become a hustling financial success rather than a creative writer. Indeed, as a reporter for the *Winesburg Eagle* George seems to focus only on the surface of life. He runs here and there "like an excited dog," writing down "little facts" about trivialities like A. P. Wringlet's shipment of straw hats or Uncle Tom Sinning's new barn (134). The teacher Kate Swift warns George that he must "stop fooling with words" and learn "what people are thinking about, not what they say" (163). And Parcival, the unsuccessful physician and frustrated novelist, says to George, "Perhaps you will be able to write the book I may never get written" (56–57). By the end of the book George has developed a hunger to see beneath the surface of life and to leave Winesburg for an unspecified city where he can pursue his growing passion for dreams. Thus *Winesburg* is also a *Kunstlerroman*, a portrait of the artist as a young man.

To the feminist reader, George's changing attitudes toward women may seem even more important than his decision to jettison business and become an artist. In "Nobody Knows" (the fifth story, if we consider "The Book of the Grotesque" an introduction), Louise Trunnion tries to communicate to George her need for love and understanding. Instead of sympathy for her impoverished and frustrating life, however, George impulsively and hurriedly has sex with her one dark night and then gloats that, since "nobody knows," she has no hold on him. In this episode he has been "wholly the male, bold and aggressive," with "no sympathy for her" (61).

In an encounter with another woman, Belle Carpenter in "An Awakening," George again tries to take advantage of the opposite sex. Feeling one night "half drunk with the sense of masculine power" (187) he goes to see Belle, a strong-willed young milliner who—though she really loves an inarticulate bartender—has occasionally let George kiss her. Convinced that she is about to "surrender herself to him," George leads her to a secluded field, expecting to have his way with her, as he had with Louise Trunnion. Suddenly, however, the jealous bartender appears, disdainfully shoves George into some bushes, and marches the unresisting Belle away. George is left feeling humiliated and used, perhaps much as Louise Trunnion had felt.

George's experience with Helen White in the book's penultimate story is not at all like his abasement of Louise or his humiliation by Belle. By this point George has begun to feel "something like reverence" for the people of his town (241). No longer so self-centered and bent on his own gratification, he thinks of Helen as a friend rather than a sexual object. "He wants to love and be loved by her" (241). Anderson ties this longing for pure love—the name "Helen White" is appropriate—to the image of hands, which appears in many of the earlier stories. George wants most of all to "come close to some other human, touch someone with his hands. . . . He wants, most of all, understanding" (235). As he and Helen sit, looking over the fairground, he "[takes] hold of her hand" (241). In this moving scene George seems to sense at last that humans can sometimes, at least momentarily, understand and love one another. When in the last story ("Departure") George leaves on a beautiful spring morning for a new life, he realizes that his years in Winesburg and the townspeople he has known there have provided him with "a background on which to paint the dreams of his manhood" (247). Continuing the metaphor of paint and canvas but on another level, we realize that this single protagonist functions as the focal point, the central figure in Anderson's group portrait of Winesburg's grotesques.

We commented earlier that *Winesburg, Ohio* is the quintessential composite novel partly because most readers are familiar with the book's form—short stories that cohere into something so like a novel that neither its author nor its audience has known quite what to call it. Even though it had such significant precursors as Mitford's *Our Village*, Turgenev's *A Sportsman's Sketches*, Daudet's *Letters from My Mill*, Jewett's *The Country of the Pointed Firs*, and Joyce's *Dubliners*, *Winesburg's* popularity makes it still the best-known composite novel. Another reason for its fame is the influence it had on other writers of composite novels in the 1920s. Jean Toomer, the author of *Cane*, remarked that he "could not have matured as an artist without having read *Winesburg, Ohio*," and Ernest Hemingway (not usually prone to acknowledging debts to other writers) admitted that *Winesburg* was his "first pattern" when he was writing *In Our Time* (Mann 7).

The Woman Warrior: Memoirs of a Childhood among Ghosts: An Outlaw Knot-maker

Notwithstanding *Winesburg's* apparent significance as a "first pattern," when we view it as a rite of passage for the protagonist George Willard, we see the book fitting comfortably into a traditional literary niche. The same cannot be said for Maxine Hong Kingston's *The Woman Warrior: Memoirs of a Childhood among Ghosts* (1976), though it, too, is a series of independent stories held together primarily by a central protagonist. Critics have been baffled about what to call this strange amalgam of autobiography, mimetic fiction, history, and myth. Estelle Jelinek, in a study of women's autobiography, calls *The Woman Warrior* a "magical chronicle" that "stretches the traditional limits of autobiography." James Olney classifies it as "autofictography," that is, autobiography in which techniques of the novelist play a prominent part. And Patricia Lin Blinde retreats into the all-inclusive phrase "a collage of genres."[9]

Perhaps this last term is the most accurate description, for in addition to being a tissue of interwoven genres, *The Woman Warrior* is also clearly a composite novel. Kingston herself has said, in an interview with Angeles Carabi, "When I started writing *The Woman Warrior* I didn't think I could write a long book, so I did the five interlocking pieces and each one was like a short story or an essay. I know the book has a very complex form but all there is is trying to take small parts and doing a mosaic with it."[10] As we look at Kingston's book we see that what ties these five "interlocking pieces" together is the narrator-protagonist, whom we take to be Kingston herself. As she commented to Carabi, "I guess it *[Woman Warrior]* is an 'I' book, it is the voices that I hear inside myself" (11).

These "voices" inside herself create five sections of memoirs that mix oral histories she has heard from her family, speculations about what might really have happened, and fiction that has no basis in fact. The juxtaposed, discontinuous sections focus on a "no-name aunt" who gives birth to an illegitimate child before killing both herself and the baby; a mythic Chinese woman-warrior named Fa Mu Lan; Kingston's mother, Brave Orchid, who in China was a respected midwife; Kingston's aunt Moon Orchid, whose wealthy Americanized husband discards her; and Maxine herself while growing up in California. Clearly this is not the chronological account typical of autobiographies.

Yet the five titled sections, which seem to focus on five different people, do indeed have a single protagonist around whom the stories cohere. As Suzanne Juhasz says, "Finding words, telling stories" is a metaphor for "achieving identity."[11] Thus, *The Woman Warrior* itself is really its author's quest for self-identity; Kingston tries to construct from fragments of "talk-story" a picture of her female relatives because she realizes that this is the best way to forge her own identity. At one point in the book Kingston, as the narrator, suggests a metaphor for this process: "Long ago in China, knot-makers tied string into buttons and frogs. . . . There was one knot so complicated that it blinded the knot-maker. Finally an emperor outlawed this cruel knot, and the nobles could not order it any more. If I had lived in China, I would have been an outlaw knot-maker" (163). In other words, as a Chinese-American caught between two cultures, she finds tying the "button" of self so complicated that she has to invent her own way of doing it, becoming in effect an outlaw knot-maker.

Part of what Kingston learns about herself is that she must refuse to be a victim like her no-name aunt, who commits suicide, and her giggling aunt Moon Orchid, who, unable to adjust to American ways, goes mad. Instead, Kingston wants to be strong like Fa Mu Lan and Brave Orchid, able to overcome her family's enemies and exorcise ghosts. Her book portrays her, the protagonist, in the process of achieving that goal. As a child she feels bewildered by her mother's stories because she can't tell what is true and what is fiction: "Night after night my mother would talk-story until we fell asleep. I couldn't tell where the stories left off and the dreams began" (19). She hears her mother say, as the other Chinese do, "Better to raise geese than girls" and "When fishing for treasures in the flood, be careful not to pull in girls" (46). Yet her mother also teaches her the song of Fa Mu Lan and makes her realize she too can be a woman warrior. The mature Kingston takes pride in being strong and independent, but she also feels bitter that no man supports her. "Even now," she thinks, "China wraps double binds around my feet" (48).

Ironically, one of the problems that this talented writer must overcome is an inability to speak. During kindergarten and the first three grades, she would not talk at school because her voice "quacked like a pressed duck" (192). At home, too, she is inarticulate: she has a list of two hundred confessions that she is never able to tell her mother. Finally, however, she finds her voice and begins to do well in school. Afraid then that her parents are going to marry her off as soon as possible, she shouts at them, "Even if I . . . talk funny and get sick, I won't let you turn me into a slave or a wife. I'm getting out of here. . . . I'm going to college" (201–2). Years later, home for a visit with her family in California, she explains to her mother that she is healthier and happier when *not* at home, and her mother agrees, "Of course, you must go, Little Dog." Suddenly, feeling that a weight has been lifted from her, Kingston thinks, "She has not called me that endearment for years—a name to fool the gods. I am really a Dragon, as she is a Dragon, both of us born in dragon years" (108–9).

Appropriately, the last talk-story in the book is produced by mother *and* daughter together. Brave Orchid tells a story of her family in China and how they loved to go to the theater. Kingston imagines that at some of these performances the family heard the songs of Ts'ai Yen, a Chinese poetess held captive by barbarians for 12 years. During that period of captivity, Ts'ai Yen heard the beautiful flute music produced by the barbarians and began composing songs about her own life. When the captive poetess was finally ransomed and returned to China, Kingston tells us, Ts'ai Yen "brought her songs back from the savage lands. One of these is called 'Eighteen Stanzas for a Barbarian Reed Pipe,' a song that Chinese sing to their own instruments. It translated well" (209). Thus Kingston suggests that like the ancient poetess, she too has had to live in a foreign culture, but that she has finally found her voice and can speak to both Americans and Chinese. The immense popularity of this unusual composite novel, with its central focus on Kingston herself, proves her right.

Qfwfq, George Willard, Maxing Hong Kingston—all are unique central figures in the composite novels for which they provide a focus. Each does indeed undergo a rite of passage, developing in some way a fuller understanding of self by learning to honor the selves of others.

Chapter 5

(E)merging Protagonist(s)

The Collective Protagonist as Concept and Connective

Protagonist is a term one can find in almost any dictionary or literary handbook, a common term that embodies a well-known concept (i.e., the protagonist is the pivotal figure, the central character). In contrast, the term *collective protagonist* is seldom encountered in literary handbooks, though the concept it embodies is often invoked by critics. Briefly, a *collective protagonist* is either a group that functions as a central character (a couple, an extended family, a special-interest group) or an implied central character who functions as a metaphor (an aggregate figure who, cumulatively, may be "typical" or "archetypal" or "the essence of" or "the developing presence of" or "the soul of"—and so on).

As we mentioned in chapter 2, some critics view Joyce's *Dubliners* as a work whose stories feature a developing collective protagonist. Susan Mann, for example, says this about *Dubliners*:

"Since there is no protagonist who reappears and develops in the process of the book, critics often fail to notice that the book presents the gradual maturation of what one might consider the archetypal Dubliner" (30). Brewster Ghiselin says in a similar vein that *Dubliners* focuses on "the one composite movement of the agonistic soul of the Irish through stage after stage of its decline."[1] Mann's "archetypal Dubliner" and Ghiselin's "agonistic soul of the Irish" imply the same concept: that is, an aggregate-character, a composite figure upon whom Joyce's narrative is centered—a collective protagonist.

In her discussion of *Dubliners* and other works, Mann *almost* uses the term *collective protagonist*, referring at various times to a "central protagonist," a "composite personality," and a "composite protagonist." Other critics use different terms. Forrest Ingram in his book about selected short story cycles, for example, talks about "co-protagonists" at some length, defining them as the individual protagonists of linked stories who are members of "a single community," which then "constitutes the central character of a cycle" (22). Rachel Blau DuPlessis, in a wide-ranging study of twentieth-century women writers, uses interchangeably such terms as "communal protagonist," "choral protagonist," "collective protagonist," "group protagonist," and "multiple protagonist." DuPlessis also, but less often, discusses "cluster protagonist" and "transpersonal protagonist."[2] One could, of course, examine at great length the subtle differences implied, both in and out of context, by the various terms used by each critic. Generally, though, all their terms have the same referent: a protagonist who is a "collective"—literally (a couple, a family, a club) or figuratively (a representative, an archetype, an ideal).

The literal collective protagonist provides connective tissue in numerous composite novels. John Updike's *Too Far to Go* (1979), for example, centers on a couple, Joan and Richard Maples, as their relationship changes (while their marriage blooms and then wilts) over a span of 20 years. Thea Astley's *It's Raining in Mango* (1987) describes itself in its subtitle as "Pictures from a Family Album," and indeed the book is album like. The collective protagonist here is a multigenerational eccentric family named Laffey, whose clan has survived since 1861 in the primitive Australian outback. In Christina Garcia's *Dreaming in Cuban* (1992), four women of the del Pino family (two in Cuba, two in

Brooklyn) share center stage as a collective protagonist. One might even call Danny and his ragtag assortment of *paisanos* in John Steinbeck's *Tortilla Flat* (1935) a "family," and certainly the 15 women (plus assorted men and children) who establish a Judeo-Christian communal habitation in Israel in E. M. Broner's *A Weave of Women* (1978) consider themselves a family by choice. Marilyn French says in the introduction to *A Weave of Women* that its "communal focus" permits "a new kind of [literary] tradition, one in which all aspects of life are interrelated, in which no figure dominates" (xiii–xv). This is exactly how a collective protagonist may function: as an element of interrelation that permits the foregrounding of several or many individuals rather than one.

Amy Tan's *The Joy Luck Club* (1989) is another work that features a literal "collective" as its protagonist, this one a transgenerational group of Chinese-American women who meet weekly to play mah-jongg, invest in stocks, eat dim sum, and talk about their lives. As the characters tell their stories the reader becomes acquainted with eight women. Their lives, like the stories in this composite novel, are "connected," as Tan maintains, by "community."[3] Yet the "community" established here is fraught with tension, because the group consists not only of Chinese immigrant mothers but also their first-generation American daughters. Thus the collective protagonist in this composite novel may be construed figuratively as well as literally—as a complex aggregate character who symbolizes the Chinese-American female torn between two cultures. In terms of its collective protagonist, then, *The Joy Luck Club* has it both ways: its protagonist is literally a "collective" (the eight "club" members who tell stories to and about each other), yet this same protagonist also reflects and embodies the tensions and conflicts experienced in the evolving consciousness of a single ethnic group *and* a "type"—a people who are moving, culturally, from displacement to assimilation.

Amy Tan's mah-jongg players, like Steinbeck's *paisanos* and Broner's weave of women, share a literal group identity. They know each other, live or work or play with each other. As members of communities, therefore, they clearly comprise "collective" protagonists. But many composite novels feature a collective protagonist who has no literal group identity whatsoever. In works such as Joe Ashby Porter's *The Kentucky Stories* (1983) and Tama Janowitz's *Slaves of New York* (1986), for example, individual stories are peopled by a variegated swatch of unrelated, mostly unacquainted characters whose only connection is that they share and are shaped by a particular place and lifestyle. Porter's archetypal Kentuckian embodies, as the author puts it, a "Kentucky state of mind" (ix), while Janowitz's typical Slave embodies the "Philistine Esthetes" who fight tooth and nail to "make it" in the Big Apple.[4] Since one lives in a backwater Eden while the other inhabits an urban Pandemonium, Porter's laid-back Kentuckian and Janowitz's frenetic New Yorker would have little to say to each other, were they to meet. Yet as collective protagonists they are identical, each embodying an ambience, a subculture, a way of life.

M. F. K. Fisher, in *Sister Age* (1983), creates a collective protagonist who is even more widely representative than Porter's Kentuckian or Janowitz's Slave. In a foreword and afterword that frame the book's 15 story-texts, Fisher explains that Sister Age is both a fanciful companion (like St. Francis of Assisi's Sister Moon and Brother Pain) and a real person—Ursula von Ott by name, an eighteenth-century German woman whose portrait Fisher bought in an antique shop. The painting itself is ragged and flaking, and Ursula, described as plain and ugly with "monkey-sad eyes" (8), was quite old when it was painted. One might expect, then, that the book's text-pieces will be peopled by the elderly, that "Sister Age" as a collective protagonist will be an aged woman, a "nagging harpy" (3). But this is not so. Fisher sees Sister Age as a companion who should be welcomed early in one's life as a friend rather than dreaded late in one's life as an enemy. Thus Fisher's characters number the young as well as the old, and the complex collective protagonist called "Sister Age" embodies the life process itself. As Fisher says, "She is my teacher and my sister, and will tell me more, in due time" (13).

Unlike Fisher's *Sister Age*, whose collective protagonist is "removed from all the nonsense and frustration" (8), Anzia Yezierska's *Hungry Hearts* (1920) features at its center the tormented figure of the immigrant from Eastern Europe. Collectively, Yezierska's Russian and Polish Jews inhabit the tenement boroughs of New York and New Jersey during the early part of this century. A few of these protagonists are acquainted with each other; fewer still are related; most are strangers. Yet they project, cumulatively, a single consciousness that embodies the fierce struggle of people caught in a cross-cultural conflict.

Two works by African-American writers also reflect cross-cultural conflict in their collective protagonists. Though there are no recurring characters in the stories that comprise Richard Wright's *Uncle Tom's Children* (1940), for example, there is clearly an implied protagonist—an evolving consciousness that moves, as one critic succinctly notes, "from victimization to self-assertion."[5] The same kind of collective protagonist who evolves, who grows, structures Ernest Gaines's *Bloodline* (1968). Though composed of only five stories (all set in Bayonne, Louisiana), *Bloodline* in its developmental strategy is reminiscent of *Dubliners*. That is, just as Joyce planned the sequence of stories in *Dubliners* so that the narrators/protagonists gradually mature (children, then adolescents, then adults, then adults in public life), so did Gaines plan the sequence of stories in *Bloodline*. Critic William Burke confidently describes the center of Gaines's book as "the changing black male" who is "reclaim[ing] his masculinity," and Gaines himself says that he "definitely arranged these stories in this order" so as to show "constant growth."[6] It is not surprising, then, that in an interview in the early 1970s, Gaines listed *Dubliners* among the books that had most influenced his writing.

In Our Time: The Archetypal Collective Protagonist

Like Gaines, Ernest Hemingway looked to *Dubliners* as a model when writing his complex composite novel *In Our Time* (1925). Although Hemingway stated to F. Scott Fitzgerald that *Winesburg* was his "first pattern" (Mann 7), Jeffrey Meyers in a recent biography cites *Dubliners* as a more important influence.[7] Most likely, both Anderson and Joyce were influential, as were others, including Gertrude Stein—who read Hemingway's manuscript and suggested significant changes.[8]

Whatever the conflation of influences that resulted in *In Our Time*, we can be sure that Hemingway saw the work as a coherent whole text. When planning the book, he envisioned a series of linked stories interwoven with 18 previously published vignettes. In a letter to Edmund Wilson he explained that the vignettes were "to give the picture of the whole between examining it in detail."[9] Because he was convinced that "there is nothing in the book that has not a definite place in its organization," he was very angry when his publisher (Boni & Liveright) insisted on deleting the sexually explicit story "Up in Michigan." Reluctantly, he agreed to substitute "The Battler," but later admitted that the substitution gave "additional unity to the book."[10] Thus *In Our Time* was published with 15 stories and 16 vignettes (two of the original vignettes had by this time been given titles and made into stories). Hemingway five years later added a prologue entitled "On the Quai at Smyrna," making a total of 32 text-pieces.

Although Nick Adams appears in only nine of these text-pieces (eight stories and one vignette),[11] some critics have insisted on seeing him as the most important unifying element in the book. This position is taken, for example, by Philip Young, who sees Nick as developing chronologically from youth to young manhood. Young argues that in each of the Nick stories ("Indian Camp," "The Doctor and the Doctor's Wife," "The End of Something," "The Three Day Blow," "The Battler," "A Very Short Story," "Cross Country Snow," and "Big Two-Hearted River") the protagonist learns something about the violence and pain in the world.[12] The problem with his argument, however, is that it ignores all stories and vignettes that are not about Nick. In a more recent publication, Debra Moddelmog also argues for the book's whole-text coherence based on the presence of Nick Adams, but she links *all* the stories and vignettes through Nick Adams's dual function as both protagonist and implied author.[13] Moddelmog's chief evidence for her position is "On Writing," a fragment that Hemingway considered publishing as part of "Big Two-Hearted River." In it, Nick, identified as a writer in "Big Two-Hearted River," asserts that the only good writing is "what you made up, what you imagined."[14] According to Moddelmog, this statement would explain why some of the vignettes and stories are about protagonists not identified as Nick. However, since Hemingway (at Stein's suggestion) decided against including the fragment "On Writing" in *In Our Time*, Moddelmog's argument remains unconvincing.[15]

What seems much more likely is that Hemingway saw his book cohering through what we call a "collective protagonist," a group of central characters who, though different individuals, are generally similar. Several critics have advanced this view. Carl Wood, for example, maintains that all the protagonists are like Nick, a "drifting and disillusioned member of the lost generation."[16] These protagonists—named Nick Adams or Harold Krebs (in "Soldier's Home") or Joe Butler (in "My Old Man") or not named at all—can be taken together as a generation that encounters the irrationality and violence of the modern world; finds religion, marriage, and family meaningless; and seeks some way to live, to make it through each day.

Certainly violence is apparent from the first story, in which Nick watches as an Indian woman goes through so much pain in giving birth that her husband can't stand it and kills himself. The first six stories, in which a gradually maturing Nick is repeatedly disillusioned, are interspersed with vignettes of war: drunken soldiers, men killing the enemy for pleasure, miserable retreats, the execution of a cabinet minister so sick that he cannot stand upright, and Nick being wounded. In the next two stories young soldiers (Krebs and an unnamed revolutionary) realize that their sacrifices are unappreciated by civilians. These two stories sandwich between them a vignette showing a young policeman in the United States who shoots two Hungarians caught in a petty robbery but argues that their deaths don't matter because they were "wops." The last five stories focus on unhappy American families—sterile married couples like the Elliots and the bored husband and wife in "The Cat in the Rain"; dissatisfied tourists like the couple in "Out of Season"; an older Nick, who is unhappy because he is about to be a father; and a boy who finds out that his "old man" is a dishonest jockey. These stories are interleaved with six vignettes showing the violent conflict, frequent shame, and inevitable death involved in bullfighting. These vignettes—in showing that the best a man can hope for is to maintain control of himself, find some escape in rituals, and meet death with dignity—encapsulate the grace under pressure expected of the Hemingway protagonist who came to be known as the "code hero." And the last story, "Big Two-Hearted River," sums all this up in the figure of Nick Adams, the psychologically wounded war veteran who finds even his beloved Michigan woods partly burned—perhaps a reminder of bomb-ravaged war zones. Nick manages to keep control of himself by concentrating on the ritual of making camp and fishing, but he knows he is not strong enough yet to fish the dark swamp.

Thus a complex collective protagonist—those members of the lost generation who reflect the cruelties of life "in our time"—is a strong cohesive factor in Hemingway's composite novel. Readers will undoubtedly notice other elements of interconnection: the fact that the first and last text-pieces ("On the Quai at Smyrna" and "L'Envoi") are set in Greece and suggest a journey's beginning and end; the fact that much of the book is set in darkness and rain; and so on. Because this book is so structurally complex, it will probably be grist for dissertation mills for years to come. Meanwhile, *In Our Time* serves as a good example of how an (e)merging protagonist links text-pieces together.

Go Down, Moses: The Extended Family as Collective Protagonist

Since its publication in 1942, critics have been bewildered about what to call William Faulkner's *Go Down, Moses* (we touched on this critical debate in chapter 1). Faulkner himself insisted that the book "is indeed a novel." Joanne V. Creighton refers to it as "a collage, a pastiche of dissimilar pieces." Dirk Kuyk, Jr. suggests that it occupies "the unfamiliar . . . middle ground between novels and collections of stories."[17] It is, in other words, a composite novel, one that achieves whole-text coherence in large part through its collective protagonist. This composite figure is not, however, an archetype like Hemingway's "lost generation" male. Rather, Faulkner's collective protagonist in *Go Down, Moses,* embodied in six generations and numerous extensions of the multitudinous McCaslin clan in Yoknapatawpha Country, is the living legacy of the Old South itself.

Briefly, *Go Down, Moses* consists of seven stories that are arranged *un*-chronologically: the first takes place in 1859; the second and third in 1941; the fourth and fifth in 1878; the sixth and seventh in 1940. All of the book's characters are yoked in some way to Mississippi's Yoknapatawpha McCaslins, and the major characters in six of the seven stories are directly descended from Lucius Quintus Carothers McCaslin, the granite-faced patriarch who hacked the McCaslin farm and property into existence in the 1840s. The McCaslin genealogical convolutions are not easily grasped, however, because they have developed for almost a century through three separate lines: through the patriarch's legitimate sons (the McCaslins); through the patriarch's legitimate daughter (the Edmondses); and through the patriarch's illegitimate slave daughter, upon whom he then sired a son (the Beauchamps). Further, as family lines will, these three have split, twisted, turned, and intertwined through the years.[18]

The first story, set in 1859, features two hunts—one by two McCaslin brothers for a missing slave (their unacknowledged half-brother), the other by a middle-aged spinster for a husband. In the next two stories, both set in 1941, African-American men prove that they are more worthy of respect than their Anglo-American opponents and counterparts. In the fourth and fifth stories Faulkner jumps back in time to the 1880s, sets most of the action in the primeval "big woods" of Mississippi, introduces Native American characters not seen in the previous stories, and demonstrates the inexorable devastation wreaked upon the land and all its dwellers by such civilizers as the McCaslins. The final two stories return us to 1940 (when Faulkner was writing the book). Here, the last hopes of the McCaslin and Edmonds lines reveal their moral corruption, and the last hope of the Beauchamps is ignominiously executed—betrayed and, like the Biblical Benjamin, "sold . . . in Egypt" (380).

This summary, of course, is a radical oversimplification. It gives no hint of the Faulknerian penchant for conceptualizing an enormous canvas (a century, a people, a cultural legacy) and fleshing it out slowly, gradually, in bits and pieces. Thus each story is dense with cross-references to other stories, with external and internal counterpoint. Relationships among the vast panorama of characters are sketchy at first, then gradually become clearer. The fifth story alone (entitled "The Bear" and often anthologized as an individual novella, in which the young Ike McCaslin learns to revere the forces of nature and to loathe his grandfather Lucius's incestuous outrages) contains innumerable narrative strands: the misadventures of three generations; the saga of an unwinnable war; the history of a displaced people and a vanishing way of life; and much, much more. As Joanne V. Creighton aptly observes, "the concentric circles of reference become larger and larger as more and more of the past which informs the present is revealed."[19] Reading a work such as this, in other words, is circular rather than linear, recursive rather than sequential.

The summary just concluded, though oversimplified, hints at Faulkner's narrative method. The jumps in time, for example (nearly a century forward to 1941, then back to the 1880s, then forward again to 1940) define and frame the book's broad historical sweep, at the same time implying the profound impact of past upon present. Plot patterns, too, imply parallel actions, as in the two hunts (to catch a slave, to catch a husband) and the two rapes (the patriarch of his slave women, white settlers of the land). To look more closely at the seven stories is to enlarge upon the methodology involved in these chronological jumps and parallel patterns. The fourth story, for example (entitled "The Old People"), features the Native American character Sam Fathers, "whose grandfathers had owned the land long before the white men ever saw it and who had vanished from it now with all their kind" (165). Thus Faulkner further expands the book's historical frame (to prehistory) while juxtaposing past with present (the previous story took place in 1940). This fourth story is also built around a hunt, during which the young Ike McCaslin is initiated into the lore of the woods by Sam Fathers. The parallel with the earlier hunts makes it clear that this is what a hunt *should* be—a dignified contest between honorable adversaries. Further, Ike McCaslin during this hunt proves himself to Sam Fathers: "Sam Fathers marked [Ike's] face with the hot blood which he had spilled and he ceased to be a child and became a hunter and a man" (177–78). Because the reader already knows (from the two future-time stories preceding this one) that such dignity and honor will die with Sam Fathers, this blood rite in the woods is heavy with irony. And when, at the end of this story, Ike's cousin says to Ike that "there is only one thing worse than not being alive, and that's shame" (186), the scene is set—two stories hence, in "Delta Autumn"—for Ike McCaslin's final, shameful humiliation.

Arthur F. Kinney has recently pointed out numerous plot parallels that are actually (when one unscrambles the chronology of the stories) contemporaneous. For example, the young Ike's repudiation of his McCaslin inheritance (in the fifth story) parallels and is contemporaneous with Lucas Beauchamp's attempt to repudiate *his* McCaslin inheritance (in the second story). In another instance, Lucas Beauchamp's temporary insanity over a treasure hunt and the near-loss of his wife, Molly (in the second story), occurs in the same year in which a millhand named Rider nearly loses his mind through grief for his dead wife (in the third story).[20] Kinney points out a number of additional counterparts, and other critics elaborate at great length upon motifs and themes that create links among the stories. Criticism of *Go Down, Moses* is so plentiful, in fact, that one can easily believe Faulkner to be the subject of more literary criticism in English than any other author besides William Shakespeare.

The point here, of course, is that all these elements contribute to a coherent vision on Faulkner's enormous canvas. Further, this coherent vision is shaped through and in the name of "McCaslin." Cleanth Brooks, who concurs in this opinion, asserts as follows: "A more useful, though more prosaic title would be *The McCaslins*, for the book has to do with the varying fortunes of the family."[21] Indeed it does. The McCaslin-Edmonds-Beauchamp influence and aura are always present, never far afield. Ike McCaslin, the character most central to the book's action and often cited as such, is the protagonist of three of the seven stories (as a young man in "The Old People" and "The Bear," and as an old man in "Delta Autumn"). It appears, in fact, that Faulkner embodies in Ike's long life span the static idealism that doomed the Old South. The young Ike (12 years old in "The Old People," 16 in "The Bear") reveres the sacred bond between the land and its people, and is so disgusted by his grandfather's exploitation of both that he disinherits himself. But the old Ike (close to 80 in "Delta Autumn") has failed through inaction, having done nothing to stop the exploitation of land and people in the intervening years. In his final opportunity to display strength of character, he fails by refusing to help or even touch the black woman who has borne Roth Edmonds's illegitimate son. The woman says to him, "Old man, have you lived so long and forgotten so much that you dont [sic] remember anything you ever knew or felt or even heard about love?" (363) And at this point Ike knows, miserably, that his grandfather's sins are his own.

In the book's final story, "Go Down, Moses," the legacy of shame comes full circle in the funeral of 26-year-old Butch Beauchamp, who had been executed for murder in Illinois. Gavin Stevens, the young lawyer who arranges the funeral, remembers that Butch had first gone to jail because of Roth Edmonds—who could have called the sheriff to handle a minor infraction, but instead called the police. Yes, Gavin thinks, this is *"something broader, quicker in scope"* (373). This is, in other words, one more failed harvest from rotten seed. Accompanied by the keening of mourners, the hearse moves "into the square, crossing it, circling the Confederate monument and the courthouse" (382). The Confederate monument, a pathetic anachronism slowly circled by a hearse that carries an unacknowledged McCaslin, is one final symbol of the Old South's impotence.

Finally one remembers the Biblical story of Benjamin, and betrayal, and a cruel pharoah, and a people held in bondage. A new story as well as an old one, it lives again in Faulkner's *Go Down, Moses* through the tragic composite figure that calls itself "McCaslin."

Love Medicine: The Tribe as Collective Protagonist

It would seem that in regard to complexity, Faulkner's and Hemingway's composite protagonists must remain unsurpassed—until one encounters Louise Erdrich's *Love Medicine* (1984), the first volume of a tetralogy of composite novels.[22] Structured as a series of separate narratives—several of which were first published as short stories—*Love Medicine* focuses on related Chippewa families on a North Dakota reservation. Covering more than 50 years, the book chronicles the complex interrelationships among four families named Kashpaw, Lamartine, Nanapush, and Morissey. The death of June Kashpaw in 1981 occurs in the first story, but the next story jumps back in time to 1934, and from that point on the stories are chronologically sequenced, ending in 1984.

The linked stories are told, Faulkner-like, from different perspectives: some in first person by six different family members, others in third person but through the eyes of various family members. Characters appear and reappear from one story to the next, and at times the same incident is described more than once but from different perspectives. Thus—and this is characteristic of many Native American narratives—*Love Medicine* suggests the connectedness of all things. In fact, working out a clear picture of the complex interrelationships among various members of the interrelated families is as difficult and time-consuming as putting together a jigsaw puzzle. As complex as it is, however, this familial composite is the primary element of interconnection among the stories.

Briefly, the patriarchs of the family are the bachelor Eli Kashpaw and his twin brother, Nector, who marries the gorgeous Marie Lazarre though he really loves the sensual (and promiscuous) Lulu Nanapush. In almost 50 years of marriage Nector and Marie rear 17 come-and-go children, one of whom is Marie's niece June Morissey. June marries her cousin Gordie Kashpaw, one of Marie and Nector's own children. By Gordie, June has a son named King—a shiftless alcoholic. June also has an illegitimate son, Lipsha Morissey, a sensitive young man reared by Nector and Marie, whom Lipsha thinks of as his grandparents. Lipsha eventually finds out that his real father is Gerry Lamartine, one of Lulu's eight children, each of whom has a different father.

All these family members figure significantly in one or more of the 14 stories. Marie Lazarre, for example, is the protagonist-narrator of "Saint Marie," a story about one day in 1934 when she went up the hill to the local convent, had a battle of wills with the passionate and possibly demented Sister Leopolda, and fled back down the hill. In the book's next story, "Wild Geese," Nector Kashpaw is the narrator-protagonist who starts up the hill to the convent to sell two wild geese that are strapped to his arms, sees Marie Lazarre running down the hill, and in a grotesque scenario (with the geese still tied to his arms) rapes the virginal Marie.

Nector is also the narrator-protagonist of "The Plunge of the Brave," set years later, in 1957. In this story, after more than 20 years of marriage to Marie and five years of weekly assignations with Lulu, Nector writes a farewell note to Marie and leaves for Lulu's house, intending to stay there permanently. However, when he arrives at Lulu's house and finds it empty, he accidentally sets it on fire and rushes back to Marie. On this same day in 1957, as described by Marie in the story "Flesh and Blood," Marie returns home from having visited the convent (this time making her peace with the dying Sister Leopolda) and finds Nector's note. But when Nector returns home and finds his note almost where he had left it, Marie never admits that she has seen it.

This same kind of cross-referencing occurs in other stories. In "A Bridge," for example, Albertine Kashpaw has a brief affair in 1973 with Henry Lamartine, one of Lulu's sons, and in "The Red Convertible" Henry's suicide a year later is described by his brother Lyman.

One wildly entertaining set of stories involves Marie, Nector, and Lulu after they have all moved to the Senior Citizens Home. The now-senile Nector tries to seduce Lulu, who, though still sexy, has been bald ever since she rushed into the fire that was burning down her house. Marie, aware that Nector is attracted to Lulu, sends Lipsha Morissey, who has a magical "healing touch," to get a wild-goose heart with which to make a love potion. Lipsha buys a frozen turkey heart instead, and when Marie puts it in Nector's sandwich, Nector chokes on it and dies. One upbeat outcome of this tragicomic episode is that Marie and Lulu forgive each other and become friends. Another is that Lipsha learns who his parents were, tracks down his father (Lulu's 6' 4", 320-pound son Gerry—whom no prison can hold), and gains a firmer sense of his own identity. As readers—following the happy Lipsha as he drives home to the reservation in the car that was purchased by his half-brother King with the insurance proceeds from June's death—we realize that the stories have brought us full circle, back to the first story, in which we saw June walking home through the snow on the night she died. June never made it, but Lipsha will: home to the heart of the family.

Thus is a kind of "closure" effected as this grandson of Lulu, this youth reared by Marie and Nector, this young man who retains some "powers" of the ancient Chippewas, completes the journey home that was begun by his mother one year before. The collective protagonist has emerged triumphant in spite of the appalling conditions of modern-day Native American life. To be sure, this four-family protagonist includes feckless characters who are alcoholics, gamblers, felons, and sex addicts. But it also includes such vital individualists as Lulu, who wins a battle with the city council by threatening to slap paternity suits against every man who might be the father of one of her children. As one observer in the council room remarks, "She's had the floor and half the council on it" (223). The family also includes such generous spirits as Marie, who feels compassion for and helps to nurse her dead husband's mistress. It includes Nector, who loves two women so much that his ghost comes back to visit each one. And it includes Lipsha, who retains and honors the magical knowledge of the tribe. Embodied in each of these figures, operative in every story, Erdrich's collective protagonist demonstrates the healing power of love medicine.

Indeed, then, as crafted by Hemingway, Faulkner, and Erdrich, each merging/emerging collective protagonist is different. In Hemingway's story-texts the protagonists are disillusioned men of the lost generation, unrelated and for the most part unacquainted, yet so similar that they coalesce into an archetypal code-hero composite. In Faulkner's story-texts the protagonists, all male and all related through Anglo- and African-American branchings on the McCaslin family tree, (e)merge as the single embodiment of a family composite. And in Erdrich's story-texts the male and female protagonists people a multiracial familial network whose ultimate empowerment and embodiment, forged through its Chippewa identity, is a tribe composite. Hemingway's code-hero collective protagonist survives, but barely, remaining disillusioned with the meaninglessness of life. Faulkner's single-family collective protagonist survives and achieves a small measure of hope, recognizing the importance of family ties and responsibilities. And Erdrich's family-tribal collective protagonist survives against all odds, challenging the future with the power of their Chippewa ancestry.

Chapter 6

Patterns and Palimpsests

Coherence through Pattern in the Composite Novel

Among Roman Jakobson's many contributions to the fields of psycholinguistics and literary criticism is his theory of the "metaphoric and metonymic poles" of language. David Lodge explains Jakobson's theory clearly and succinctly: "According to Jakobson, a discourse connects one topic with another either because they are in some sense similar to each other [metaphoric], or because they are in some sense contiguous to each other in space-time [metonymic]. . . . Stated most baldly, Jakobson's theory asserts that any discourse must connect its topics according to either similarity or contiguity, and will usually prefer one type of connection to the other."[1] In other words, metaphor establishes connection through resemblance, metonymy establishes connection through location and context, and most coherent texts use one more than the other. This idea has a profound impact upon literature. Seen broadly, it means that poetry is primarily metaphoric while prose (Jakobson calls it "pragmatical prose")[2] is primarily metonymic. Poetry, then, is more likely than prose to depend on metaphor for textual links and less likely to contain such space-time contextual connections as chronology, locale, sustained action or characterization, and so on. On a somewhat less expansive scale, Jakobson's theory means that the disjunctive texts of modernism rely primarily on metaphoric elements for coherence while the conjunctive texts of realism rely primarily on metonymic elements for coherence. As Lodge explains it, "Modernist texts, like *The Waste Land*, look discontinuous only as long as we fail to identify their metaphorical unity" (14).

Jakobson's theory is also highly relevant to a particular type of composite novel: those in which pattern is a primary element of interrelationship. A significant early text of this type is Gustave Flaubert's *Three Tales* (published in 1877 in French as *Trois contes*),[3] which we mentioned briefly in chapter 2. The book's three stories (or novellas), respectively, are about a simple French peasant woman named Félicité, St. Julien of medieval legend, and John the Baptist. Félicité's story, set in eighteenth-century Normandy, tells of her dreary life as a servant and her ignominious death; St. Julien's life story of sin, penance, redemption, and glorious death is idealized and recast in medieval France; John the Baptist's story concerns only his last day of life, when Salome dances for him and he loses his head. Flaubert himself conceived of the volume's three "tales" as a single entity and published them as a whole text, yet most critical discussions of *Three Tales* mention whole-text coherence more in passing than as a point in itself. Even so, such "passing" comments have clear implications. One critic writes, for example, that "each of the three tales tells the story of an immolation and a sacrifice." Another says that "the great difference in period between the stories is less important than the close similarities between three central characters, who are all in their different ways martyrs and saints."[4] Indeed, the implication here is clear. Each "tale" contains the same pattern of action ("an immolation and a sacrifice"), and these similar plot patterns (or life patterns) function metaphorically to link the stories.

This is, of course, a gross oversimplification. *Three Tales* is dense with repeated details and motifs. There are, in other words, many intertextual elements that contribute to whole-text coherence, as there are in most composite novels. Thus even critics who are not arguing for whole-text coherence may recognize it and comment accordingly. For example, Fredric Jameson discusses at length the book's "peculiar form," which he calls a "triptych." According to Jameson, this form embodies an "impossible triangular relationship" whose function is to subvert interpretation (an end point) and invite meditation (a continuum).[5] Although Jameson's overall argument concerning *Three Tales* is that it reveals an aspect of Flaubert's political unconscious, his point concerning the form of the book is relevant to its generic designation as a composite novel: the three stories exist in a dynamic relationship, much like that among the elements in a lyric poem that resists synopsis and refuses line-by-line explication.

Jameson's point thus produces unexpected reverberations. Flaubert was a scholar who was well aware of and constantly challenged the conventions and prescriptions of genre. He believed that prose should aspire to qualities analogous to those possessed by poetry, and it is quite possible that he planned this triptych form as an analogue to a poem, that is, as a poem-in-prose or a prose-poem. If Jakobson's theory of metaphoric and metonymic poles is valid, then the three texts of *Three Tales*—connected primarily not by elements of contiguity but rather by elements of similarity—achieve in prose the metaphoric, palimpsestic coherence of nonnarrative poetry. And like such poetry, dense and many-layered, the book invites continued consideration while resisting closure.

Three Lives and *Palimpsest*: Altered Patterns

While early critics persisted in assessing Flaubert's "three tales" individually, the public bought the book. *Three Tales,* in fact, was to be one of the most successful of Flaubert's works during his lifetime, popular and income-producing. And it influenced one, possibly two later three-part composite novels to which it bears a striking resemblance: Gertrude Stein's *Three Lives* (1909) and H. D.'s *Palimpsest* (1926). Stein wrote "The Good Anna," the first story in *Three Lives,* after translating for her brother Leo the first of Flaubert's three "tales" (Flaubert's character Félicité in "A Simple Heart" and Stein's character Anna in "The Good Anna" share remarkably similar life stories).[6] Stein's other two stories are "Melanctha" and "The Gentle Lena," and each story (again like Flaubert's) focuses on one life. Though all three stories share a common setting (a city called Bridgeport that closely resembles Baltimore, Maryland, at the turn of the century), the setting is resolutely indeterminate and creates few if any links between or among the stories.

Flaubert's composite novel so influenced Stein that, as Jayne L. Walker puts it, "the original title of Stein's book was "*Three Histories*, in deliberate homage to Flaubert's *Trois Contes*."[7] Whether Flaubert's composite novel directly influenced H. D.'s *Palimpsest* is not certain, yet H. D. read and spoke French, and she would certainly have been familiar with the highly popular *Trois contes* (as well as with Stein's *Three Lives*). H. D.'s three stories, like Flaubert's, share no common setting. "Hipparchia," the first story, focuses on a reluctant courtesan in ancient Rome. "Murex," the second story, focuses on a poet named Raymonde Ransome who lives in post–World War I London. "Secret Name," the third story, focuses on an unmarried American historian named Helen Fairwood who is on a short holiday in Egypt in the 1920s. Setting, then, offers few if any metonymic connections, and the focus of each story is, like Flaubert's and Stein's, the trajectory of a single life.

The "palimpsest" of H. D.'s title is a concept that had long fascinated her, and it is an image that occurs frequently throughout her work as a symbol for recurring patterns of human experience. Literally, a palimpsest is a parchment on which incompletely erased earlier writing is partially visible underneath present writing. Outlines of other "stories," in other words, can be glimpsed through a present story. Looked at in this sense, Flaubert's *Three Tales* is (metaphorically) a palimpsest that reveals through the superimposed life stories of three "martyrs and saints" one common life pattern that can be described as "an immolation and a sacrifice." *Three Lives* and *Palimpsest* are also "palimpsests," but the life patterns that they reveal are far from sacrificial. In fact, though Stein's and H. D.'s women live the three traditionally "female" plots (the spinster, the tart, and the wife), both authors change traditionally accepted lines of plot development.

In Stein's *Three Lives*, the pattern of each woman's life appears to be one of victimization and defeat. Spinster-Anna is a servant woman from the lower classes (like Flaubert's Félicité) who spends a long lifetime caring for others and dies alone. Tart-Melanctha in Stein's middle story, finding nothing but rejection in her desperately promiscuous search for love, develops consumption and dies. And Wife-Lena in the last story agrees reluctantly to an arranged marriage, fades quickly, and dies giving birth to her fourth child. Each story, however, contains a twist on its apparently dreary plot. Anna deliberately chooses an unmarried life, which, though arduous, permits her the occasional pleasure of women friends. Melanctha gives in to despair because she loses her women friends, not because of her rejection by men. And Lena is profoundly though quietly happy as long as she is single; her decline begins after her marriage, not before. Yes, these synopses are oversimplifications, but their outlines are clear: the three women share a common life pattern of achieving happiness as long as they remain unmarried and enjoy the friendship of other women.

Palimpsest's three stories, like those in *Three Lives*, focus on a tart, a wife, and a spinster, all of whom are writers. Tart-Hipparchia in the first story is the mistress of several high-ranking Roman officials; rejections by these men cause a breakdown, after which she recovers and begins to write. Wife-Raymonde in the second story is mired in the pain of her husband's rejection and betrayal of her; when she is able to purge her pain through writing, she recommences her life as a poet. And middle-aged Spinster-Helen in the third story is rejected by an ex–army captain with whom she becomes infatuated while vacationing; when she regains her senses, she returns to America and her career as a historian. Again, these synopses are oversimplifications, but a recurrent life-pattern shows clearly through: each of H. D.'s three women rises above rejection by men and moves forward into a creative life.[8]

From Palimpsests to Patchwork—Six Composite Novels

The tripartite composite novels by Flaubert, Stein, and H. D. are remarkably similar in that each work is composed of three novellas that focus on one life apiece, and that each work's three novellas are linked by similar life patterns. The same palimpsestic design aesthetic structures Mary Gordon's recent *The Rest of*

Life (1993), composed of three novellas, each of which focuses on one woman who appears to be living a full life. Unlike Flaubert's Félicité and Stein's Lena, who are doomed to be victims, Gordon's women develop interesting careers, have children, and carry on love affairs. Each successful life pattern ultimately reveals itself to be deeply and similarly flawed, however. In the words of Alison Lurie, Gordon's three protagonists are "strong, interesting and admirable women who have been deeply damaged by their dependence on men."[9]

Similar in tone to Gordon's composite novel but varied in novella-pattern is Simone de Beauvoir's *The Woman Destroyed* (published in 1967 in French as *La Femme rompue*). This book, too, is composed of three novellas, but de Beauvoir moves the venue to France and focuses in each novella on a middle-aged Parisian woman. Each woman is temporarily living alone, feeling betrayed by the family around whom she built her life and to whom she is not very important anymore. The women all try to come to terms with their situations, but only one is successful— the first of the three, the woman who had all along maintained an emotional and intellectual life of her own, independent of her husband and children. De Beauvoir, then, creates three life patterns that appear at first to be parallel (single woman, rejected and alone, tries to cope). But after establishing the outlines of the first life pattern, she then varies the second and third in midtrajectory, using the kind of metaphoric connection that David Lodge would describe as "ironic contrast, a negative kind of similarity" (Lodge 11). This deviation in pattern is indeed an ironic connective, making clear in the contrast between an initial success and two subsequent failures the point that one woman's success story is not all women's, that the culturally prescribed immersion of a woman's life in family alone is more likely than not to end in disappointment and resentment.

Though we have been using a palimpsest metaphor as a way of visualizing these pattern-related composite novels, we could just as well use a quilt metaphor. In fact, many pattern-related composite novels reveal design affinities to the nineteenth-century "patchwork" tradition that we described in chapter 2. Albert Camus's *Exile and the Kingdom* (published in 1957 in French as *L'Exil et le royaume*), for example, utilizes a design aesthetic remarkably similar to that of a "log cabin" quilt. By definition, a "log cabin" quilt uses light-dark contrast as its structural aesthetic and unifying motif. In other words, the light-versus-dark motif is worked into some kind of geometric design (there are many possibilities), and this design is repeated exactly in each square. To look at a completed log cabin quilt-top is a curious experience, however, because it requires a dual focus: close up, to see individual squares; and distanced, to see the overall design. The quilt-top and its component squares, like the whole text and text-pieces of a composite novel, exist in a dynamic relationship.

In Camus's composite novel, "exile" and "kingdom" comprise the "light-dark" motif—opposites that connote isolation *("solitaire")* and belonging *("solidaire")*. Throughout the book Camus sets up character-pairs, situation-pairs, and image-pairs that reflect this "kingdom vs. exile" binary opposition. Like the light-dark surface-squares of a "log cabin" quilt, then, Camus's text-pieces are all constructed upon an exile-kingdom motif pattern. And like a "log cabin" quilt-top, which reflects an overall design, Camus's composite novel, as a whole text, reflects its "exile-kingdom" pattern. As Forrest Ingram explains, "There is a dynamic interplay of 'exile' and 'kingdom' on every level" (38).

Also reflecting the patchwork tradition but using a different design aesthetic, Ntozake Shange's *Sassafrass, Cypress & Indigo* (1982) and Angela Carter's *The Bloody Chamber* (1979) might well be visualized as "motif" quilts, that is, quilts that feature image or symbol repetition. In Shange's book (called a "novel" on its title page) the sassafrass leaf signifies a poet-daughter, the cypress leaf signifies a dancer-daughter, and the indigo leaf signifies a musician-daughter. The three daughters' many "squares" (recipes, rituals, stories, journal entries, remedies) carry their signifiers, creating motifs through repetition, and all the daughter-squares are enclosed within one weaver-mother's border (their mother's name is "Hilda Effania"), stitched with the book's ubiquitous and final words, "Mama was there." In Carter's book (called "stories" on its title page) each story-square is an adaptation of a folk- or fairy tale, and each foregrounds at least one symbol traditionally associated with women and love stories: roses, lilies, hearts, gentle beasts, beauties (some sleeping, some not). But each symbol is yoked to violence. Roses drip blood; lilies are cobra-headed; heart-shaped stains burn like fire; gentle beasts sneer and slink; beauties are raped and murdered (some sleeping, some not); and all is starkly rendered in snow white, ruby red, and pitch black. Thus Carter develops, in essence, a tricolor quilt-text whose story-squares reveal, *en collage,* a motif: the sex-violence subscript encoded in folk tales.

As these composite novels demonstrate, an image or symbol or plot pattern may become a motif through repetition, and vivid motifs may effect and enhance whole-text coherence. Walter M. Miller, Jr.'s *A Canticle for Leibowitz* (1959) presents an intriguing variation on such pattern-effected coherence. The book is composed of three novellas, all set in the same place (the Abbey of the Albertian Order of Leibowitz) but at different times: the first takes place 600 years after a nuclear holocaust, the second 600 years later, and the third 600 years after that. The point, of course, is simple—everything that goes around, comes around. Or, as Eric Rabkin puts it, "The novel [is] about repetition, about the cyclic nature of history, about the fatedness of human affairs." Further, says Rabkin, each novella is structured by a myth, and myths are "the persistent truths which describe the universe into which we are born and against which, by our seeking after wealth and power and even science, we struggle vainly."[10] Miller's composite novel, in other words, uses myth-pattern as a structural motif—to illustrate the ineluctability of pattern itself in human life and affairs.

The Golden Apples: The Power of Myth

Whole-text coherence as effected through pattern repetition is, in some composite novels, highly complex. One such work is Eudora Welty's composite novel *The Golden Apples* (1949), which presents an intriguing study in pattern connection through myth, or what Welty describes as "a shadowing of Greek mythological figures, gods and heroes that wander in various guises, at various times, in and out."[11] A vision of mythological gods and heroes who "wander in and out" may seem somewhat out of place in a sleepy little southern hamlet. Nevertheless, Morgana, Mississippi, is the setting for six of the book's seven stories, which span 40 years of village life (the one non-Mississippi story, though it takes place in San Francisco, focuses on a MacLain from Morgana). Three Morgana families are of major importance (the Raineys, Starkses, and Morrisons), and one family, the MacLains, is featured in four stories: "Shower of Gold," "Sir Rabbit," "The Whole World Knows," and "Music from Spain."

Welty says that she "discovered only part way through" the writing of this book that "the stories were connected," that "[one] story's people were [another] story's people at a different period in their lives."[12] Once discovered, however, this intertextuality of her stories apparently satisfied what Barbara Harrell Carson calls Welty's "passion for connection."[13] Welty herself admits that of all the books she has written, "*The Golden Apples* is, on the whole, my favorite." What she especially likes, she continues, is the way the stories "exist on their own as short stories. . . . They don't have to be connected, but I think by being connected there's something additional coming from them as a group with a meaning of its own" (*Conversations* 192). Indeed, these stories are "passionately" connected—by setting and collective protagonist; by binary images like sun-and-moon, apples-and-pears; by themes like loneliness and wandering; by character foils like Virgie Rainey and Cassie Morrison; by episode-foils like the conception of the twins in the first story and the funeral of Katie Rainey in the last story, and so on. All these elements provide layer upon layer of connection until *The Golden Apples* resembles nothing so much as a textual baklava. Critics seem to have been most interested in one particular aspect of the book, however: its treasure trove of mythological allusions.[14]

It is not surprising that mythological allusions abound in the work of someone who says of herself, "I lived with mythology all my life. It is just as close to me as the landscape" (*Conversations* 224). In the same vein, Welty has said that *The Golden Apples* "does draw freely on myths—all kinds of myths, Greek, Norwegian, anything—just because I feel they do permeate life and endure in our imagination" (*Conversations* 313). Certainly Joseph Campbell would agree with Welty that myths "permeate" our lives. While enumerating the mythical vestiges that are part of our everyday lives (e.g., club and society initiations, marriage ceremonies, the wearing of uniforms, funeral rites, processions of all kinds), Campbell argues that "myth opens the world . . . to the realization of the mystery that underlies all forms."[15] We need ritual, in other words, because we need myth, and myth appeals to us through mystery, exerting an ever-present power through stories of immortal heroes who transcend normal rules and expectations, perform magic, and perpetrate violence without guilt and often without punishment.

Welty invokes this power in *The Golden Apples*. By creating character relationships and situations whose patterns are eternal, archetypal, she fashions a mythical palimpsest. On one level are the everyday lives of Morgana's folk, but underneath, on another level, are the lives lived by gods and goddesses, lives that are at once familiar and strange. Thus each of Welty's seven stories contains shadow patterns of other stories from other narrative worlds. Though the shadow patterns may differ from story to story, all are somehow related in a complex mythic tapestry whose interwoven patterns tease the mind and memory.

The mythmaking impulse apparent in Welty's composite novel may be part of what Kathryn Lee Seidel describes as "the urge to mythicize" that is "strong in the South." Seidel explains that after the Civil War the South needed some affirmation that life had meaning. Creating a myth, she continues, "was the perfect answer to that need."[16] According to Seidel, the central answer for the South was the Edenic myth, centering around the plantation and the unfallen Eve (anyone who has ever heard an old-time southerner talk **about** "damyankees"—one word—knows who the snake was). Welty modifies the Edenic myth, however, by focusing not on the plantation but on a pastoral world peopled by innocent bucolics who are as free of guilt as the Olympian immortals.

Thus in one episode in *The Golden Apples* Welty describes how 15-year-old Mattie Will Sojourner rather complacently acquiesces in her seduction by the MacLain twins in Morgan's Woods, then a few years later acquiesces in her seduction in those same woods by the twins' father, King MacLain. All of this is told playfully—the twins are described as "two gawky boys" who, as Mattie remembers later, are "like young deer . . . gamboling now she knew not where" (111). The white-suited King has a reputation for seducing young girls in the woods, but because his shoulders "twinkled in the glade" and his smile was "like a little boy's," Mattie Will dubs him "Sir Rabbit" (107, 111) and welcomes his advances. Clearly these episodes in Morgan's Wood are presented as innocent high jinks. Just as clearly, Mattie's "fall" is not going to get her thrown out of Eden.

In short, the Morgana that Welty creates is inhabited by citizens who are rapists, murderers, and suicides, and by characters who experience loneliness, jealousy, and greed. Yet the reader's lasting impression of Morgana is of a world of innocence, mystery, and beauty. This impression is created partly through mythic parallels, but Welty's method of creating it is not easily divined. Indeed, although Welty says that in writing *The Golden Apples* she used myth "as freely" as "salt and pepper," she also states, "I had no system about it" (*Conversations* 331). A look at other obvious mythological allusions shows why the image of unsystematically sprinkling myths like "salt and pepper" on the stories is apt.

One of the most obvious mythical motifs involves the Celtic god described by W. B. Yeats in "The Song of Wandering Aengus" as searching throughout his adult life for a beautiful maiden he has glimpsed in his youth. Aengus longs to pluck for this maiden "the silver apples of the moon, the golden apples of the sun." In "June Recital," Cassie Morrison thinks of a few lines from this poem while she is tie-dyeing a scarf. After she wakes in the middle of that night with another line in her head, she sees in her dreams the "grave, unappeased, and radiant face" of Aengus (97). This clear allusion to Yeats's poem not only gives Welty's book its title but also introduces the theme of an insatiable longing to wander that is clearly evident in all of the stories.

Another network of mythical parallels involves several stories about Zeus. In "Sir Rabbit," already described, King MacLain's rape of Mattie Will allusively reenacts Yeats's "Leda and the Swan." His monarchical name, his "grandeur" in his white linen suit, the statement that "she had to put on what he knew with what he did," and the fact that a feather floats down into her hand after King leaves, all point to allusive parallels (108). Welty in her inimitable way, of course, is parodying the Olympian seduction: King is "an old rascal," his white shoulders remind Mattie of the back of a goose rather than a swan, and the floating feather is a dove's.

In the book's first story, "Shower of Gold," Welty makes other alterations to this particular myth. There King also appears as Zeus, this time impregnating his wife, Snowdie. When Snowdie tells her neighbor that she is expecting, the neighbor thinks

Snowdie looks "like a shower of something had struck her, like she had been caught out in something bright" (7). Readers may recognize the allusion to the myth of Danae's being impregnated by a "shower of gold" from Zeus, the outcome of which was the birth of Perseus. Again Welty avoids following the myth too closely by having Snowdie give birth not to one son but to twin boys, as Leda did when she bore Castor and Pollux after Zeus impregnated her.

To complicate things further, Welty's allusions to Perseus are not connected with the MacLains, as logic would dictate, but rather with a lad named Loch Morrison and an elderly piano teacher named Miss Eckhart, a German lady who rooms with Snowdie MacLain. Loch Morrison is an important character in both the second and fourth stories, "June Recital" and "Moon Lake." In "Moon Lake" the teenager, who is working as a lifeguard at a summer camp for girls, rescues a drowning orphan by snatching "the hair of Easter's head" (142), just as Perseus had seized the Gorgon's snaky hair. When Loch later stands in his candlelit tent looking like the victorious Perseus, Welty undercuts his heroic stance by having two sniggering girls outside comment to each other about the "little tickling thing hung on him like the last drop on the pitcher's lip" (155).

The myth of Perseus appears again in the last story, "The Wanderers," which, like "The Dead" in *Dubliners* and "Big Two-Hearted River" in *In Our Time,* functions to provide a final integration of the composite novel. In this story, which climaxes *The Golden Apples,* Virgie Rainey thinks of Miss Eckhart, a major actor in "June Recital." Virgie remembers that in the MacLains' house, near the piano Miss Eckhart used for her lessons and recitals, there was a picture of the vaunting Perseus holding the decapitated head of Medusa. As Virgie remembers this picture, she realizes that Miss Eckhart had hung it there because she "had absorbed the hero and the victim and then, stoutly, could sit down to the piano with all Beethoven ahead of her" (276). The point seems to be that the mythical hero and victim must be integrated in the mind of the artist, who then is able to see the contrarieties and complexities of the world and from that vision create art. As Virgie concludes, "Every time Perseus struck off the Medusa's head, there was the beat of time, and the melody. Endless the Medusa, and Perseus endless" (276).

Critics have identified many other mythological allusions in *The Golden Apples*. Kathryn Etter, for example, suggests that the name "Morgana" alludes to the powerful enchantress Morgan Le Fay, that Arthurian legend lies behind the name "Guenevere" given to Katie Rainey's cloth doll, and that a similar connection applies to Katie's deathbed, which looks like "a vast King Arthur shield that might have concealed a motto."[17] We could continue tracing allusions, but critics have already done this. Anyway, as Welty warns her readers, she had "no system" because she was just using myth as freely as "salt and pepper." In discussing further her own use of mythology she added, "It's kind of frightening to think that people see ponderous and allegorical meanings" (*Conversations* 189).

We certainly don't want to belabor any "ponderous allegorical meanings," and yet we contend that there *is* a pattern in Welty's use of myth. What? How? The answer lies in what T. S. Eliot called "mythical method." In reviewing James Joyce's *Ulysses* for the *Dial* in 1923, Eliot spoke of Joyce as "manipulating a continuous parallel between contemporaneity and antiquity."[18] Whereas the parallel in *Ulysses* is between one day in the life of Leopold Bloom in modern Dublin and 10 years in the epic voyage of Odysseus in ancient Greece, the parallel in *The Golden Apples* is between one 40-year chronicle set in Morgana, Mississippi, and timeless tales set in various mythical worlds. In each case, Joyce's and Welty's, the "parallel between contemporaneity and antiquity" exists, evoking what Welty calls the "spaciousness and mystery" of life, "something perhaps bigger than ordinary life allows people to be sometimes" (*Conversations* 307). Indeed, as effected through Eudora Welty's mythic vision, the world of the marvelous is contemporaneous with the world of the ordinary—at least in the hamlet called Morgana, in the state of Mississippi.

Italo Calvino contends that myth is "the hidden part" and "the underground part" of stories,[19] an idea that is certainly reflected in the "hidden" worlds of myth that gird Welty's Morgana. In another respect, though, Calvino's comment is relevant to Stein's and H. D.'s composite novels, to Gordon's and de Beauvoir's, to Miller's and many others. Ultimately, myth is story—story pattern, to be exact. Some authors, like Stein in *Three Lives*, use one story pattern; other authors, like Welty in *The Golden Apples*, appropriate many. Though their works are very different, their method is the same—a method that illustrates the connective power of pattern in the composite novel.

Chapter 7

Storytelling

The Process of Fiction Making as Focus in the Composite Novel

Leslie Marmon Silko begins *Storyteller*, her 1981 composite novel, with this dedication:

> . . . to the storytellers as far back as memory goes and to the telling which continues and through which they all live and we with them.

"The telling which continues" aptly describes *Storyteller*'s elusive structure. It is an assemblage of short stories, anecdotes, poems, folktales, excerpts from letters, autobiographical and historical notes, and photographs, in which many text-pieces have titles but others do not. At first glance the book appears to be an uncentered, unfocused collage. But in reading it one becomes immediately aware of a unifying voice, a "telling which continues." An early review described this "telling" as "a continuing verse narrative [that] is interspersed with the stories."[1] But this is misleading: it implies identifiable narrative text-pieces. Instead, the "telling" voice in *Storyteller* runs throughout the book, interrupting here, remembering there, commenting briefly somewhere else. Perhaps the best description of Silko's method (which is indistinguishable from the book's structure, if that is possible) occurs in one fragment of an untitled text-piece that follows a story that is part of a letter: "I've heard tellers begin 'The way I heard it was. . . .' and then proceed with another story purportedly a version of a story just told but the story they would tell was a wholly separate story, a new story with an integrity of its own, an offspring, a part of the continuing which storytelling must be" (227; ellipsis in original). This excerpt by itself appears confusing, run-on, impossibly incoherent. But taken in context, encountered where it occurs in *Storyteller* (near the end), it describes what the reader understands full well to be the "structure" of this book, which, in telling many versions of many stories, tells one. And what is this "one" story? It is, says the voice of *Storyteller*, "the whole story / the long story of the people" (7).

In a 1979 address, Silko explained to an academic audience the conventions of her Laguna Pueblo oral tradition: "For those of you accustomed to a structure that moves from point A to point B to point C, this presentation may be somewhat difficult to follow because the structure of Pueblo expression resembles something like a spider's web—with many little threads radiating from a center, criss-crossing each other. As with the web, the structure will emerge *as it is made* and you must simply listen and trust" (italics ours). Throughout her presentation Silko stressed the importance of "the one thing—which is the 'telling,' or the storytelling." Further, she went on to emphasize "storytelling" as an experience in which the audience plays a crucial role: "The storytelling always includes the audience and the listeners, and, in fact, a great deal of the story is believed to be inside the listener."[2]

Silko's concept of "storytelling," then, is experiential and transactional. In such aspects it is remarkably similar to the kind of reading experience postulated by some reader-response literary critics. When Stanley Fish explains how a sentence carries meaning, for example, he emphasizes the active role of the reader in creating that meaning. Thus the sentence, says Fish, is not an object "but an *event*, something that *happens* to, and with the participation of, the reader," and this event is a "temporal experience" rather than a "spatial one."[3]

Critics like Fish place less emphasis on the writer than they do on the interaction between reader and text. Silko, however, makes it clear that "the telling" is a three-part transaction: "The *storyteller's* role is to draw the *story* out of the *listeners*. This kind of shared experience grows out of a strong community base" (italics ours).[4] As Silko sees it, then, "storytelling" is a communal experience involving teller, tale, and audience—a multivalent transaction that echoes Roman Jakobson's model of linguistic communication, often diagrammed as follows:

$$\text{addresser} \underline{\quad} \underset{\substack{\text{code} \\ \text{context}}}{\overset{\text{contact}}{[\text{ message }]}} \underline{\quad} \text{addressee}$$

According to Jakobson's model, all communication consists of six elements: a *contact* that occurs within a *context*, so that a *message* formulated in mutually understood *code* is delivered from an *addresser* to an *addressee*. And the point is that the message itself (the book, the text, the story) is not enough, that meaning is transmitted through a dynamic and interactive process. Thus, though the diagram looks simple, its ramifications are profound. As Terence Hawkes encapsulates them, "'Meaning' in short resides in the *total* act of communication."[5]

Storytelling as a "total act of communication" is indeed Silko's structuring principle in *Storyteller*, which replicates as much as possible in a print medium the experiential-communal act of "telling." Thus, the addresser (the book's first-person voice) immediately invokes the context (the Hopi of Laguna Pueblo) and explains the code ("the photographs are here because they are part of many of the stories") while launching into a description of "Aunt Susie," then telling how Aunt Susie would tell a story, then telling a story that Aunt Susie told, then telling how Aunt Susie would change a story during storytelling, and so on.

If there is a progression in the book, it is spiral-like rather than linear. In this regard, Silko's description of the storytelling process as a "web" is fitting because the archetypal figure for poets and storytellers in many Native American cultures (including the Hopi) is affectionately known as Grandmother Spider.

"Grandmother Spider," writes Susan Scarberry, "spins her thoughts into existence" in a web that is "symbolic of the coherence of all experience." Further, "the most prevalent image of the spiderweb, the orb web, is an orderly arrangement of threads radiating out from a central hub and linked to one another in a spiral."[6] Thus, the spiderweb is an intricate form, but ultimately an orderly one. In much the same way, storytelling itself is the focus of *Storyteller*, bringing together diverse text-pieces in "an entire vision of the world" (6).

The Way to Rainy Mountain: Another Way of Telling

Structurally, N. Scott Momaday's *The Way to Rainy Mountain* (1969) presents an interesting contrast to *Storyteller*, yet Momaday's book is just as reflective of Native American tradition and was as self-consciously planned as Silko's. At the center of Momaday's symmetrically crafted composite novel are three kinds of narratives: Kiowa myths that he learned from his grandmother and tribal elders, commentaries on Kiowa history, and reminiscences from his own childhood. Thus, *The Way to Rainy Mountain* contains three narrative voice-tracks—the mythic, the historical, and the personal. The three voice-tracks, rendered in different typefaces, are divided into 24 pieces, with one piece from each voice-track (a myth-piece, a history-piece, and a reminiscence-piece) comprising a three-part section. The 24 three-part sections are arranged into three divisions entitled "The Setting Out," "The Going On," and "The Closing In." Framing the three divisions are three lyrical essays (prologue and introduction, and epilogue) and two poems ("Headwaters" at the beginning and "Rainy Mountain Cemetery" at the end).

Kenneth Lincoln describes *The Way to Rainy Mountain* as "a carefully structured personal history . . . within a whole narrative sequence of tribal life."[7] Lincoln's description is apt. The book's structure was obviously deliberate, very carefully planned to reflect the many "journeys" contained therein. On a literal level, the journeys described are the tribal migration of the Kiowas from Montana to the southern Great Plains, and the retracing by Momaday himself of the Kiowa migration route from its beginning at the headwaters of the Yellowstone River to its end (and his grandmother's grave) at the foot of Rainy Mountain, near the

Wichita Range in Oklahoma. On a symbolic level, the journeys in *The Way to Rainy Mountain* are many: a factual journey through Kiowa history; a mythic journey through Kiowa legend and culture; an empathetic, imaginary journey through the life of Momaday's family, especially his grandmother; and a personal journey (Momaday's) in search of identity.

"All of this and more," says Momaday in the book's epilogue, was a "quest" (88). Indeed, then, "the way to Rainy Mountain" embodies a composite quest with complementary but separate tracks, each having a beginning and an end. The Kiowa migration and Momaday's retracing of it, of course, had geographic origins and end points. Similarly traceable through linear progression in space-time, the Kiowa people developed from nomadic outsiders to Lords of the Plains to displaced persons, their final displacement represented in the vestiges of tribal memory and language that lie buried with Momaday's grandmother at the foot of Rainy Mountain. Even Momaday's own memory-identity as a Kiowa is traceable from its beginning through events that he remembers and stories he has heard to glories that he imaginatively re-creates. But there is one journey in *The Way to Rainy Mountain* that adumbrates all others, and this journey is a continuum, having neither beginning nor end. Momaday explains in the prologue: "The journey herein recalled *continues to be made anew* . . . for that is peculiarly the right and responsibility of the imagination. It is a whole journey, intricate with motion and meaning; and it is made with the whole memory, that experience of the mind which is legendary as well as historical, personal as well as cultural" (italics ours) (4). All of this is a "miracle," Momaday continues, because the journey "continues to be made anew." As Silko would say, the journey continues in "the telling."

In one regard, then, the meticulously crafted linear structure of Momaday's composite novel is fundamentally different from the loosely collaged, weblike structure of Silko's. To some extent this difference reflects each author's respective Native American culture: the agricultural Hopi lived in permanent communities that stressed weblike cooperation and interdependence, unlike the nomadic Kiowa, who ranged over the plains and prized questlike individual achievement in their hunter-warriors. Feminist critics might note at this point that the web and the quest carry gender-specific figural connotations in all cultures, that in all symbologies the web (essentially the circle) is traditionally female while the quest (essentially the straight line) is traditionally male. Certainly this is the case in most Native American cultures. Paula Gunn Allen in *The Sacred Hoop* affirms this gender-specific distinction in the two symbols, discussing them in the context of "the complementary traditions of women and men" in Native American cultures, where "women's traditions are largely about continuity [the circle], and men's traditions are largely about transitoriness or change [the straight line]."[8] Allen deals at length with the writings of Silko and Momaday, and it is surely no accident that the Silko chapter is subtitled "Healing and Ritual" while the Momaday chapter is subtitled "Transition and Transcendence."

Undoubtedly, then, there are many complex factors that influenced the contrasting composite forms of *Storyteller* and *The Way to Rainy Mountain,* including the life aesthetic of each author as well as the respective ties of each to Native American tribal cultures. Yet in one point of comparison the two works are identical, and this may in fact be the most important connection of all: the focus of each is "the telling which continues," the process of storytelling itself.

Obabakoak and *Pricksongs & Descants*: Like Paella and Apple Pie

Another composite novel that shares this focus is Bernardo Atxaga's *Obabakoak* (first published in Spanish in 1989). Atxaga (a nom de plume pronounced "*Otch*-ga") is a Basque; Obaba is the name of the Basque village that serves as a centering device in the book, and *Obabakoak* is a Basque word meaning "the people and things of Obaba." Once a reader understands this (thus defusing the threat inherent in the book's peculiar-sounding and intimidating title), Atxaga's composite novel reveals a treasure trove of stories as one might hear them while attending a *tertulia*—a village storytelling session. Because a *tertulia*'s offerings are neither preset nor prescriptive, one may hear tales from all generic traditions (including crime stories, romances, personal memoirs, and fairy tales) by one tale-teller or many (the book's text-pieces are grouped into three sections, only one of which features a common narrator). Actually, Atxaga manages to fuse the hometown aspects of *Winesburg* (tales, tellers, and/or characters are somehow connected with Obaba) with the far-flung adventure and fantasy aspects of *Cosmicomics* (stories may carry one anywhere within or beyond space-time). And Atxaga is able to do this precisely because the focus and organizing principle of his book is, as Eugenio Suarez-Galban explains it, an *"obsession with storytelling"* and "with tale-telling in all its forms."[9] Further, Atxaga incorporates a "telling" twist on metafiction (literally, fiction about itself) by including among his stories brief essaylike text-pieces that discuss aspects of storytelling (*Obabakoak,* says Suarez-Galban, is a "manual on storytelling"). Like Silko and Momaday, then, Atxaga emphasizes a dynamic, interactive process in which teller(s), tale(s), and audience (the components of a *tertulia*) are essential entities. Interestingly, the American edition of *Obabakoak* is called a novel. We, of course, would call it a composite novel or, in Suarez-Galban's more colorful phrase, "a delicious literary *paella*" (20).

At first glance Robert Coover's *Pricksongs & Descants* (1969) appears less cohesive than Atxaga's *Obabakoak* because *Pricksongs,* composed of 21 short fictions, has no interconnective reference point similar to Atxaga's Basque village and culture. Yet Coover himself said his book is structured upon an "organizing principle,"[10] a principle that is surely reflected in the title's musical terms *pricksongs* and *descants.* Medieval in origin ("pre-Monteverdian," as Coover puts it), the terms refer, respectively, to a printed song (in early music, notes were literally "pricked" on paper) and to unprinted variations on a song (early descants were improvised, constantly changing) (Gado 83).

In literary terms, we might say that "pricksongs" correspond to culturally inscribed texts while "descants" correspond to uninscribed variant texts. That this analogy is appropriate is borne out by such critics as Larry McCafferty and Richard Andersen who affirm that the fictions in *Pricksongs and Descants* are generally of two types: (1) stories that tell "a familiar story from an unfamiliar point of view" (as in "The Brother"—the story of Noah, told by his brother who is left behind to drown in the flood); and (2) stories that "present fiction as a variety of narrative possibilities" (as in "The Babysitter"—the story of an everyday family event, told in 107 fragments that include mutually incompatible and outrageous plot possibilities).[11] To rewrite a familiar story, then, is to challenge prevailing truths (what manner of lowlife scum was Noah, that he could consign his own brother to a miserable death?) And to stuff a story full of incompatible happenings is to question the nature of reality (did the babysitter strangle the baby? or will she? or does she wish she could? or is she fantasizing about it? or is she dreaming? or is she in someone else's dream?) Further, both "types" of stories in Coover's book contain pricksong elements *and* descant elements. As Coover explains it, "A pricksong *is* a descant" in the sense that musicians eventually "pricked" (printed) the descants as well as the basic musical line, and when that happened, "the idea of a counterpoint, of a full, beautiful harmony emerged" (italics ours) (Gado 83).

Counterpoint and harmony are process-effected and process-dependent, and thus Coover makes it clear that *Pricksongs* takes as its "organizational principle" a process: the process of fiction making. This process, as narratologist Seymour Chatman describes it, depends upon two crucial elements that Chatman calls "story" and "discourse." "Precisely," says Chatman, "story is the content of the narrative expression, while discourse is the form of that expression," and he goes on to explain in even simpler terms that, in any narrative, "story is the *'what'*" while "discourse is the *'how.'*"[12] Chatman's what/how duo is remarkably similar to Coover's pricksong/descant duo in that "pricksong" exemplifies the "what" of fiction making while "descant" exemplifies the "how" of it, the two elements of each duo always working together in a process that creates both counterpoint and harmony.

The crucial point here—that "what" cannot exist independent of "how"—demonstrates Chatman's conviction concerning the profound importance of narrative making. Coover is equally convinced. Roughly in the middle of *Pricksongs & Descants* is a "Dedication and Prologue" in which the author talks about storytelling and addresses Miguel de Cervantes *("maestro apreciadisimo")*, in whose work "narrative fiction . . . became a process of discovery" and whose "exemplary adventures of the Poetic Imagination" Coover hopes to emulate (78). In this text-piece, in essence, Coover explains that by focusing on fiction making (metaphorically, a descant in ongoing improvisational motion with and against a pricksong), he seeks to explore the essential counterpoints and harmonies of life itself.

In many aspects, then, Coover's *Pricksongs & Descants* is similar to Bernardo Atxaga's *Obabakoak*. Both are clearly composite novels; both draw on and transform a variety of genre sources; both are linguistically effulgent and playful; and both find their method, structural aesthetic, and focus in the process of fiction making. If the ingredients in Atxaga's composite novel render it a "literary *paella*" (it is "very Spanish," emphasizes Suarez-Galban), then Coover's is surely a literary apple pie—crusty, filling, quintessentially American. And both pie and paella, at least as Coover and Atxaga serve them up, are heavily spiced and hot to the tongue.

The hoary traditions that inform the works of Silko and Momaday seem far removed from the avant garde self-consciousness of Coover and Atxaga, as well as such other metafictional iconoclasts as Ishmael Reed and Claribel Alegría, Donald Barthelme and John Barth, and many more. Jim Ruppert suggests an intriguing connection, however, between metafictional works and works springing from the Native American oral tradition. Referring to what he calls the "story reality" of Native American fiction, Ruppert explains (echoing Momaday) that "the telling of the story creates a reality," and (echoing Silko) that "the performance of the story becomes part of the story." Finally, says Ruppert, there is "the reality of the story-in-the-making,"[13] a phrase that could describe not only the career of John Barth, but also and most particularly his best-known work, the composite novel *Lost in the Funhouse*.

Lost in the Funhouse: "On with the Story"

Silko's concept of "the telling which continues" is apparent from the first text-piece of John Barth's *Lost in the Funhouse* (1968).[14] This text-piece, entitled "Frame-Tale," reads simply, "Once upon a time there was a story that began" (1) and is juxtaposed with instructions about cutting and fastening that will result in a "moebius strip" that repeats these words endlessly. Clearly Barth is sending two signals to the reader: (1) this book is circular and continous (like the Möbius strip that is its frame tale) rather than teleological, and (2) story rather than character is the book's central focus.

This same idea, expressed by Momaday as the metaphor of a "journey that continues to be made anew," is embedded in the second text-piece, "Night-Sea Journey." In this strange little story the narrator-protagonist is a spermatozoan who begins to believe, as he swims up the Fallopian tube, that he may be the "sole survivor" of this long journey and thus become "tale-bearer of a generation" (9). He is considering a hypothesis he has heard: that "makers and swimmers each generate the other" so that what is immortal is "the cyclic process of incarnation" (8). In other words, the "journey continues to be made anew."

Because three of the five stories that follow "Night-Sea Journey" are about a boy named Ambrose Mensch, a reader may be tempted to see the night-sea journey as Ambrose's conception, but another explanation is suggested by the fourth text-piece, entitled "Autobiography: A Self-Recorded Fiction." Barth states unequivocally in the prefatory "Author's Note" that in "Autobiography" the first-person pronoun refers to "the story, speaking of itself," and, further, that he (Barth) is the father while a recording machine is the mother (x). This idea—that the story itself is the narrator-protagonist—helps one appreciate some of the outrageous puns in "Autobiography." For example, the "I" speaks of being upset but having to "compose myself" (33), of having a mother who was "a mere novel device . . . to which Dad resorted one day when he found himself by himself with pointless pen" (34). The "I" had expected to be "beautiful, powerful. . . . Anyhow, human," but is instead a "Basket case. Waste" (36–37). Using "Autobiography" as a key, one can easily see that "story" is the protagonist in several other text-pieces as well. For example, in "Echo," the eighth text-piece, the protagonist cannot speak for herself but instead repeats the "tongue-tried tales" of others (97). Similarly, "Menelaid" begins, "This voice *is* Menelaus, all there is of him" (127).

This emphasis on voices and the story they tell, of course, suggests the need for a listener/reader. Thus Story, the speaker, says pointedly in "Autobiography": "You who listen give me life in a manner of speaking" (33). And if we have a Story and a listener/reader, then we must also have a speaker/writer—for, as the spermatozoan has pointed out, "makers and swimmers each generate the other." The same is true of storytellers and stories, and this explains why three of the most often reprinted stories in *Lost in the Funhouse* focus on Ambrose Mensch, creating a scaled-down portrait of the storyteller as a young man. In the best of these, the title story "Lost in the Funhouse," 13-year-old Ambrose visits a funhouse in Ocean City. This is a family outing that includes a lovely 14-year-old named Magda, about whom Ambrose has sexual fantasies throughout the story. Intermingled with these fantasies are thoughts about fiction so that the funhouse becomes a metaphor for both life—particularly sex—and writing. When Ambrose gets separated from the others, lost in the labyrinthine funhouse, confused by distorting mirrors and disembodied voices, he entertains himself by making up stories and longing for Magda. He finally decides that he "will construct funhouses for others and be their secret operator—though he would rather be among the lovers for whom funhouses are designed" (94).

Ambrose is not mentioned again in *Lost in the Funhouse*, though both he and Magda are developed further in later books by Barth. However, the final *Funhouse* story, "Anonymiad," is told by an unnamed Greek writer (perhaps Homer, father of fiction) who becomes inspired while drinking wine from nine amphorae named after the Muses. He then fills the amphorae with sperm and fiction written on goatskin and throws them into the water to float like spermatozoa on a long night-sea journey. This text-piece is obviously a reminder, then, of the frame tale (since the story seems to be beginning again), and of the story "Night-Sea Journey." But it is also a reminder of the fifth text-piece, "Water Message," in which Ambrose, while playing along the seashore, finds a bottle with a message in it.

Lost in the Funhouse ends with Anonymous uncertain as to whether his message in the bottle will ever be found. Nevertheless, he thinks with satisfaction, "My tale's afloat." He imagines it bumping the wharves of Mycenae and moving out to sea again, drifting for age after countless age, perhaps never picked up and read by anyone. "No matter," he thinks. "Upon this noontime of his wasting day, . . . on a lorn fair shore a nameless minstrel"—the text stops abruptly here and then continues on a new line: "Wrote it" (193–94). The emphasis on these last two words—"Wrote it"—is the same emphasis that was apparent from the beginning in "Author's Note"—"On with the story. On with the story" (ix). *Lost in the Funhouse* begins and ends, in other words, with a telling that continues.

"How can we know the dancer from the dance?" asks W. B. Yeats in his well-known poem "Among School Children." This may be an unanswerable question for some people, but not for Leslie Marmon Silko, N. Scott Momaday, Bernardo Atxaga, Robert Coover, or John Barth. They know full well that the dancer *is* the dancing, the teller *is* the telling. And we, too, live—dancing and telling—through the composite novels that they write.

Chapter 8

Testing Boundaries

Exploring Generic Variety in the Composite Novel

Janette Turner Hospital, in a recent review article, commented on the limitations that the traditional novel places on a writer. At times, Hospital says, one wishes for "a different literary form, a new kind of polemic"—"perhaps something akin to Pascal's *Pensees,* an episodic collage of documentary fact, scholarly opinion and lyrical monologue."[1] Certainly some composite novels exhibit the collagelike structure and generic smorgasbord that Hospital describes. One thinks, for example, of recent works such as George Garrett's *Whistling in the Dark: True Stories and Other Fables* (1992), a pastiche of stories, lectures, poems, anecdotes, family histories, and reminiscences. Or Barry Gifford's *A Good Man to Know: A Semi-Documentary Fictional Memoir* (1992), an assemblage of magazine pieces, newspaper clippings, a few maps, an FBI report, and personal stories (Gifford in an author's note calls his book a *shoset-*

su, which is "a rather more flexible and generous and catholic term than 'novel.'") Or Gilbert Sorrentino's *Under the Shadow* (1991), which is self-described on its dust jacket as a "novel" that "takes the form of fifty-nine brief sketches with simple nouns as titles." Or Judith Ortiz Cofer's *Silent Dancing: A Partial Remembrance of a Puerto Rican Childhood* (1990), a carefully orchestrated composition of alternating *"ensayos"* (essays of a life) and poems, all of which its author describes as nonfictional fiction—"that combination of memory, imagination, and strong emotion that [results] in 'poetic truth' " (11).

It is surely significant that works like these can announce outright their generic miscegenation, the implication being that they expect their self-designation to be accepted rather than contested. In this regard they illustrate how attitudes toward generic hybridization have changed since the early 1940s, when the editors of the *Partisan Review* hesitated to publish one of Mary McCarthy's stories because it mixed journalism and fiction.[2] Even during the 1960s and 1970s, which were characterized by a flurry of literary experimentation, these books would have been generic outlaws—at best labeled "experimental" and consigned to the hinterlands, at worst overlooked completely. Why? For two reasons: first, because of their "collagified" structures, and second, because they transgress the traditionally accepted boundaries of "fiction."[3]

As we have mentioned in previous chapters, however, critics and reviewers have gradually become more aware and accepting of books that exhibit composite-novel structure, even though they don't what what to call them. Further, the traditional genre-bound distinctions between fiction and nonfiction have virtually been left by the wayside. Certainly we have discourse theorists such as Foucault to thank for this, but we also must give credit to those twentieth-century writers, particularly in America and Europe in the early years but throughout the world in later years, who have tested traditionally held concepts concerning the nature of fiction and the parameters of form all along. Not all boundary-testing works were composite novels, of course, but many of them were, including two significant texts that have not been highlighted in previous chapters—*Tender Buttons* by Gertrude Stein and *Cane* by Jean Toomer.

Characteristically audacious, Stein's book self-consciously defines itself in its title: *Tender Buttons: Objects, Food, Rooms—*

Studies in Description (1914). The three sections are composed of titled pieces (some several pages in length, others merely six or seven words) that are indeed prose "studies" describing objects, foods, and rooms. *Tender Buttons* so nonplussed early readers and critics that it was virtually ignored; it is only recent critics who have made any attempt at genre designation, describing it as a "melange," "a little book of still lifes," a "verbal collage," and a "linguistic collage" while affirming it as an "artfully structured" and "cohesive" work.[4]

Jean Toomer's *Cane* (1923), too, has always caused similar problems. Briefly, *Cane* is a three-section assemblage of sketches, stories, poems, and a short drama, with the first and last sections set in the South and the middle section set in Washington, D.C. In the introduction to Liveright's 1975 paperback edition, Darwin T. Turner discussed the problem of *Cane's* "puzzling" structural aesthetic and concluded that "the name given to the form of *Cane* probably does not matter" (xxi). Apparently it does matter, though. Charles Larson claimed just a year later, in 1976, that *Cane* is "*sui generis*—a unique piece of writing in American literature as well as in the entire scope of Third World writing." And the debate continues, exemplified by the judgments of two recent critics (in 1992) concerning *Cane's* generic status: that *Cane* (and Alice Walker's *Meridian*) "are examples of literary collage," and that *Cane* is "certainly not genre-specific" but rather "a unique avant-garde work."[5] Claims for *Cane's* status as a one-of-a-kind literary text may well depend upon the sample used in making comparisons. For *Cane* is actually far from unique, certainly in light of the many such montagelike books that have succeeded it, but also in light of those that preceded it—including W. E. B. DuBois's *The Souls of Black Folk* in 1903.[6]

Singular composite novels appeared early, then, and they have continued to appear ever since. One thinks, for example, of the works of Willa Cather, who quite self-consciously tested the limits of form, preferring to call many of her later works "narratives" rather than "novels." Cather's composite novels include *The Professor's House* (1925), a three-part text compared by James Schroeter to "an Indian bracelet" that embeds "turquoise" in "dull silver"; *Death Comes for the Archbishop* (1927), whose stylized structure Merrill Maguire Skaggs compares to "the stations of the cross" and "its own gallery containing many pieces"; *Shadows on the Rock* (1931), described by Deborah Carlin as a "palimpsest" on which one encounters "different story genres: legends, hagiography, personal histories, miracles, adventure stories, dreams, visions, and historical vignettes"; and *Obscure Destinies* (1932), whose three-novella structure was influenced by and is highly reminiscent of Flaubert's *Trois Contes*.[7]

In a broad-sweep survey, one also cannot overlook the genre-boundaries tested by William Faulkner. *Go Down, Moses* (1942) has already been highlighted in chapter 5 (of all Faulkner's books, *Go Down, Moses* is the one whose genre designation has been most keenly contested). But Faulkner wrote other composite novels, including *The Unvanquished* (1938), a sequenced group of stories with a developing protagonist; *The Wild Palms* (1939), a text that interleaves two novellas; and *The Hamlet* (1942), whose four sections chronicle four branches of the Snopes family. It is possible, too, that *The Sound and the Fury* (1929), a four-section text that experiments with point of view, might be better designated as a "composite novel" than a "novel."

The works of Italo Calvino are similarly self-conscious in their structural innovations. In addition to *Cosmicomics* (1965), which was highlighted in chapter 4, Calvino's composite novels include *Our Ancestors* (1960), a three-novella fantasy-text; *Marcovaldo or the Seasons in the City* (1963), whose stories, set in a grimly unchanging city and featuring a similarly static protagonist, are arranged ironically according to seasonal cycles; *The Castle of Crossed Destinies* (1973), divided into two parts, entitled "The Castle" and "The Tavern," each serving as a frame for its guests' stories, which are told by means of a tarot deck (the guests are mute); and *Mr. Palomar* (1983), a series of camera-eye vignettes arranged in three major sections.

The composite novels just discussed, from Stein's *Tender Buttons* to Calvino's *Mr. Palomar*, are obviously works that explore generic limits regarding form and structure. They vary greatly in that each has its own structural aesthetic and its own combination of unifying elements. Yet they are all alike, generally speaking, in that they eschew linear narration (at least in part) and achieve whole-text coherence through the principle of juxtaposition. These works are also alike in another way. Their component pieces all fall within the purview of traditionally accepted "literary" categories: stories, sketches, poems, vignettes, plays, novellas, frame pieces bearing such titles as "prologue" and "epilogue," and so on. In addition, in all of these works, the boundary line between fiction and autobiography, or fiction and essay, or fiction and historical fact is rarely tested, and, if at all, gently so.

Other composite novels are more pugnacious in testing the generic boundaries of "fiction" and even "literature." Here one thinks of those recent works (discussed at the beginning of this chapter) by Garrett, Gifford, Sorrentino, and Cofer—all of which announce quite clearly that they are defying traditional genre divisions between fiction and fact, fiction and autobiography, fiction and journalism. Certainly there are many other composite novels that flirt in some way with generic transvestism, however. Claribel Alegría's *Luisa in Realityland* (1987), for example, described on its dust jacket as an "autobiographical prose/verse novel," is composed of 89 titled passages (52 in prose, 37 in verse) that feature a protagonist, some recurring characters, and several sequel narratives. Ntozake Shange's *Sassafrass, Cypress & Indigo* (1982) is a sharply sectioned but novel-like work that incorporates poems, magical incantations, recipes, letters, dreams, and drama criticism. And Clarence Major's *Emergency Exit* (1979) is an assembled text that self-consciously tests conceptions of "fiction" and "the novel" by including in its adumbrating family saga an assortment of schedules, catalogs, incident reports, double-column passages, questions, charts, episodes, poems, paintings, and lists.

The generic innovation continues, startling in its variety. E. M. Broner's *Her Mothers* (1975), for instance, is a seven-part concoction of stories and incidents, running jokes and refrains, "Q & A"s and quotations, described on its back cover as a "serial montage" and in an introduction by Marilyn French as a woman's version of "the Jewish novel" (x). Ishmael Reed's *Mumbo Jumbo* (1972) is a verbal-cum-visual collage text that includes drawings, photos, and posters as well as graphs, newspaper clippings, dictionary definitions, symbols, and anagrams. And Peter Handke's *The Inner World of the Outer World of the Inner World* (1969) is another verbal-cum-visual assemblage that includes photographic and newsprint collages among its stories and prose texts.

The roll call continues backward in time, through a roster of fiction-testing composite novels, including Mary McCarthy's *Memories of a Catholic Girlhood* (1957), Edmund Wilson's *Memoirs of Hecate County* (1946), Antoine de Saint-Exupéry's *Wind, Sand*

and Stars (1939) (which won France's Grand Prix du Roman as the best "novel" of 1939 and was also named the best "non-fiction book" of 1939 by the American Booksellers Association), Michael Gold's *Jews Without Money* (1930), Djuna Barnes's *Ladies Almanack* (1928), Sui Sin Far's *Mrs. Spring Fragrance* (1912), and Joseph Conrad's *The Mirror of the Sea* (1906). Just as those composite novels that are structurally innovative span the twentieth century, so too do these, which test, in one way or another, traditionally accepted boundaries of fiction.

But the point here is to be representative, not comprehensive. Thus the twentieth-century genre-testing composite novels mentioned so far in this chapter are but a few examples, a selection chosen to illustrate the variety of works that have explored the aesthetics of structure and the nature of fiction. To conclude by illustrating another kind of variety, we will discuss five contemporary composite novels: *Like Water for Chocolate* (1992 in English), *A Certain Lucas* (1984 in English), *Borderlands/La Frontera* (1987), *A Yellow Raft in Blue Water* (1987), and *How to Make an American Quilt* (1991). Each of these books in its own way has broken new ground and tested boundaries; taken together they reflect the range and possibilities of the composite-novel form. Not coincidentally, these books have been chosen because they illustrate distinctive variations on the five primary principles of organization through which whole-text coherence in the composite novel may be effected.

The Importance of Place: Esquivel's Magical Village

A term that most appropriately describes Laura Esquivel's composite novel *Like Water for Chocolate: A Novel in Monthly Installments with Recipes, Romances and Home Remedies* (1992) is *femmage*, coined by American artist Miriam Schapiro in the early 1970s to describe her own works, which incorporated through collage techniques the materials and images of women's lives. In speaking of Schapiro's femmages, art critic Norma Broude describes "the exploding vitality of Schapiro's fabrics and patterns, which she harmonizes within a lucid structural order."[8] No better description of Esquivel's composite novel could be devised. Though the book's recipe-of-the-month frame epitomizes "lucid structural order," its magical realism gives it an "exploding vitality." And underlying it all, providing the essential backdrop for this cookbook-and-fireworks femmage, is turn-of-the-century Mexico—its history, culture, and flavor.

Like Water for Chocolate is composed of 12 chapters, each designated by a month of the year and a recipe from a cookbook-diary left by the narrator's great-aunt Tita. Within this structure unfolds a fable of four women (Tita, her tyrannical mother, and her two older sisters), a tale as comic and cruel as any collected by the brothers Grimm and with the same propensity for magic. Thus, hundreds of guests become violently ill after eating wedding cake because copious tears had been shed in the batter; a woman eats until she explodes; a virgin's breasts flow with milk; blood from thorn pricks turns pink roses red, and those rose petals, cooked in a wine sauce with quail, provoke a sexual frenzy so overwhelming that body heat ignites rose-scented flames.

Esquivel's femmage-tale of food and fancy focuses on indoor life, on women's lives as they were circumscribed by home and family. Yet it is clear from the outset that this is a particular country, culture, and time, a place-specific way of life. Thus the recipes themselves, as one reviewer notes, "are rich with Mexican history": chocolate for drinking is made as it was in Montezuma's day, for example, and all the recipes combine "pre-Columbian basics" such as corn, chilies, and beans with "Spanish extras" like cinnamon, sesame, and pomegranate seeds.[9] Since this is a rural setting in a pre-Cuisinart era, the recipe-tales also include such helpful instructions as how to castrate chickens, wring the necks of quail, and feed turkeys with walnuts to insure that their flesh will be sweet.

The "home remedies" referred to in the book's title are also grounded in the region and the time. One needed, for instance, to know how to poison bedbugs (with a preparation of alcohol, turpentine, and powdered camphor); how to swaddle a newborn so that he is "wrapped up like a taco" (73); how to treat severe burns with a potato plaster and then prevent scarring by applying "the bark of the tepezcohuite tree" (202).

Most of all, this is a Mexico rich in folklore but hobbled by tradition—where children are frightened into obedience by stories about the night-wailing witch *La Llorona;* where the women of a house work for months embroidering the white wedding-sheet that modestly hides the bride while permitting intimate relations through an aperture in the center; where the lives of females are controlled by the age-old rule that the youngest daughter of a family can have no life of her own other than caring for her mother. When this rule was applied to the narrator's great-aunt Tita, it ruined her life so thoroughly that "Tita was literally 'like water for chocolate'—she was on the verge of boiling over" (151).

Indeed, the cooking pots and characters in this composite novel are always "on the verge of boiling over," until they blaze up in a final conflagration that lights the night skies over neighboring towns with a dazzling display of multicolored lights. As if to complement these fireworks in the sky, Esquivel's literary femmage is grounded in a culture-specific referential field as colorful as the enormous bedspread that Tita crochets through her insomniac nights: "a kaleidoscopic combination of colors, textures, and forms" (101). Although Mary Russell Mitford might not recognize it, this is "Our Village" rendered in magical realism.

Rites of Passage: He/I Is/Am Lucas/Cortázar

Julio Cortázar's *A Certain Lucas* (1984 in English) is described on its dust jacket as "a kaleidoscopic *jeu*" (*jeu* is French for "game" or "sport") composed of a "series of eccentrically interlocking pieces." Obligingly, the dust jacket also tells us other things: that the book "reveals the essence of one particular man's life"; that the book is divided into three major sections whose mission is to reveal Lucas's life, then his world, then his life again; finally, that the many text-pieces are "glimpses" and "aspects" through which we compile "a complete picture of a complete man." In essence, then, this all-knowing dust jacket defines *A Certain Lucas* as a composite novel (a "series" of "interlocking pieces" that cohere into "a complete picture") and identifies the primary principle of organization ("one particular man's life," i.e., a single protagonist as focus).

What the dust jacket most assiduously avoids, however, is *calling* the book anything ("kaleidoscopic *jeu*" is not very specific as a genre designation). Most reviewers did the same. In a review, Paul West called it "an assembly of slices and glimpses" and concluded, "The book is both a whole without parts and parts without a whole—an impossible object." And though "collage" is a term used occasionally for Cortázar's essay books, it has seldom if ever been used to describe *A Certain Lucas*.[10]

Cortázar himself (a Brussels-born Argentine who lived his last 30 years in Paris) is well known for his self-conscious experimentations in literary genres. "The truly revolutionary novel," he once said, "does not merely have revolutionary 'content,' but also seeks to revolutionize the novel itself, the novel form."[11] Does he do this in *A Certain Lucas?* Consider. The book's many short text-pieces are gathered into three major sections that differ primarily in narrative point of view: Pieces in the first and last sections are in the third person, while pieces in the middle section are in the first person. It is made clear that the book's *he* and *I* are writers, and it requires only cursory knowledge of Cortázar's life and career to recognize in all three sections autobiographical facts as well as his distinctive ideas on literature and politics, his love of city life, and his wacky sense of humor. The *he*s and *I*s coalesce, then, and all the text-pieces contribute to a composite picture of one man who is Lucas (in fiction) and Cortázar (in fact).

Further, because this pieced-together text makes no promise of linear narration, it easily incorporates in a relatively short book a generic mixture: the facts of auto/biography, the philosophical reflections of prose essay, and the fancies of fiction. In other words, the fact that "Lucas was once operated on for appendicitis" need bear no causal relation to the reflection that "Somewhere there must be a garbage dump where explanations are piled up," and neither fact nor reflection need bear a causal relation to the story about "Mrs. Cinamomo," who squashes snails in her slippers with a hammer before she realizes that in doing so she is ruining her slippers. Nevertheless, the picture one gets of this protagonist is not fragmented; it is sympathetic and three-dimensional.

Indeed, though *A Certain Lucas* maintains a tone of ironic detachment, it is an intensely personal work whose text-pieces cohere around and in the process fully flesh its central figure. In essence, this ingenious composite novel is an associational interior/exterior monologue that permits us to watch "a certain Lucas/Cortázar" as he watches himself.

(E)Merging Protagonist(s): Anzaldua's New Mestiza(s)

Author Gloria Anzaldua announces in the preface to *Borderlands/La Frontera: The New Mestiza* (1987), "I am a border woman," and then refers to herself as "this *mestiza.*" But by the end of the preface that single voice has become the choral voice of "the new mestizas," and Anzaldua's collective protagonist has been identified: each and all who live "on borders and in margins" while maintaining a "shifting and multiple identity and integrity" (n.p.). For Anzaldua herself, the borderlands are both literal and figurative. Her homeland is Hidalgo County in Texas ("the most poverty-stricken county in the nation"), and she is Chicana by birth—"a kind of dual identity—we don't identify with the Anglo-American cultural values and we don't totally identify with the Mexican cultural values" (98, 63). As a Chicana and poor, then, she is suspect by both Anglo and Mexican standards. Further, she is marginalized even within Chicano culture because she has left its enclave and speaks out against its traditional oppression of women. And in American society at large, where homophobia is almost universal, Anzaldua as a lesbian is once again marginalized, exiled to a no-man's-land (no pun intended) on the borders.

Thus, Anzaldua speaks with authority and compassion for this collective protagonist, and she does so through a composite novel that, in itself, is a structural reconfiguration of its embodied focus. The book, in other words, in both design and organization, reflects the consciousness of a borderlands dweller who is always aware of the border ("this thin edge of / barbwire") that paradoxically divides and unites its adjacent territories (13).

Signifying the concept of a line that divides, *Borderlands* itself parts, in the middle, into two distinct, titled sections. Spatially, this text arrangement replicates the geography of Anzaldua's homeland: "The U.S.-Mexican border *es una herida abierta* where the Third World grates against the first and bleeds. And before a scab forms it hemorrhages again, the lifeblood of two worlds merging to form a third country—a border culture" (3). There is, then, a geographic demarcation between the two countries (reflected in the division between the two book sections), a "border" that is precisely definable on a map in terms of latitude and longitude.

But in the "border culture" (made up of the territory on *both sides* of the border), all is a hemorrhagic mixture, even language. Thus does Anzaldua explain in the book's introduction

109

that a reader, like a borderlands dweller, will continually segue from one tongue to another, "from English to Castillian Spanish to the North Mexican dialect to Tex-Mex to a sprinkling of Nahuatl to a mixture of all these: the language of the Borderlands" (n.p.). Echoing these language shifts in Anzaldua's book are genre shifts. Again the structural aesthetic is the segue, a shift form in which one encounters, in no discernible order, academic prose, scholarly citations, stories, poems, history and myth, aphorisms, Anzaldua's on-and-off personal narration, instructions, dual-language translations, epigraphs, and dedications. To comprehend this text is to listen attentively to the voice(s) that speak(s) throughout, just as one would listen to a madrigal or a cantata.

Obviously, *Borderlands* is a juxtapositional text rather than a linear one. Yet it is also centered and coherent—a composite novel—and it is ultimately Anzaldua herself who provides the best description of it: "In looking at this book that I'm almost finished writing, I see a mosaic pattern (Aztec-like) emerging, a weaving pattern, thin here, thick there. . . . This almost finished product seems an assemblage, a montage, a beaded work with several leitmotifs and with a central core" (66). The "central core" of the book, of course, is the collective protagonist, all those who by virtue of *mestizaje* are caught in *los intersticios* between worlds. Anzaldua speaks for these people, but she also speaks to them. And in this final regard, the text as polemic, Anzaldua continues to test boundaries. For she proposes a new world, a global consciousness that can be effected only by action and activism, by "theory in the flesh":[12]

Cuando vives en la frontera	[When you live on the border]
you're a *burra, buey,* scapegoat,	[donkey, oxen]
forerunner of a new race,	

To live in the Borderlands means to
put *chile* in the borscht,
eat whole wheat *tortillas,*
speak Tex-Mex with a Brooklyn accent;

To survive the Borderlands	
you must live *sin fronteras*	[without borders]
be a crossroads. (194–95)	

"You," then, must "be a crossroads" while you live "without borders." The back cover of *Borderlands* suggests that "the work of the 21st century will be about the coming together of diverse cultures." Gloria Anzaldua has begun that work.

Pattern and Palimpsest: A Lifeline for Dorris's Yellow Raft

Michael Dorris's *A Yellow Raft in Blue Water* (1987) tells in separate novellas the stories of three Native American women: teenaged Rayona; her mother, Christine; and Ida (known as "Aunt Ida"), who raised Christine. Each woman speaks in the first person in her own novella, and, because their lives are intertwined, each figures prominently in the other two novellas. Thus, the reader gets three perspectives on the life events of a family, with the end result that the book's three sections cohere into one multigenerational saga.

Numerous cross-references connect the book's three parts, as each narrator in turn describes events and relationships that the three women have in common. Each woman's perspective is skewed in some areas and incomplete in others, however, so that a reader participates in constructing a whole story by merging all three. Thus the book may be visualized as three "layers" that cohere through superimposition, a kind of textual sandwich made from three slices of bread.

Significantly, the image here is one of depth, of a text entity that is structurally like the title's "yellow raft in blue water," which appears only once, in the first section, when Rayona swims to it. Deceptively visible, the yellow raft seems a simple contraption as long as one stays on its *Rayona*-surface. But daylight filters through the *Rayona*-slats, making visible in half-light the barely submerged *Christine*-platform, and hinting not only of the *Ida*-beams that gird the frame but also of the mucky, oozy lake-bottom in which the entire structure rests. It is only by diving down—by settling one's feet "into plants and soft mud that squeezes out between [your] toes" (59) and then looking up from the bottom to see all the pieces—that it is possible to comprehend the raft structure in its entirety.

In one way, then, the three sections of *A Yellow Raft in Blue Water* are layered, palimpsestically pattern-coherent, making Dorris's composite novel appear similar to the three-part texts that we discussed in chapter 6 (*Three Lives* and *Palimpsest,* among others). But the novellas in *Yellow Raft* are also connected through an image that begins the book, ends it, and recurs throughout it—an image of three strands, braided together. This image is occasionally static, as in the "bracelet made of three different kinds of metals—iron, copper, and brass—twisted together" that Rayona's father, Elgin, wears (183). But it is most often dynamic, couched in the action of hands that pull, catch, blend, and weave, and it resonates in the final scene (and words) of the book, as Ida muses on "the rhythm of three strands, the whispers of coming and going, of twisting and tying and blending, of catching and of letting go, of braiding" (372).

In discussing *Yellow Raft,* Adalaide Morris applauds its plural focus on "the greedy, sticky-fingered, endlessly complicated family." Then Morris goes on to explain why this focus is so timely, so crucial: "The family is the one force in our culture that regularly binds together people of different ages, genders, interests, skills, and sexual preferences and sometimes also people of different ethnic traditions, racial or religious backgrounds, and economic classes."[13] A family, in other words, is not like a club whose members we can choose; our relatives may be the only people we connect with in life *in spite of* diversity and heterogeneity.

Thus, when Michael Dorris anchors his narrative in family, when he reveals the enormous tensile strength that comes from braiding a three-generational lifeline, he creates an ethos of connection. In terms of the book's structural aesthetic, the two controlling patterns are the raft and the braided triple strand. The raft pattern is augmented by the braid pattern, both triply strong, one of depth and one of distance—a synergy of perspectives that reflects the complex layering and interweaving of family ties.

Storytelling: Whitney Otto on Quilt (Story) Making

Whitney Otto's *How to Make an American Quilt* (1991) is composed of eight titled stories that alternate with sets of quilting instructions, all connected through a frame story contained in a prologue and an epilogue. The narrator is Finn Bennett-Dodd, 26 years old and at a crossroads in her life. In order to think things out, she spends the summer at her grandmother's house in a small California town, where she observes an eight-member quilting circle that has been meeting, on and off, for 35 years.

Judging from a quick survey, it appears that this composite novel prompted most reviewers into a profusion of needlework metaphors. Just for fun, we "pieced together" the following metareview entirely from "fragments and scraps" of reviews that are included as prefatory blurbs in the 1992 paperback edition:

> [In prose] "as careful and precise as needlework," [Whitney Otto] "stitches together the lives of eight women" [whose stories]—"like the sashing that binds together the blocks"—"alternate with sets of quilting 'instructions.' | " [The women's] "lives are the squares, their words the designs, their gestures the stitches" [that create] "this tapestry of feelings." [Chronicling] "the ways in which our lives border, overlap and are stitched together," [Otto's book reveals] "a larger pattern of female culture."

> (from eight review-blurbs)

This metareview is meant not in parody but rather to point out the ubiquity of writing-as-sewing and book-as-quilt tropes. As we discussed in chapter 2, such metaphors are as ancient as needle-and-cloth work itself, and appropriately so. And if, as Sandra Gilbert and Susan Gubar so convincingly demonstrate in *The Madwoman in the Attic*, the pen in modern times is construed as a metaphoric penis, then surely the needle is fittingly construed as a metaphoric pen.[14] Thus, it is inviting, as many reviewers do, to visualize *How to Make an American Quilt* metaphorically, as a quilt—with a border (the prologue-epilogue frame tale) and a pieced top composed of alternating instruction blocks and story blocks.

Such a metaphor is misleading, however. For the primary focus in *How to Make an American Quilt* is not the quilt itself but the quilting, not the stories themselves but the telling and the listening. The stance of the narrator is significant here. She "tells" the eight stories quite conventionally, using third-person narration. The prologue, in which she sets up the frame story, is told in the first person. But the "instruction" pieces are detached and musing, spoken in timeless second person to an unidentified "you." This "you" is multiple: the reader(s); women in history; women in the quilting circle whose stories the narrator is writing; the narrator herself as she is writing. In this way the narrator speaks *for* women ("I"), *about* women ("she/they") and *to* women ("you").

Indeed, this is a voice that knows well the history of women and women's culture in America, where until quite recently all women were denied a voice, and where many women are still silenced. Speaking to/of women silenced in history, unable to vote or hold property, the narrator says, "Save your opinions for your quilt. Put your heart and voice into it. Cast your ballot; express your feelings regarding industrialization, emancipation, women's suffrage, your love of family" (13). Speaking to/of women silenced by poverty, racism, and ageism, she says, "Make yourself heard in a wild profusion of colors, shapes, themes, and dreams with your fingertips" (168). As if in answer, one of the quilters (in the story "Tears Like Diamond Stars") says, "I learned to speak with needle and thread long before society finally 'gave' me a voice—as if society can give anyone a voice; it can only take a voice away" (175).

The telling, then, the telling through quilting, is the focus. As if in affirmation, Jill McCorkle concludes a review of Otto's book in this way: "It is a tribute to an art form that allowed women self-expression even when society did not."[15] Indeed, the vitality of this art form is as evident today as it ever was. Quilts bloom in bright colors at roadside stands and on backyard clotheslines, spread warmth and comfort across narrow bunks and splendid four-posters, announce their prestige and priciness in trendy galleries and vaulted museums. "Quilt art," in other words, is alive and well,[16] and Otto's book is, as McCorkle asserts, a "tribute" to it. But *How to Make an American Quilt* is also a tribute to the power of voice, to the driving need of every individual to tell and talk and say. "Say it with your hands," the narrator admonishes each silenced self (92).

And thus the telling continues.

Esquivel's, Cortázar's, Anzaldua's, Dorris's, Otto's—these five composite novels reflect the exciting variety of contemporary fiction, incorporating magical realism, subject-object pronoun conflation, polyglot prose/verse synthesis, three-dimensional structure metaphors, and triple-stanced narrative point of view. In earlier years, each might have been called something else: *Like Water for Chocolate* a "loose-leaf novel," perhaps; *A Certain Lucas* a "prose collection"; *Borderlands* a "miscellany"; *A Yellow Raft in Blue Water* a "triptych"; and *How to Make an American Quilt* a "story cycle" or "framed cycle." Perhaps, like *Cane,* one or more might have been declared sui generis, a one-of-a-kind text. The fact that now all of these may be designated as composite novels implies in broad terms a shift in critical attitude and stance— away from product and toward process, away from narrow specialization and toward cross-disciplinary expertise, away from boundary making and toward networking. If, as Jonathan Culler has averred, "a genre . . . is a set of expectations,"[17] then the genre designation of "composite novel," in its embodied "expectations," reflects the diversity, multiplicity, and exhilaration of our fin de siècle era.

Chapter 9

Looking to the Future

Conclusion and Speculations

As the narrator of Whitney Otto's *How to Make an American Quilt* is explaining her fascination with history, she notes that she realized very early on that a linear "time line" is deceptive because it is too reductive, that such a scheme leaves out "the small odd details" and "historical gossip" that characterize the human dimension of history ("I mean, is it true that Catherine the Great died trying to copulate with a horse? And if not, what a strange thing to say about someone"). Then she makes this most significant statement: "The construction of the time line [must be] both horizontal and vertical, both distance and depth" (2, 3). She is saying, in other words, that when we think horizontally, as is the case when we identify and isolate fixed time points on a line, we lose sight of the connectedness of life. To achieve and maintain a sense of connectedness, we must also think vertically, three-dimensionally.

The narrator's point, and Otto's, reflects an ongoing critical inquiry into the concept of "spatialization" as it relates to the process of reading, to the interaction that occurs when a reader engages a text and derives meaning therefrom. Drawing on the theoretical work of Julia Kristeva and M. M. Bakhtin, Susan Stanford Friedman suggests that readers who "spatialize" when they read—that is, readers who conceptualize what they're reading in terms of depth as well as surface—are better able "to construct a 'story' of the fluidly interactive relationship between the surface and palimpsestic depths of a given text" than readers who do not. Then, in making a crucial point, Friedman quotes Kristeva: "Spatialization suggests an interpretive strategy that regards a text as 'a dynamic . . . *intersection of textual surfaces* rather than a *point.*'"[1]

It occurs to us that the metaphors we have worked with in various ways throughout this book are related in principle to the idea that spatialization is an efficacious reading strategy. To visualize "the village" spatially when one is reading Anderson's *Winesburg, Ohio,* for example, is to construct—mentally—in three dimensions. True, *Winesburg* offers an element of linearity in that a reader can "follow" George Willard's developmental trajectory through the individual text-pieces. But to focus in such fashion on an individual is to shift one's perspective away from the surrounding field, and in a text such as *Winesburg,* the field (village *and* villagers) is also important. Thus, each text-piece is a story-space, and as we read one text-piece after another, we see a first story-space intersecting with a second story-space and a third and fourth and so on. In addition, the story-spaces overlap, some more and others less, so that a depth field develops—or what we are calling a "village" develops—or what Kristeva calls "an intersection of textual surfaces" develops. This is not to refute the importance of George Willard in *Winesburg* (or any protagonist, single or collective, in any text). Rather, we are simply pointing out the significance of perspective in regard to depth perception, that is, in regard to three-dimensional reading.

The quilt is another such metaphor, in fact a particularly apt metaphor in regard to visualizing in three dimensions. Each quilt has a surface/horizontal dimension in its decorative top, which may itself exhibit a number of depth areas by virtue of trapunto work (in which areas of the top are "stuffed" from behind) or appliqué. But all quilts also have a depth/vertical dimension in that they are composed of three layers: a base (usually plain cloth, muslin of some kind); a midsection composed of cotton batting; and the top itself, the decorative layer. Indeed, quilters are well aware of the importance of depth. A quilt top, no matter how beautifully designed and executed, is a poor limp layabout without its depth layers. If one were to visualize *The Woman Warrior* in terms of a quilt, then, one might see an America-top whose many life pieces are contributed by Kingston, her mother and aunt, her friends and schoolmates, and so on. Underneath would be a China-base for stability and strength, and in the middle would be myth-batting for depth and warmth. Indeed, to visualize Kingston's composite novel in this way is to realize that the "woman warrior" herself is, again to quote Kristeva, "a dynamic intersection of textual surfaces rather than a point."

In her discussion of spatialization, Susan Friedman refers to the palimpsest, another metaphor that we have used for the composite novel. H. D.'s *Palimpsest* is a three-layer text, as are some others that we discussed. However, the palimpsest as a metaphor for spatialization is not limited to any specific number of "layers" and may in fact connote a deep delving into historical time. Thus the palimpsest may be a helpful metaphor for visualizing such works as *Go Down, Moses,* whose "textual surfaces" are as many and as finely layered as the shale beds that lie beneath the Mississippi woods and mucklands.

Another trope that we have discussed, especially in chapter 7, is the web or spiderweb. Like the quilt-as-text metaphor, this too is deceptive in that it appears to be a "surface" trope. But we made the point (citing Susan Scarberry's definition of an "orb" web) that the web is a spiral structure that defeats closure and implies continuous motion. In the process of "spatializing" a text via web-metaphor, a reader would also realize that one "sees through" a web-surface into the space beyond it, as if one were looking through an old-fashioned Victorian window that contains tiny diamond-shaped panes of beveled glass. In this way the web-metaphor also contains depth. It is, in fact, an appropriate metaphor for visualizing *The Golden Apples,* whose surface stories are so backlit by mythic torchlight that one sees, as if through a gossamer web, the eternal twilight dance of the gods.

One final metaphor, the borderlands, illustrates the importance of perspective in spatialization. As we discussed in chapter 8, the borderlands metaphor is a paradox. Though positioned by a line-that-divides, it is nevertheless defined as one territory, that is, as the combined territories adjacent to *both* sides of the border. Thus "borderlands" is a metaphor of *con*vergence as well as *di*vergence. In regard to spatialization, in fact, it has interesting possibilities in relation to *The Country of the Pointed Firs*. As we mentioned in chapter 3, Jewett's *Pointed Firs* is anchored firmly in Maine's rural Dunnet area. But because the summer visitor comes from "another country," the city to which she will return, a dividing line is always implied between rural and urban, between trees and concrete. In the course of her summer at Dunnet, however, the visitor-protagonist becomes a borderlands dweller: henceforth she will always have a foot in both worlds. Thus, a reader who spatializes *Pointed Firs* by means of this dichotomous borderlands trope will foreground country life and place city life in the background. And the perception will always be one of depth—once again, "a dynamic intersection of textual surfaces."

The idea of approaching a text through spatialization, through metaphor, is not really new, of course—just newly rediscovered. Louise Rosenblatt in 1978 proposed a trope much like the "referential field" (Wolfgang Iser's term) that we used in chapter 3. In Rosenblatt's metaphor the text is visualized as "a meshed woven curtain, a mesh of flexible strands that hold a certain relationship to one another, but whose total shape and pattern changes as any one part is pulled or loosened." Further, Rosenblatt goes on to picture "the reader peering through the curtain, affecting its shape and the pattern of the mesh by the tension or looseness with which he is holding it, and filling in the openings from his own palette of colors."[2] Although her point was to illustrate the importance of the reader in the reading process, Rosenblatt's trope is directly applicable to the structural aesthetic of the composite novel and a reader's involvement in it.

Friedman (through Kristeva), then, uses spatialization to emphasize depth as well as surface; Rosenblatt uses spatialization to emphasize the porous and malleable nature of a text. In essence, the principle underlying each critic's metaphor is that a reader's perspective must shift from distance to depth, from the individual to the field, and back again, in a dynamic process. Again, in essence, the composite novel facilitates such a dynamic process because of its structural aesthetic—the fact that its text-pieces are both autonomous and interconnected. And this is, after all, a paradigm of how we live our lives: constantly shifting our focus from past to future to present, from others to ourselves and back again, with autonomy *and* interconnection, in fits and starts.

Certainly women will attest that this has always been the shape of their experience. Suzanne Juhasz speaks for countless generations when she describes the "dailiness" of women's lives, a "repetitive, cumulative, cyclical structure" that Juhasz finds reflected in women's writing.[3] But is a "repetitive, cumulative, cyclical" life structure really gender-specific? Or class-specific? Or race-specific? The Victorians (white-anglo-saxon-protestant-eminent ones, at least) lived leisurely lives that paralleled and were reflected in their big, long, linear novels. But our lives are different from theirs, and it stands to reason that our books should be different. Ronald Sukenick could well be in conversation with Juhasz when he insists that "instead of reproducing the form of previous fiction, the form of the novel should seek to approximate the shape of our experience."[4]

We believe that the composite novel does this. It is, in other words, user-friendly. It fits our lives.

Alain Robbe-Grillet knew well that "there is no question . . . of establishing a theory, a pre-existing mold into which to pour the books of the future."[5] What happens, happens. And we who are fortunate enough to be able to look back in retrospect on an entire century can see what *has* happened—in our particular case, proposing a generic term *(composite novel)* for a form that has long been developing. Literature will continue, just as story itself will continue, because human beings need connectedness in their lives. Perhaps the composite novel is a reflection—possibly it is even a result—of this essential fact.

Notes

Chapter 1

1. Elizabeth Jordan, ed., *The Sturdy Oak: A Composite Novel of American Politics by Fourteen American Authors* (New York: Holt, 1917).

2. Alfred Bendixen, "Introduction: The Whole Story behind *The Whole Family,*" in *The Whole Family: A Novel by Twelve Authors* (1908; reprint, New York: Ungar, 1986), 1. Bendixen also mentions *Six of One by Half a Dozen of the Other* (1872), whose contributors included Harriet Beecher Stowe and Edward Everett Hale; *Bobbed Hair* (1925), whose contributors included Dorothy Parker, Alexander Woollcott, and Rube Goldberg; and *A House Party* (1901), whose contributors included Sarah Orne Jewett and George Washington Cable (li).

3. See Eric S. Rabkin, *The Fantastic in Literature* (Princeton: Princeton University Press, 1976), 133; Robert Scholes and Eric S. Rabkin, *Science Fiction: History, Science, Vision* (New York: Oxford University Press, 1977), esp. 61 and 221–26; and Eric S. Rabkin, "To Fairyland by Rocket: Bradbury's *The Martian Chronicles,*" in *Ray Bradbury,* ed. Joseph D. Olander and Martin Harry Greenberg (New York: Taplinger, 1980), esp. 110.

4. Joseph Warren Beach, *The Twentieth Century Novel* (New York: D. Appleton-Century, 1932), 475. Beach includes one chapter entitled "Composite Views" (470–84).

5. Malcolm Cowley, "Faulkner Stories, in Amiable Mood," review of *Knight's Gambit*, by William Faulkner, *New York Herald Tribune Books*, 6 Nov. 1949, p. 7; and Malcolm Cowley, Introduction to *Winesburg, Ohio*, by Sherwood Anderson (New York: Viking, 1960), 15.

6. Complete source information for all genre terms is included in the back of this book in "Survey of Scholarship: A Bibliographic Essay." Regarding the argument against the term *short story cycle*, see Robert Michael Luscher, *American Regional Short Story Sequences* (Ph.D. diss., Duke U, 1984), esp. 3–8.

7. Forrest L. Ingram, *Representative Short Story Cycles of the Twentieth Century: Studies in a Literary Genre* (The Hague: Mouton, 1971); hereafter cited in the text as Ingram.

8. Ian Reid, *The Short Story* (New York: Methuen, 1977), 46–49.

9. Susan Garland Mann, *The Short Story Cycle: A Genre Companion and Reference Guide* (New York: Greenwood, 1989); hereafter cited in the text as Mann.

10. An excellent discussion of Bakhtin's work can be found in Tzvetan Todorov, *Mikhail Bakhtin: The Dialogical Principle*, trans. Wlad Godzich (Minneapolis: University of Minnesota Press, 1984), 85.

11. Ingram refers to the "cyclical habit of mind" a number of times, the first on page 24; Levi-Strauss's "symbolic function" is explained contextually in Teresa De Lauretis, "Narrative Discourse in Calvino: Praxis or Poiesis?" *PMLA* 90 (1975): 420–21.

12. E. M. Forster, *Aspects of the Novel* (New York: Harcourt, Brace, 1927), 213 ff.

13. George Levine, "Victorian Studies," in *Redrawing the Boundaries: The Transformation of English and American Literary Studies*, ed. Stephen Greenblatt and Giles Gunn (New York: Modern Language Association, 1992), 145–46.

14. Anais Nin, *Collages* (Denver: Alan Swallow, 1964); Sharon Spencer, *Space, Time and Structure in the Modern Novel* (New York: New York University Press, 1971), 199; and "The Art of

Ragpicking," in *Anais, Art and Artists: A Collection of Essays,* ed. Sharon Spencer (Greenwood, Fla.: Penkevill, 1986), 165.

15. As to "short story composite," see Warren French, *John Steinbeck,* 2d ed. (Boston: Twayne, 1975), esp. 54–75; as to "short story cycle," see Ingram, 39–43 and Mann, esp. 93–106; Steinbeck is quoted in Peter Lisca, *The Wide World of John Steinbeck* (New Brunswick, N.J.: Rutgers University Press, 1958), 57.

16. Ingram (who cites a personal letter from O'Connor's literary executor) and Mann differ on this point: see Ingram, 18 n. 13, and Mann, 156, 166 n. 1.

17. Raman Selden explains *gestalt* in *A Reader's Guide to Contemporary Literary Theory* (Lexington: University Press of Kentucky, 1985), 106.

18. As "short story cycles," Susan Mann includes Sherwood Anderson's *Death in the Woods and Other Stories* and Horacio Quiroga's *The Exiles: And Other Stories* (187, 203).

19. John Dos Passos, *U.S.A.,* 3 vols. (1938; reprint, Boston: Houghton, 1946); James Herriott, *All Creatures Great and Small, All Things Bright and Beautiful, All Things Wise and Wonderful, The Lord God Made Them All* (New York: St. Martin's, 1970, 1974, 1977, 1981); Edith Wharton, *Old New York: The Edith Wharton Omnibus* (1924; reprint, New York: Scribner's, 1978).

20. *Murasaki: A Novel in Six Parts,* ed. Robert Silverberg (New York: Bantam, 1992), vii. As the dust jacket of this "shared world anthology" explains, two of its six authors, Poul Anderson and Frederik Pohl, "constructed the working mechanics of a real star system, projecting the atmosphere, geology, chemistry, flora, and fauna of the two planets on which the work is set." Anderson and Pohl were then joined by four others (Greg Bear, Gregory Benford, David Brin, and Nancy Kress), and all six used the Anderson-Pohl essays as source material for stories that, together in this one volume, comprise an epic tale set in "the Murasaki star system— which actually exists."

21. Robert Coover, "The End of Books," *New York Times Book Review,* 21 June 1992, p. 24; see also Robert Coover,

"Hyperfiction: Novels for the Computer," *New York Times Book Review*, 29 Aug. 1993 pp. 1, 8–13.

22. Katherine Neville, *The Eight* (New York: Ballantine, 1988).
23. Italo Calvino, *Invisible Cities,* trans. William Weaver (1972; reprint, New York: Harcourt, 1974).
24. A. N. Wilson, Introduction to *The Four Men: A Farrago,* by Hilaire Belloc (1911; reprint, Oxford: Oxford University Press, 1984), xii.
25. Oates is quoted in Sanford Pinsker, "Speaking about Short Fiction: An Interview with Joyce Carol Oates," *Studies in Short Fiction* 18 (1981): 241.

Chapter 2

1. Mary Russell Mitford, *Our Village* (1819–24; reprint, London: MacMillan, 1906). Josephine Donovan, in *New England Local Color Literature: A Women's Tradition* (New York: Ungar, 1983), says unequivocally that Mitford "pioneered" the village sketch (esp. 23). Sandra Zagarell, however—in "'America' as Community in Three Antebellum Village Sketches," in *The (Other) American Traditions: Nineteenth-Century Women Writers,* ed. Joyce W. Warren (New Brunswick, N.J.: Rutgers University Press, 1993)—gives equal credit for "inspiring" the village sketch to Mitford and to Washington Irving (159–60 n. 1). The difference in opinion may derive from the way in which one defines "village sketch." Mitford's narrator looks only within the parameters of Reading, a village outside London. In contrast, Irving's Geoffrey Crayon extends his "sauntering gaze" to both England and America.
2. Elizabeth Gaskell, *Cranford* (1853; reprint, New York: Thomas Y. Crowell, n.d.); George Eliot, *Scenes of Clerical Life,* ed. Thomas A. Noble, Clarendon Edition (1858; reprint, New York: Oxford University Press, 1985); Jane Barlow, *Irish Idylls* (1893; reprint, Freeport, N.Y.: Books for Libraries Press, 1968); George Moore, *The Untilled Field* (1903; reprint, Freeport, N.Y.: Books for Libraries Press, 1970).
3. Sarah Josepha Hale, *Sketches of American Character* (1829; reprint, Boston: Freeman Hunt, 1831).

4. Augustus Baldwin Longstreet, *Georgia Scenes* (1835; reprint, New York: Sagamore Press, 1957); Mary Clavers [Caroline Kirkland], *A New Home—Who'll Follow? Or, Glimpses of Western Life* (1839; reprint, New York: Garrett, 1969); George Washington Cable, *Old Creole Days* (1879; reprint, Miami: Mnemosyne Publishing, 1969); Constance Fenimore Woolson, *Rodman the Keeper: Southern Sketches* (1880; reprint, New York: Garrett, 1969); Hamlin Garland, *Main-Travelled Roads* (1891; reprint, New York: Harper & Row, n.d.).

5. Jane Barker, *A Patch-Work Screen for the Ladies* (London: E. Curll and T. Payne, 1723).

6. Caroline Lee Hentz, *Aunt Patty's Scrap Bag* (Philadelphia: Carey and Hart, 1846); Louisa May Alcott, *Aunt Jo's Scrap-Bag*, in 4 vols: *My Boys, Shawl Scraps, Cupid and Chow-Chow,* and *My Girls* (Boston: Roberts, 1872–78); Maley Bainbridge Crist, *Patchwork: The Poems and Prose Sketches* (Atlanta: Martin & Hoyt, 1898).

7. Eliza Southgate's letter to her father is quoted in part in Jean Taylor Federico's "American Quilts 1770–1880," in *The Artist and the Quilt,* ed. Charlotte Robinson (New York: Knopf, 1983), 21.

8. Hannah Farnham Sawyer Lee, *Three Experiments of Living* (Boston: William S. Damrell, 1837).

9. [Louisa Caroline H. Tuthill], *The Belle, the Blue, and the Bigot; or, Three Fields for Woman's Influence* (Providence, R.I.: Samuel C. Blodget, 1844).

10. Marion Harland [Mary Virginia Terhune], *Husbands and Homes* (1865; reprint, New York: G. W. Dillingham, 1889).

11. Mary Eleanor Wilkins Freeman, *Understudies* (1901; reprint, Freeport, N.Y.: Books for Libraries Press, 1969), and *Six Trees* (1903; reprint, Freeport, N.Y.: Books for Libraries Press, 1969).

12. See, e.g., John Michael Vlach, *The Afro-American Tradition in Decorative Arts* (Cleveland: Cleveland Museum of Art, 1978), 55–75; see also Cynthia Elyce Rubin, ed., *Southern Folk Art* (Birmingham, Ala.: Oxmoor House, 1985), esp. 195.

13. Frances E. Watkins Harper's *Sketches of Southern Life* (Philadelphia: Ferguson Bros., 1891) is very difficult to find,

although it is available on microfilm (University Microfilms International: Ann Arbor, Mich.). But Susie King Taylor's book, originally published as *Reminiscences of My Life in Camp with the 33rd U.S. Colored Troops, Late 1st South Carolina Volunteers* (Boston: self-published, 1902), has been reissued as *Reminiscences of My Life: A Black Woman's Civil War Memoirs,* ed. Patricia W. Romero and Willie Lee Rose (New York: Markus Wiener, 1988). The description of Taylor's book as "random recollections" is from the 1988 edition's introduction by Willie Lee Rose (7).

14. Mrs. A. J. Graves, *Girlhood and Womanhood; or, Sketches of My Schoolmates* (Boston: T. H. Carter & Co. and Benjamin B. Musey, 1844).

15. Louisa May Alcott, *Hospital Sketches* (1863; reprint, Boston: Roberts Brothers, 1895).

16. Harriet Beecher Stowe, *Sam Lawson's Oldtown Fireside Stories* (Boston: James R. Osgood & Co., 1871).

17. Donald George Mitchell, *Reveries of a Bachelor; or, A Book of the Heart* (1850; reprint, New York: Scribner's, 1889).

18. See Arlin Turner, *Nathaniel Hawthorne: A Biography* (New York: Oxford University Press, 1980), 49–58.

19. See Michael Millgate, *Thomas Hardy: A Biography* (New York: Oxford University Press, 1982), 305.

20. See Stephen Crane, *Tales of Whilomville,* ed. Fredson Bowers (Charlottesville: University Press of Virginia, 1969).

21. Ivan Turgenev, *A Sportsman's Sketches,* trans. Constance Garnett (London: Heinemann, 1917).

22. Frank O'Connor, *The Lonely Voice: A Study of the Short Story* (Cleveland: World Publishing, 1963), 46.

23. Alphonse Daudet, *Letters from My Mill,* trans. John P. MacGregor (London: George G. Harrap, 1962).

24. David Stouck, "Willa Cather and the Impressionist Novel," in *Critical Essays on Willa Cather,* ed. John J. Murphy (Boston: G. K. Hall, 1984), esp. 55–57.

25. Gustave Flaubert, *Three Tales,* trans. Robert Baldick (Baltimore: Penguin Books, 1961).

26. David Roe, *Gustave Flaubert* (New York: St. Martin's, 1989), 87.
27. Alexander Pushkin, *The Tales of Ivan Belkin*, trans. Ivy and Tatiana Litvinov (Moscow: Foreign Languages Publishing House, 1954); Nikolai Gogol, *Evenings Near the Village of Dikanka*, trans. Ovid Gorchakov (New York: Ungar, n.d.); Mikhail Lermontov, *A Hero of Our Time*, trans. Martin Parker (Moscow: Foreign Languages Publishing House, n.d.).
28. Selma Lagerlof, *The Story of Gosta Berling*, trans. Pauline Bancroft Place (Garden City, N.Y.: Doubleday, 1941).

Chapter 3

1. Eudora Welty, "Place in Fiction" (1956), reprinted in *A Modern Southern Reader*, ed. Ben Forkner and Patrick Samway, S.J. (Atlanta: Peachtree Publishers, 1986), 538, 541.
2. Wolfgang Iser, *The Act of Reading: A Theory of Aesthetic Response* (Baltimore: Johns Hopkins University Press, 1968), esp. 128.
3. George Wickes, "Henry Miller: Down and Out in Paris," in *Critical Essays on Henry Miller*, ed. Ronald Gottesman (New York: MacMillan, 1992), 123; originally published in Wickes's *American in Paris* (Garden City, N.Y.: Doubleday, 1969).
4. See, e.g., Alan Trachtenberg, "'History on the side': Henry Miller's American Dream," in *American Dreams, American Nightmares*, ed. David Madden (Carbondale: Southern Illinois University Press; 1970), 136–48, and Wallace Fowlie, *Age of Surrealism* (New York: Swallow Press, 1950), esp. 185–87.
5. Editors' Preface to *The Martian Chronicles*, by Ray Bradbury, special ed. (1950; reprint, New York: Time, 1963), xii.
6. Arnold E. Davidson, "Regions of the Mind and Margaret Gibson Gilboord's *The Butterfly Ward*," in *Regionalism and the Female Imagination: A Collection of Essays*, ed. Emily Toth (University Park, Penn.: Pennsylvania State University Press, 1985), 168.
7. Sarah Orne Jewett authorized only one version of *The*

Country of the Pointed Firs—the 1896 version. Our page citations are to the text as it appears in a contemporary paperback edition that follows the format of Jewett's 1896 text and
is readily available for classroom use: *Short Fiction of Sarah
Orne Jewett and Mary Wilkins Freeman,* ed. Barbara H.
Solomon (New York: Meridian-NAL, 1979). Because readers
may use some version other than the Solomon text, we list
here, in sequence, the chapter numbers and titles according
to Jewett's 1896 table of contents:

After publication of the 1896 text—at Henry James's suggestion that she write more about "the dear country of the

Pointed Firs"—Jewett wrote four related stories: "A Dunnet Shepherdess," "The Queen's Twin," "The Foreigner," and "William's Wedding" (unfinished when she died in 1909). Many subsequent editions of *The Country of the Pointed Firs*, therefore, included these last four stories, which, though related, were not part of the whole text that Jewett planned with such care. Solomon also includes the four later stories but makes clear that they are "related stories." For the James-Jewett correspondence, see *The Selected Letters of Henry James*, ed. Leon Edel (New York: Farrar, Straus and Cudahy, 1955), 202–3.

8. Francis Otto Matthiessen, *Sarah Orne Jewett* (Boston: Houghton, 1929), 101; and Barbara H. Solomon, Introduction to *Short Fiction of Sarah Orne Jewett and Mary Wilkins Freeman*, 6.

9. The hiatus between the completion and the publication of *Dubliners'* was due to skittishness on the part of publishers as well as Joyce's reluctance to revise and emend. See, e.g., Richard Ellmann, *James Joyce*, rev. ed. (Oxford: Oxford University Press, 1982), 214—254.

10. Susan Mann, in *The Short Story Cycle*, argues for the importance of "the archetypal Dubliner" (30–32). Also see Florence L. Walzl, "A Book of Signs and Symbols: The Protagonist," in *The Seventh of Joyce*, ed. Bernard Benstock (Bloomington: Indiana University Press, 1982), 117–23.

11. For an analysis of Homer's *Odyssey* as external pattern for *Dubliners*, see Richard Levin and Charles Shattuck, "First Flight to Ithaca—A New Reading of Joyce's *Dubliners* (1944), reprinted in *James Joyce: Two Decades of Criticism*, ed. Seon Givens, 2d ed. (New York: Vanguard, 1963), 47–94. For analysis of Dante's *Inferno* as external pattern for *Dubliners*, see Mary T. Reynolds, "Joyce and Dante: The Shaping Imagination" (1981), reprinted in *The Seventh of Joyce*, ed. Bernard Benstock (Bloomington: Indiana University Press, 1982), 124–30. For analysis of recurrent internal patterns in *Dubliners*, see James S. Atherton, "The Joyce of *Dubliners*," in *James Joyce Today: Essays on the Major Works*, ed. Thomas F. Staley (Bloomington: Indiana University Press, 1966), esp. 40–53.

12. Robert Scholes and A. Walton Litz, Editors' Preface to *"Dubliners" by James Joyce: Text, Criticism, and Notes*, ed. Robert Scholes and A. Walton Litz (New York: Viking, 1969), 1.

13. Helen Fiddyment Levy, *Fiction of the Home Place: Jewett, Cather, Glasgow, Porter, Welty, and Naylor* (Jackson: University Press of Mississippi, 1992), 199. Fiddyment Levy calls *The Women of Brewster Place* a "cautionary tale" because, unlike Naylor's later novel *Mama Day*, its women characters have no stable maternal "home place," no way to forge their personal identities apart from "the Big Man social order" (12).

14. Barbara Christian, "Gloria Naylor's Geography: Community, Class, and Patriarchy in *The Women of Brewster Place* and *Linden Hills*," in *Reading Black, Reading Feminist: A Critical Anthology*, ed. Henry Louis Gates, Jr. (New York: Meridian-Penguin, 1990), 349, 353.

15. Susan Bolotin, review of *The Women of Brewster Place*, by Gloria Naylor, *New York Times*, 13 July 1982, sec. C, p. 10; Annie Gottlieb, "Women Together," review of *The Women of Brewster Place*, by Gloria Naylor, *New York Times Book Review*, 22 Aug. 1982, p. 11.

Chapter 4

1. Gore Vidal, for example, referred to *Cosmicomics* simply as "stories" and then elaborated that into "a super strip cartoon" in "Fabulous Calvino," *New York Review of Books*, 30 May 1974, p. 17.

2. John Gatt-Rutter, "Calvino Ludens: Literary Play and Its Political Implications," *Journal of European Studies* 5 (Dec. 1975): 335.

3. See, for example, Frank MacShane, "A Novel within a Novel Within. . . ," *New Republic* 184 (9 May 1981): 34.

4. Even though it is composed of 30 short pieces, Saltzman's *Iron and Silk* reads smoothly and chronologically—exactly like a traditional linear narrative. Yet the review excerpts on the dust jacket stress "a series of lightly sketched-in episodes" and "wonderfully observed anecdotes and sketch-

es." Similarly, even though Cisneros's *The House on Mango Street* is composed of 46 short pieces, it reads like a novel. Yet its dust-jacket describes it as "a series of vignettes." In both cases, reviewers avoid words like *novel* and just say *book*.

5. John H. Randall III chooses "double protagonists" who lead "parallel lives" in "Interpretation of *My Ántonia*" (1960); reprinted in *Willa Cather and Her Critics*, ed. James Schroeter (Ithaca: Cornell University Press, 1967), esp. 273–76.

6. Dorothy Tuck McFarland, *Willa Cather* (New York: Ungar, 1972), 40.

7. *Sherwood Anderson's Memoirs*, ed. Paul Rosenfeld (New York: Harcourt Brace, 1942), 289. Significantly, critics are still arguing about *how* the stories are connected. See, for example, John S. Reist, Jr., "An Ellipse Becomes a Circle: The Developing Unity of *Winesburg, Ohio*," *CEA Critic* 55 (Spring/Summer 1993): 26–38.

8. Malcolm Cowley, Introduction to *Winesburg, Ohio* (New York: Viking, 1960), 11–12.

9. Estelle Jelinek, *The Tradition of Women's Autobiography: From Antiquity to the Present* (Boston: Twayne, 1986), 189; James Olney is quoted in Elizabeth W. Bruss, *Autobiographical Acts: The Changing Situation of a Literary Genre* (Baltimore: Johns Hopkins University Press, 1976), 11; Patricia Lin Blinde, "The Icicle in the Desert: Perspective and Form in the Works of Two Chinese-American Women Writers," *MELUS* 6 (Fall 1979): 52.

10. The Kingston-Carabi interview is printed as "Special Eyes: The Chinese-American World of Maxine Hong Kingston," *Belles Lettres* 4 (Winter 1989): 11.

11. Suzanne Juhasz, "Narrative Techniques and Female Identity," *Contemporary American Women Writers: Narrative Strategies*, ed. Catherine Rainwater and William J. Scheick (Lexington: University Press of Kentucky, 1985), 175.

Chapter 5

1. Brewster Ghiselin, "The Unity of *Dubliners*" (1956); reprinted in *Twentieth Century Interpretations of "Dubliners": A Collection*

of Critical Essays, ed. Peter K. Garrett (Englewood Cliffs, N.J.: Prentice-Hall, 1968), 69.

2. Rachel Blau DuPlessis, *Writing beyond the Ending: Narrative Strategies of Twentieth-Century Women Writers* (Bloomington: Indiana University Press, 1985). The interchangeability of terms is made explicit in DuPlessis's index, which includes this entry: "Communal (choral, collective, group, multiple) protagonist" (248). DuPlessis uses all these terms synonymously throughout chapters 10 and 11 (162 ff.), and in addition refers to a "cluster protagonist" (182) and "transpersonal protagonist" (185). Other feminist critics who invoke the concept of a collective protagonist include Elizabeth Abel, Marianne Hirsch, and Elizabeth Langland, in their editors' introduction to *The Voyage In: Fictions of Female Development* (Hanover, N.H.: University Press of New England, 1983), 12, in which they define a "collective protagonist" as a group engaging in "psychological relationships" and whose members "assume equal status as protagonists." See also Elizabeth Abel in "(E)merging (I)dentities: The Dynamics of Female Friendship in Contemporary Fiction by Women," *SIGNS* 6 (Spring 1981): 413–35; and Judith Kegan Gardiner, "The (US)es of (I)dentity: A Response to Abel's '(E)merging (I)dentities,'" *SIGNS* 6 (Spring 1981): 436–42.

3. Barbara Somogyi and David Stanton, "Amy Tan: An Interview," *Poets & Writers* (Sept./Oct. 1991): 24–31.

4. The term "philistine esthetes" is Jay McInerney's, in "I'm Successful and You're Not," review of *Slaves of New York,* by Tama Janowitz, *New York Times Book Review,* 13 July 1986, p. 7.

5. Dan McCall, *The Example of Richard Wright* (New York: Harcourt Brace Jovanovich, 1969), 26.

6. William Burke, "*Bloodline:* A Black Man's South," *College Language Association Journal* 19 (1976): 545; Ernest Gaines is quoted in "Ernest J. Gaines," *Interviews with Black Writers,* ed. John O'Brien (New York: Liveright, 1973), 91.

7. Jeffrey Meyers, *Hemingway: A Biography* (New York: Harper, 1985), 82–83.

8. Critics continue to worry the bone of "influences" on

Hemingway. Most recently Joseph M. Flora, in "Saving Nick Adams for Another Day," *South Atlantic Review* 58 (1993): 620, suggested that Hemingway, especially in *In Our Time*, tried to "write the way Cezanne had painted."

9. Carlos Baker, ed., *Ernest Hemingway: Selected Letters 1917–61* (New York: Scribner's, 1981), 128.

10. Ibid., 154–55.

11. We are counting "A Very Short Story" as a "Nick" story. The vignette immediately preceding tells of Nick's being wounded, and "A Very Short Story" describes a wounded soldier in a hospital.

12. Philip Young, *Ernest Hemingway: A Reconsideration* (University Park: Pennsylvania State University Press, 1986), 41.

13. Debra Moddelmog, "The Unifying Consciousness of a Divided Conscience: Nick Adams as Author of *In Our Time*," *American Literature* 64 (1988): 591–610; reprinted in Jackson J. Benson, ed., *New Critical Approaches to the Short Stories of Ernest Hemingway* (Durham, N.C.: Duke University Press, 1990), 18–32.

14. Ernest Hemingway, *The Nick Adams Stories*, ed. Philip Young (New York: Scribner's, 1972), 327.

15. See Joseph M. Flora's "Saving Nick Adams for Another Day" for a fuller refutation.

16. Carl Wood, "*In Our Time:* Hemingway's Fragmentary Novel," *NM* 74 (1973): 722.

17. Faulkner is quoted in Joseph Blotner, *Faulkner: A Biography* (New York: Random House, 1974), 1102; in Joanne V. Creighton, *William Faulkner's Craft of Revision: The Snopes Trilogy, "The Unvanquished," and "Go Down, Moses"* (Detroit: Wayne State University Press, 1977), 85; in Dirk Kuyk, Jr., *Threads Cable-Strong: William Faulkner's "Go Down, Moses"* (East Brunswick, N.J.: Associated University Presses, 1983), 14.

18. For further elaboration and clarification, see these appendix articles in Arthur F. Kinney, ed., *Critical Essays on William Faulkner: The McCaslin Family* (Boston: G. K. Hall, 1990):

Robert W. Kirk with Marvin Klotz, "The McCaslin-Edmonds-Beauchamp Family" (262–63); Harry Runyan, "[Family Members]" (264–68); and Meredith Smith, "A Chronology of *Go Down, Moses*" (269–77).

19. Creighton, *William Faulkner's Craft of Revision*, 113.
20. Arthur F. Kinney, Introduction to *Critical Essays on William Faulkner: The McCaslin Family*, 36–37.
21. Cleanth Brooks, *William Faulkner: The Yoknapatawpha Country* (New Haven: Yale University Press, 1963), 244.
22. Erdrich's composite novel tetralogy includes *The Beet Queen* (New York: Holt, 1986), which covers the years 1932–72; *Tracks* (New York: Holt, 1988), which covers the years 1912–24; and *American Horse* (forthcoming), which covers the years from 1972 to the present.

Chapter 6

1. David Lodge, *Working with Structuralism* (Boston: Routledge and Kegan Paul, 1981), 11, 13.
2. Roman Jakobson, "The Metaphoric and Metonymic Poles," in *Critical Theory since Plato*, ed. Hazard Adams (New York: Harcourt Brace Jovanovich, 1971), 1116.
3. Gustave Flaubert, *Three Tales*, trans. Robert Baldick (Baltimore: Penguin Books, 1961).
4. Stratton Buck, *Gustave Flaubert* (New York: Twayne, 1966), 104; David Roe, *Gustave Flaubert* (New York: St. Martin's, 1989), 88.
5. Fredric Jameson, "Flaubert's Libidinal Historicism: *Trois Contes*," in *Flaubert and Postmodernism*, ed. Naomi Schor and Henry F. Majewski (Lincoln: University of Nebraska Press, 1984), 77.
6. Though the life stories are similar in so many other respects, an interesting contrast can be found in the deaths of the two women. According to Stein, "The good Anna with her strong, strained, worn-out body died" (82). According to Flaubert, "[Félicité] closed her eyes. Her lips smiled. Her heart-beats grew slower and slower, each a little fainter and gentler, like a fountain running dry, an echo fading away.

And as she breathed her last, she thought she could see, in the opening heavens, a gigantic parrot hovering above her head" (56).

7. Jayne L. Walker, *The Making of a Modernist: Gertrude Stein from "Three Lives" to "Tender Buttons"* (Amherst: University of Massachusetts Press, 1984), 19.

8. For a detailed comparison of *Three Lives* and *Palimpsest*, see Margaret M. Dunn, "Altered Patterns and New Endings: Reflections of Change in Stein's *Three Lives* and H. D.'s *Palimpsest*," *Frontiers* 9 (1987): 54–59.

9. Alison Lurie, "Love Has Its Consequences," review of *The Rest of Life*, by Mary Gordon, *New York Times Book Review*, 8 Aug. 1993, p. 25.

10. Robert Scholes and Eric S. Rabkin, *Science Fiction: History, Science, Vision* (New York: Oxford University Press, 1977), 221.

11. Eudora Welty, *One Writer's Beginnings* (New York: Warner, 1983), 108.

12. Peggy Whitman Prenshaw, ed., *Conversations with Eudora Welty* (Jackson: University Press of Mississippi, 1984), 192. This volume collects 40 years of Welty interviews. Because it is easily available while the individual interviews themselves are not, we will use it for all further Welty quotations and hereafter cite it in the text as *Conversations*.

13. Barbara Harrell Carson, *Eudora Welty: Two Pictures at Once in Her Frame* (Troy, N.Y.: Whitston, 1992), 7.

14. See, particularly, Ruth M. Van de Kieft, *Eudora Welty* (Boston: Twayne, 1962), 111–49; Thomas L. McHaney, "Eudora Welty and the Multitudinous Golden Apples," *Mississippi Quarterly* 26 (1973): 589–624; Merrill Maguire Skaggs, "Morgana's Apples and Pears," in *Eudora Welty: Critical Essays*, ed. Peggy Prenshaw (Jackson: University Press of Mississippi, 1979), 220–41; and Michael Kreyling, *Eudora Welty's Achievement of Order* (Baton Rouge: Louisiana State University Press, 1980), 77–105.

15. Joseph Campbell, *The Power of Myth* (New York: Doubleday, 1988), 31.

16. Kathryn Lee Seidel, *The Southern Belle in the American Novel* (Tampa: University of South Florida Press, 1985), 137.

17. Kathryn Etter, *Genre of Return: The Short Story Volume* (Ph.D. diss., University of Iowa, 1985), 102.
18. T.S. Eliot, "Ulysses, Order, and Myth," *Dial* (Nov. 1923); reprinted in *James Joyce: Two Decades of Criticism*, 2d ed., ed. Seon Givens (New York: Vanguard, 1963), 201.
19. Italo Calvino, "Myth in the Narrative," *Surfiction: Fiction Now and Tomorrow*, 2d ed., ed. Raymond Federman (Chicago: Swallow Press, 1981), 76–77.

Chapter 7

1. James Polk, "Books: 'Storyteller,'" review of *Storyteller*, by Leslie Marmon Silko, *Saturday Review* (May 1981): 72.
2. Leslie Marmon Silko, "Language and Literature from a Pueblo Indian Perspective," in *English Literature/Opening Up the Canon: Selected Papers from the English Institute, 1979*, ed. Leslie A. Fiedler and Houston A. Baker, Jr. (Baltimore: Johns Hopkins University Press, 1981), 54–55, 57. Silko's essay, an edited transcript, was originally an oral presentation.
3. Stanley E. Fish, "Literature in the Reader: Affective Stylistics," in *Reader-Response Criticism: From Formalism to Post-Structuralism*, ed. Jane P. Tompkins (Baltimore: Johns Hopkins University Press, 1980), 72, 83. Fish's essay first appeared in 1970.
4. Silko, "Language and Literature," 61.
5. Terence Hawkes, *Structuralism and Semiotics* (Berkeley: University of California Press, 1977), 83.
6. Susan J. Scarberry, "Grandmother Spider's Lifeline," *Studies in American Indian Literature: Critical Essays and Course Designs*, ed. Paula Gunn Allen (New York: MLA, 1983), 100, 104.
7. Kenneth Lincoln, *Native American Renaissance* (Berkeley: University of California Press, 1983), 104.
8. Paula Gunn Allen, *The Sacred Hoop: Recovering the Feminine in American Indian Traditions* (Boston: Beacon, 1986), 82.
9. Eugenio Suarez-Galban, "A Village in the Palm of One's Hand," review of *Obabakoak*, by Bernardo Atxaga [Joseba

Irazu Garmendia], *New York Times Book Review*, 20 June 1993, p. 20.

10. Coover interview in Frank Gado, *First Person: Conversations on Writers and Writing* (Schenectady, N.Y.: Union College Press, 1973), 151.

11. Larry McCafferty, "Robert Coover," in *Dictionary of Literary Biography* (Detroit: Gale Research), 113; Richard Andersen, *Robert Coover* (Boston: Twayne, 1981), 17.

12. Seymour Chatman, *Story and Discourse: Narrative Structure in Fiction and Film* (Ithaca: Cornell University Press, 1978), 23, 19.

13. Jim Ruppert, "Story Telling: The Fiction of Leslie Silko," *Journal of Ethnic Studies* 9 (Spring 1981): 56–57.

14. This text-piece, we believe, is the key to the book's whole-text identity—which critics have debated for 25 years. For example, Robert Scholes in *Fabulation and Metafiction* (Urbana: University of Illinois Press, 1979) describes *Lost in the Funhouse* as "a collection of short pieces" (114). Yet Barth argues up-front in the "Author's Note" that the book "is neither a collection nor a selection, but a series" and adds that although some of the 14 stories had been published prior to inclusion in the book, he means for the series to be received "all at once and in this order" (ix). This announcement of intention and sequence, as well as the fact that the stories are so obviously interconnected, has led a number of critics to argue for the whole-text coherence of *Lost in the Funhouse*, even though, once again, they don't know quite what to call it. See, for example, Beverly Gray Bienstock, "Lingering on the Autognostic Edge," *Modern Fiction Studies* 19 (Spring 1973): 69–78; Gerald Gillespie, "Barth's *Lost in the Funhouse*: Short Story Text in its Cyclic Context," *Studies in Short Fiction* 12 (1975): 223–30; and Michael Hinden, "*Lost in the Funhouse*: Barth's Use of the Recent Past," *Twentieth Century Literature* 19 (1973): 107–18. Jan Marta even speaks of the book as "a novel comprised of short stories," in "John Barth's Portrait of the Artist as a Fiction: Modernism through the Looking-Glass," *Canadian Revue of Comparative Literature* 9 (June 1982): 215.

Chapter 8

1. Janette Turner Hospital, "What They Did to Tashi," review of *Possessing the Secret of Joy*, by Alice Walker, *New York Times Book Review*, 28 June 1992, p. 12.

2. One of Mary McCarthy's first stories, "The Man in the Brooks Brothers Shirt" (later included in *The Company She Keeps*, her 1942 composite novel), scandalized the editors and readers of the *Partisan Review*—the editors because it was "journalism, not fiction," and the readers because of its explicit sex-on-a-train episode. See Jean Strouse, "Making the Facts Obey," review of *Intellectual Memoirs: New York 1936–38*, by Mary McCarthy, *New York Times Book Review*, 24 May 1992, pp. 3, 16–17. Also see chapter 9, esp. 170–74, in Louis Auchincloss, *Pioneers and Caretakers: A Study of 9 American Women Novelists* (Boston: G.K. Hall, 1985), for a discussion of the genre boundaries tested by McCarthy in *The Company She Keeps* and *Memories of a Catholic Girlhood*.

3. Sven Birkerts says that he is "coining" the term "collagified" in "Who Deconstructed Adam Snell," review of *Book: A Novel*, by Robert Grudin, *New York Times Book Review*, 6 Sept. 1992, p. 5. On a related point, Robert Scholes and Sharon Spencer both assert that critics, journalists, and the reading public have often overlooked experimental works precisely because they did not know how to read them and talk about them. See Scholes, "For Nonrealistic Fiction," *New York Times Book Review*, 22 Oct. 1967, p. 2; and Spencer, *Space, Time and Structure in the Modern Novel* (New York: New York University Press, 1971), esp. xiii–xvi and 227–28.

4. Richard Bridgman, *Gertrude Stein in Pieces* (New York: Oxford University Press, 1970), 125 ("cohesive"), 127 ("melange"); Michael J. Hoffman, *Gertrude Stein* (Boston: Twayne, 1976), 66 ("still lifes"), 67 ("verbal collage"); Jayne L. Walker, *The Making of a Modernist*, 127 ("artfully structured"); Ellen G. Friedman and Miriam Fuchs, "Contexts and Continuities: An Introduction to Women's Experimental Fiction in English," in *Breaking the Sequence: Women's Experimental Fiction* (Princeton: Princeton University Press, 1989), 16 ("linguistic collage").

5. Charles R. Larson, "*Cane* by Jean Toomer," *New Republic* (19 June 1976): 30; Rudolph P. Byrd, "Shared Orientation and Narrative Acts in *Cane, Their Eyes Were Watching God,* and *Meridian,*" *MELUS* 17 (Winter 1991–92): 55n8; Frederik L. Rusch, "Form, Function, and Creative Tension in *Cane:* Jean Toomer and the Need for the Avant-Garde," *MELUS* 17 (Winter 1991–92): 15, 26.

6. See Robert B. Stepto, *From behind the Veil: A Study of Afro-American Narrative* (Urbana: University of Illinois Press, 1979). Stepto discusses *The Souls of Black Folk* as a "generic narrative," asserting that "it is not merely an assembled text, but also an orchestrated one" and that its text-pieces "are far more written, metaphorical, and archetypal than they are edited, prosaic, or documentary" (52–53); Stepto also asserts that DuBois's book is "the precursor text" for *Cane* (66).

7. James Schroeter, "Willa Cather and *The Professor's House,*" in *Willa Cather and Her Critics,* ed. James Schroeter (Ithaca: Cornell University Press, 1967), 370; Merrill Maguire Skaggs, *After the World Broke in Two: The Later Novels of Willa Cather* (Charlottesville: University Press of Virginia, 1990), 122; Deborah Carlin, *Cather, Canon, and the Politics of Reading* (Amherst: University of Massachusetts Press, 1992), 88, 64. Carlin deals extensively with Cather's genre "experiments," especially in the late texts. See also Elizabeth Ammons, in *Conflicting Stories: American Women Writers at the Turn into the Twentieth Century* (New York: Oxford University Press, 1992), who focuses at length on Cather's "manipulation of narrative form" (131, chapter 8). Flaubert's influence on Cather (suggesting *Trois Contes*'s influence on *Obscure Destinies*) is affirmed by numerous critics. In one related point, James Woodress, in a variorum edition of Cather's 1905 *The Troll Garden* (Lincoln: University of Nebraska Press, 1983), asserts that even this early collection is generically innovative: "*The Troll Garden* is not simply a collection of stories all having something to do with art and artist. There is overall design and meaning and a careful arrangement of the tales to support the themes woven into the fabric of the text" (xvi).

8. Norma Broude, "Miriam Schapiro and 'Femmage': Reflections on the Conflict between Decoration and

Abstraction in Twentieth-Century Art," in *Feminism and Art History: Questioning the Litany,* ed. Norma Broude and Mary D. Garrard (New York: Harper, 1982), 324. The clearest definition and explanation of "femmage" appears in Melissa Meyer and Miriam Schapiro, "Waste Not Want Not: An Inquiry into What Women Saved and Assembled: FEMMAGE," *Heresies: A Feminist Publication on Art and Politics* 4 (1978): 66–69. After defining and discussing *collage, assemblage, decoupage,* and *photomontage,* Meyer and Schapiro enumerate 14 "criteria" that determine a "femmage" (to qualify, any work should include at least seven of the criteria):

1. It is a work by a woman.
2. The activities of saving and collecting are important ingredients.
3. Scraps are essential to the process and are recycled in the work.
4. The theme has a woman-life context.
5. The work has elements of covert imagery.
6. The theme of the work addresses itself to an audience of intimates.
7. It celebrates a private or public event.
8. A diarist's point of view is reflected in the work.
9. There is drawing and/or handwriting sewn in the work.
10. It contains silhouetted images which are fixed on other material.
11. Recognizable images appear in narrative sequence.
12. Abstract forms create a pattern.
13. The work contains photographs or other printed matter.
14. The work has a functional as well as an aesthetic life. (69)

Even though these criteria were devised for visual artworks, a number of composite novels, including *Like Water for Chocolate,* clearly qualify as "femmages." Interestingly, although the term *femmage* appears not to have been appropriated by any visual artist other than Schapiro (who refers to herself a "femmagist"), the term *has* been applied by folklorist Kay F. Turner to home altars *("altarcitos")* created by Mexican-American women because these altars exemplify an "aesthetic of connection and relation" ("Mexican American Home Altars: Towards Their Interpretation," *Aztlan* 13 [1982]: 309, 323). See also Jose E. Limon, "Legendry, Metafolklore, and Performance: A Mexican-American Example," *Western Folklore* 42 (1983): 201.

9. Suzanne Ruta, "In Grandmother's Kitchen," review of *Like Water for Chocolate,* by Laura Esquivel, *Women's Review of Books* 10 (Feb. 1993): 7.

10. Paul West, "Julio Cortázar's *A Certain Lucas,*" *Sheer Fiction* (New Paltz, N.Y.: McPherson, 1987), 111, 113; West's review was originally published in the *Washington Post.* See also E. D. Carter, Jr., *Julio Cortázar: Life, Work, and Criticism* (Fredericton, New Brunswick: York Press, 1986), and Steven Boldy, *The Novels of Julio Cortázar* (Cambridge: Cambridge University Press, 1980).

11. Julio Cortázar, quoted in West, "Julio Cortázar's *A Certain Lucas,*" 112.

12. The phrase "theory in the flesh" was coined by Cherrie Moraga and Gloria Anzaldua as a section title in *This Bridge Called My Back: Writings by Radical Women of Color* (New York: Kitchen Table/Women of Color Press, 1983). Moraga, in *"La Guera,"* explains: "The danger lies in attempting to deal with oppression purely from a theoretical base. Without an emotional, heartfelt grappling with the source of our own oppression, without naming the enemy within ourselves and outside of us, no authentic, non-hierarchical connection among oppressed groups can take place" (29). Shane Phelan, in "(Be)Coming Out: Lesbian Identity and Politics," *Signs* 18 (1993), uses "theory in the flesh" to describe "the leap from theoretical understanding to visceral reaction" that characterizes Anzaldua's stance in her life and in *Borderlands:* "Anzaldua's 'new mestiza' does not transcend race but transgresses it, refusing to collude in the homophobic demands of some Chicanas/os or in the racist invisibility that is too much a part of white lesbian communities" (780–82). Teresa de Lauretis, in "Eccentric Subjects: Feminist Theory and

Historical Consciousness," *Feminist Studies* 16 (Spring 1990), uses the phrase to encapsulate the risky "dis-placement" and "self-displacement" necessary "to sustain the feminist movement itself." Anzaldua's *Borderlands,* says Lauretis, is about "a remapping of boundaries between bodies and discourses, identities and communities—which may be a reason why it is primarily feminists of color and lesbian feminists who have taken the risk" (138–39).

13. Adalaide Morris, "First Persons Plural in Contemporary Feminist Fiction," *Tulsa Studies in Women's Literature* 2 (Spring 1992): 18–19.

14. The first words of Sandra M. Gilbert and Susan Gubar's *The Madwoman in the Attic: The Woman Writer and the Nineteenth-Century Literary Imagination* (New Haven: Yale University Press, 1979) are "Is a pen a metaphorical penis?" (3) From that point on they proceed to demonstrate that the nineteenth century's answer was "yes."

15. Jill McCorkle, "Cover Stories," review of *How to Make an American Quilt,* by Whitney Otto, *New York Times Book Review,* 24 Mar. 1991, p. 10. Although McCorkle's review is "blurbed" on the inside front cover of the book's paperback edition, it is not one of the "scraps" in our metareview.

16. The now classic article that sparked contemporary interest in quilt art is Patricia Mainardi's "Quilts: The Great American Art," *Feminist Art Journal* 2 (Winter 1973): 1, 18–23; enlarged and reprinted in *Feminism and Art History: Questioning the Litany,* ed. Norma Broude and Mary D. Garrard (New York: Harper, 1982), 331–46.

17. Jonathan Culler, "Towards a Theory of Non-Genre Literature," in *Surfiction: Fiction Now and Tomorrow,* 2d ed., ed. Raymond Federman (Chicago: Swallow Press, 1981), 255.

Chapter 9

1. Susan Stanford Friedman, "Spatialization: A Strategy for Reading Narrative," *Narrative* 1 (Jan. 1993): 20.

2. Louise Rosenblatt, *The Reader, the Text, the Poem* (Carbondale: Southern Illinois University Press, 1978), 76.

3. Suzanne Juhasz, "Towards a Theory of Form in Feminist Autobiography: Kate Millet's *Fear of Flying* and *Sita;* Maxine Hong Kingston's *The Woman Warrior*," *International Journal of Women's Studies* 2 (1979): esp. 63–64.

4. Ronald Sukenick, "The New Tradition in Fiction," in *Surfiction: Fiction Now and Tomorrow*, 2d ed., ed. Raymond Federman (Chicago: Swallow Press, 1981), 40.

5. Alain Robbe-Grillet, *For a New Novel: Essays on Fiction*, trans. Richard Howard (Freeport, N.Y.: Books for Libraries Press, 1965), 12.

Survey of Scholarship: A Bibliographic Essay

Ours is the first critical work—book or article—to (1) propose the name *Composite Novel* for, (2) define the genre specifications of, and (3) trace the history and development of this genre through the nineteenth and twentieth centuries. Thus there is no prior scholarship that is precisely on point. However, as the subtitle of this book, "The Short Story Cycle in Transition," indicates, many of the works we identify as "composite novels" have been called "short story cycles" more than they have been called anything else. In addition, two critical works on the "short story cycle" anticipated and broke ground for our study.

The first was Forrest L. Ingram's *Representative Short Story Cycles of the Twentieth Century: Studies in a Literary Genre* (The Hague: Mouton, 1971). Ingram defines the "short story cycle" as "a book of short stories so linked to each other by their author that the reader's successive experience on various levels of the pattern of the whole significantly modifies his experience of each of its component parts" (19). This is an intriguing definition, but it is devilishly hard to apply because of its insistence on a reader's "experience" of a text. Although Ingram focuses primarily on Franz Kafka's *A Hunger Artist* (50 pages of discussion) and devotes an equal amount of space to Sherwood Anderson's *Winesburg, Ohio,* he also discusses James Joyce's *Dubliners,* Albert

Camus's *Exile and the Kingdom,* John Steinbeck's *The Pastures of Heaven,* and William Faulkner's *The Unvanquished,* identifying each as a "short story cycle" and explaining the elements that (according to his genre specifications) contribute to whole-text coherence. Although Ingram's analyses of what he calls "the dynamic patterns of recurrence and development" (20) are confusing, his book breaks significant ground, and Ingram's familiarity with Continental literature is impressive. Incidentally, this book is long out of print and difficult to obtain through interlibrary loan.

Ingram's book was not only significant in itself, but also indicative of a widespread interest in what we are now calling "the composite novel." Warren French made this point clear, writing that same year (1971) in *American Literary Scholarship* about Ingram's book. Said French, "Ingram is not the only one concerned about defining the form of a work like *Winesburg.*" Then he went on to discuss dissertations that "deal with the same problem and propose other labels for a new genre" (221). French also made the point that there was at this time a virtual outpouring of articles and books that focused on individual composite works such as *Winesburg.* Many of these, he wrote, discussed tangentially the "problem" of "a new genre," but few if any proposed "a label," much less a genre hypothesis.

Following Ingram, Susan Garland Mann in 1989 published *The Short Story Cycle: A Genre Companion and Reference Guide* (New York: Greenwood). A revised and enlarged version of Mann's 1984 dissertation, this book gives copious credit to Ingram for his "terminology and incipient genre theory" (x) and goes on to analyze (in addition to *Dubliners, Winesburg, The Pastures of Heaven,* and *The Unvanquished,* which had earlier been discussed by Ingram), Ernest Hemingway's *In Our Time,* William Faulkner's *Go Down, Moses,* Eudora Welty's *The Golden Apples,* Flannery O'Connor's *Everything That Rises Must Converge,* and John Updike's *Too Far to Go: The Maples Stories.* Mann's book is a bibliographic treasure trove in regard to the nine major texts that she discusses, and she includes as an appendix a long annotated list of "short story cycles." Like Ingram, however, Mann has definitional problems. She says quite simply in the book's introduction that "there is only one essential characteristic of the short story cycle: the stories are both self-sufficient and interrelated" (15).

But in elaborating upon a "cycle" ("there is generally some conscious effort on the part of the writer to make the stories work together") and a "short story" ("a narrative that contains some kind of development"), Mann clouds her otherwise trenchant discussions of specific works (16–17).

The term *composite novel* had itself appeared around the turn of the century in connection with collaborative works (literary "gimmicks," some called them) such as *The Sturdy Oak: A Composite Novel of American Politics by Fourteen American Authors,* which was published in 1917. The best known of these may be *The Whole Family: A Novel by Twelve Authors,* published in 1908, whose contributors included Henry James, William Dean Howells, and Mary E. Wilkins Freeman. To our knowledge, all of these early "collaborative composites" are out of print and difficult to find, except *The Whole Family,* which was reissued by Ungar in 1986 in an edition whose introduction by Alfred Bendixen discusses the star-crossed history of *The Whole Family's* composition and includes helpful information about other such early collaborative works (xi–li).

Thus an early precedent was set for the use of the term *composite novel* as a generic label—one denoting collaboration by a large number of authors. But few of these collaboration-composites were published, and fewer still achieved much popularity. It is not surprising, then, that the term *composite novel* is nowhere to be found in literary handbooks, literary dictionaries, and the like. In fact, when Eric S. Rabkin in the late 1970s referred to Isaac Asimov's *I, Robot* and Ray Bradbury's *The Martian Chronicles* as "composite novels," he believed that he had coined the term. In one way Rabkin *was* coining it: he was using it in a completely new way that did not at all connote collaborative authorship. Specifically, Rabkin's published remarks are in *The Fantastic in Literature* (Princeton: Princeton University Press, 1976); Robert Scholes and Eric S. Rabkin, *Science Fiction: History, Science, Vision* (New York: Oxford University Press, 1977); and Eric S. Rabkin, "To Fairyland by Rocket: Bradbury's *The Martian Chronicles,*" in *Ray Bradbury,* ed. Joseph D. Olander and Martin Harry Greenberg (New York: Taplinger, 1980).

Long before Rabkin's 1970s sci-fi commentaries, critics had realized the need for genre designation of such works as *Dubliners, Winesburg,* and *Go Down, Moses.* These books weren't "novels," but they weren't mere "collections" either, and over the course of years perplexed critics have proposed numerous terms for them. Again, though, few of these terms were proposed in connection with genre theory, and those that did carry theoretical underpinnings were most often buried in dissertations. Many terms, too, were merely mentioned, "tossed off" in passing, as it were, especially in connection with the oft-discussed *Dubliners, Winesburg,* and *Go Down, Moses.*

Nevertheless, *short story cycle* is the generic label that has been most widely used, beginning with Malcolm Cowley and others in the 1940s and 1950s (Cowley was particularly interested in the generic innovations of William Faulkner), and receiving its credentials through the works of Ingram in 1971 and Mann in 1989. Cowley, in fact, advised Ingram and corresponded with him about the need for a theoretical genre study, Cowley saying at one point that Faulkner's *The Hamlet* is "more a cycle of stories than a novel" (Ingram 16). In addition, Ian Reid in his book *The Short Story* (New York: Methuen, 1977) devoted a short subsection to the "cycle." Reid leads off by citing Forrest Ingram and then briefly discussing *Winesburg, Dubliners,* and *Go Down, Moses*—along with a strange choice: Frank Moorhouse's *Futility and Other Animals.* To us, Reid's brief discussion of a subgenre that he calls the "framed miscellany" is most relevant because his comments about Alphonse Daudet's *Letters from My Mill* anticipate our own points concerning generic miscegenation in certain composite novels.

Others who proposed the term *short story cycle* for this "incipient genre" include Warren French in "Naturalism—The Story Cycles," in *John Steinbeck,* 2d ed. (Boston: Twayne, 1975) and Harlan Harbour Winn III, in his 1975 dissertation entitled "Short Story Cycles of Hemingway, Steinbeck, Faulkner, and O'Connor" (University of Oregon). In his discussion of John Steinbeck's *The Pastures of Heaven,* French emphasizes the book's experimental structure (self-sufficient stories that are interrelated) and then acknowledges his dependence upon Ingram for analysis. Also drawing heavily upon Ingram, Winn emphasizes the genre implications inherent in "cycles" and "the cyclical habit of mind" (5). In an introduction, Winn describes both the process of genre evolution and critics' reaction to it quite succinctly: "Many writers have amalgamated the aesthetics of the novel and short story to construct groupings of interrelated stories that do not fit into either genre. Criticism of this resulting hybrid has generally failed to recognize the existence of a new genre" (2).

Winn could hardly be more on target. And it is surely an indication of critics' difficulty with this "new genre" that they have proposed so many names for it. Consider D. H. Lawrence's critical reaction to Ernest Hemingway's *In Our Time* in a 1927 review: "*In Our Time* calls itself a book of stories, but it isn't that. It is a series of successive sketches from a man's life, and makes a fragmentary novel." Lawrence's review is reprinted in *Hemingway: A Collection of Critical Essays,* ed. Robert Weeks (Englewood Cliffs, N.J.: Prentice-Hall, 1962), 93–94. Another early "term coiner" was Hugh Kenner, who fell upon *multi-faceted novel* as a descriptive term for *Dubliners* in his 1956 book entitled *Dublin's Joyce* (Bloomington: Indiana University Press). According to Kenner, the stories in *Dubliners* cohere "at a minimal level of organization," one that is *not* "the sort of organization that fuses in a single action or demands a single narrative" (48).

Still another descriptive term was suggested by Olga W. Vickery, who coined *story-novel* and applied it to *The Unvanquished* in *The Novels of William Faulkner: A Critical Interpretation* (Baton Rouge: Louisiana State University Press, 1959). Vickery's focus is on Faulkner's work as a whole rather than his composite novels. Nevertheless, she does note that *Knight's Gambit, Go Down, Moses,* and *The Hamlet,* as well as *The Unvanquished,* represent a new form, and she stresses the interconnections among text-pieces (she calls them "stories") in these particular works. Another Faulkner critic, Stanley Tick, in "The Unity of *Go Down, Moses,*" *TCL* 8 (July 1962): 67–73, proposed the term *short story blend* while suggesting that *The Unvanquished* and *Go Down, Moses* are representative texts in a subgenre of the novel (but Tick does not go on to delve into genre theory).

One can surely not ignore Michael Millgate's *The Achievement of William Faulkner* (New York: 1963; Vintage-Random, 1971), in which Millgate discusses *The Unvanquished* and *Go Down, Moses* as "novels," while dubbing *The Wild Palms* a "double-novel" (175). Millgate's focus in this book is not at all upon hypotheses regarding genres, however, and therefore is of limited relevance to the composite novel. Moving into the 1970s, Joseph W. Reed, Jr. contributed another broad survey of the work of William

Faulkner in *Faulkner's Narrative* (New Haven: Yale University Press, 1973), 176. Reed uses the term *short story compound* for both *The Unvanquished* and *Go Down, Moses,* but he lauds only the latter work as "command[ing] the respect due a novel's unity and cohesion and at the same time conform[ing] to the standards of cohesion and impact in its short stories" (186).

Floyd C. Watkins in "Faulkner's Inexhaustible Voice," in *The Flesh and the Word* (Nashville: Vanderbilt University Press, 1971), 234–53, seemed to encapsulate much Faulkner criticism devoted to individual works when he stated that "Faulkner wrote many books which are not sufficiently unified to be termed a novel nor diverse enough to be regarded as separate stories" (241). But note the negative slant of Watkins's comment. The implication is that such works as *Go Down, Moses* are too disjointed to qualify as "real" novels, while their component text-pieces are too similar to qualify as "real" short stories. The problem here, we contend, is not with literary works like Faulkner's that were experimenting with a structural aesthetic but rather with critics who were unable to think in terms of a "new genre."

Joanne V. Creighton was one of the first critics to move beyond terminology and into genre theory when she proposed the term *short story composite* in her 1969 dissertation entitled *"Dubliners* and *Go Down, Moses:* The Short Story Composite" (University of Michigan)—part of which Creighton revised and published in 1977 as *William Faulkner's Craft of Revision: The Snopes Trilogy, "The Unvanquished," and "Go Down, Moses"* (Detroit: Wayne State University Press). In her book Creighton defines "short story composite" as "a form between that of the novel and the collection of short stories" and then describes *Go Down, Moses* as "an audacious attempt at collage" (16). Creighton also enumerates other critics' attempts to describe the structural aesthetic of *Go Down, Moses:* "a remarkably unified novel" (Edmond Volpe); "a single novelistic structure" (Michael Millgate); "a loosely constructed novel" (Olga Vickery); "an experimental novel" (Lawrance Thompson); "a hybrid: a loosely jointed but ambitious novel masking as a collection of short stories" (Malcolm Cowley); "if not exactly a novel, then at least a narrative which begins, develops, and concludes" (Lionel Trilling); "a mosaic in which not only the sequence but the very presence of all seven stories is meaningful" (Stanley Sultan); "a set of variations upon two major themes" (dust jacket blurb); and "a book of related short stories" (William Van O'Connor) (Creighton 85). Creighton's genre term of choice, however, *short story composite*, seems not to have been adopted by many others, even though Susan Mann cites Creighton as a significant influence on her own (Mann's) work. Ultimately, Creighton's book may have had limited influence on genre theory because it focuses only on a few works by Faulkner rather than a diverse group of representative texts.

Creighton did receive thanks for her input and advice regarding Raymond Joel Silverman's 1970 dissertation at the University of Michigan (Creighton's dissertation was also from Michigan, a year before Silverman's). In his dissertation, "The Short Story Composite: Forms, Functions, and Applications," Silverman defines "short story composite" as "a group of stories, written by one author, arranged in a definite sequence, and meant to be read as a whole" (1). Silverman also proposes "structural diagrams" (drawings) of the three works upon which he focuses: *The Pastures of Heaven* (57), *Winesburg, Ohio* (142), and *In Our Time* (199). All three diagrams show some variation on small circles enclosed by a large circle—as if dimes, pennies, and/or nickels were arranged around the edge of a dinner plate. Ironically, these circular diagrams imply the cyclical structure that Silverman explicitly eschews when he chooses the term *short story composite* rather than *short story cycle* to describe this genre.

Complete dissertations (in contrast to the printed abstracts available in *DAI*) are available only through purchase or travel to a collection, meaning that only the most committed (and financially supported) scholars can gain access to them. Nevertheless, much of the theoretical ground broken in this area of genre theory is encompassed in dissertations, and we therefore mention several more that are relevant and helpful.

In his 1970 dissertation, Stephen Lee Sniderman proposed and applied the term *composite* ("The 'Composite' in Twentieth Century American Literature," University of Wisconsin) to a variety of works, including (in addition to those much-discussed ones by Anderson, Faulkner, and Hemingway) *Pnin* by Vladimir Nabokov and *Pictures of Fidelman* by Bernard Malamud. Sniderman limits his analyses to works whose text-pieces are interrelated through setting or a single protagonist. Another 1970

151

dissertation, by Dallas Marion Lemmon, Jr., is interesting for its terminology and for its discussions of *A Hero of Our Time* by Mikhail Lermontov and *Das Sinngedicht* by Gottfried Keller. Lemmon proposed for these works and others the term *rovelle* and also included, as a secondary term, *novel of interrelated stories* ("The Rovelle, or the Novel of Interrelated Stories: M. Lermontov, G. Keller, S. Anderson," Indiana University).

One final spate of dissertations underscores the importance of naming in genre theory. Consider again the fact that critics since the 1920s have been coming up with names for this incipient genre because available names (*novel* and *story collection*) did not fit. Also consider the fact that in proposing a name, one also implies a definition—as Dallas Lemmon does above when he proposes *novel of interrelated stories*. Thus, when we encounter the term *integrated short-story collection*, proposed in a 1974 dissertation at Indiana University by Pleasant Larus Reed III ("The Integrated Short-Story Collection: Studies of a Form of Nineteenth- and Twentieth-Century Fiction"), we infer the definition that stands behind the term. Further, in considering the terms proposed by Lemmon and Reed, we suppose (correctly) that Lemmon's demands more connection among text-pieces (the emphasis is on "novel") while Reed's demands less connection (the emphasis is on "collection"). To choose a term that reflects structure, then, is to define; but to survey the variety of possible terms is to broaden our awareness of structural possibilities and subtleties.

The term *anthology novel* was coined by James Michael Grimwood in his dissertation entitled "Pastoral and Parody: The Making of Faulkner's Anthology Novels" (Princeton University, 1976). Keith Carabine, who also used the term *short story cycle*, proposed the term *hybrid novel* in his 1978 dissertation entitled "'A Pretty Good Unity': A Study of Sherwood Anderson's *Winesburg, Ohio* and Ernest Hemingway's *In Our Time*" (Yale University). And Kathryn Etter focused on an unusual trio of works—Eudora Welty's *The Golden Apples*, Renata Adler's *Speedboat,* and Alice Munro's *The Beggar Maid*—while proposing *genre of return* and *short story volume* in "Genre of Return: The Short Story Volume" (University of Iowa, 1985).

Robert Michael Luscher, in an extremely cogent and convincing dissertation that focuses on Garland's *Main-Travelled Roads,*

Jewett's *The Country of the Pointed Firs,* Freeman's *Six Trees,* Anderson's *Winesburg, Ohio,* and Welty's *The Golden Apples,* argued against the term *short story cycle* and proposed instead *short story sequence* in "American Regional Short Story Sequences" (Duke University, 1984). In a short story sequence, argues Luscher, "the author has consciously structured the collection in an attempt to create an internal consistency and coherence similar to that of the novel" (4). More to the point, and emphatically underscoring our insistence on the importance of naming, is Luscher's admonition that "the most basic difficulty the form must contend with is the lack of a collective and adequately descriptive name which can focus discussion on these works and their dynamics" (6).

Returning to published sources, the term *paranovel* is used by Richard Cary in *Sarah Orne Jewett* (New York: Twayne, 1962) as a generically descriptive term for Jewett's *The Country of the Pointed Firs.* A paranovel, as Cary suggests, contains "unifying factors" that are "continuously at work" so that "an over-all pattern" becomes discernible (149). Also referring to Jewett's *Pointed Firs* and to her earlier work *Deephaven,* Louis Auchincloss coined the term *loose-leaf novel* in 1965 in an essay that is reprinted in *Pioneers and Caretakers: A Study of 9 American Women Novelists* (Boston: G.K. Hall, 1985). As Auchincloss defines it, "loose-leaf novel" is "a literary form" in which "a narrator gives the reader sketches of persons and places in a small . . . village" (7).

In a somewhat tangential context but one that focuses on *Winesburg* as a major text, Joseph R. Millichap proposed the peculiar term *modernist grotesque* in "Distorted Matter and Disjunctive Forms: The Grotesque as Modernist Genre," *Arizona Quarterly* 33 (1977): 339–47. In this article, Millichap proposed that grotesquerie in characterization and disjunction in form conflate in a "structural principle" that reflects "fragmentation and alienation" (342, 347). Similar in direction to Millichap's idea is Andre le Vot's theory concerning a "disjunctive mode" and "conjunctive mode" in literary works, a theory he worked out in great detail in "New Modes of Story-Telling in Recent American Writings: The Dismantling of Contemporary Fiction," in *New French Criticism on Modern American Fiction,* ed. Ira D. Johnson and Christiane Johnson (Port Washington, N.Y.: Kennikat Press, 1978: 110–29, 223–34). The "conjunctive principle," le Vot argued, "gives coherence and unity" to such works as *Winesburg, In Our Time*, and *Go Down, Moses* (116).

Like Millichap and LeVot, other critics were beginning to propose unusual genre terms for these works that we call composite novels; they were also supporting their choices with sophisticated theoretical and pedagogical underpinnings. Craig Hansen Werner, for example, in *Paradoxical Resolutions: American Fiction since James Joyce* (Urbana: University of Illinois Press, 1982), discusses a number of works that he calls *short story volumes*, maintaining that *Dubliners* pioneered a new "technique" based on three elements: (1) "focusing on one well-defined setting"; (2) "developing a group of central thematic issues"; and (3) "manipulating narrative stance to reflect shifting authorial attitude toward the subject matter" (35). *Story chronicle* was the term Werner Berthoff chose to designate the composite works around which he built a college course; Berthoff's materials are listed and his course is outlined in "The American Story-Chronicle," in *Reconstructing American Literature: Courses, Syllabi, Issues*, ed. Paul Lauter (Old Westbury, N.Y.: The Feminist Press, 1983), 141–45. And Fredric Jameson proposed, for Gustave Flaubert's *Three Tales*, the term *triptych*, in "Flaubert's Libidinal Historicism: *Trois Contes*," in *Flaubert and Postmodernism*, ed. Naomi Schor and Henry F. Majewski (Lincoln: University of Nebraska Press), 76–83. The triptych, as Jameson explains it, is "a peculiar form" that subverts interpretation because of "the impossible triangular relationship" among its three text-pieces. Thus, continues Jameson, the triptych is "an object of endless meditation, like the mandala, across which the eye and the mind trace seemingly interminable paths" (77).

Sandra A. Zagarell, in a study that relates primarily to composite novels in the "village sketch" tradition (Elizabeth Gaskell's *Cranford* and Jane Barlow's *Irish Idylls*, among many others), proposed the generic designation *narrative of community* in "Narrative of Community: The Identification of a Genre," *Signs: Journal of Women in Culture and Society* 13 (1988): 498–527. Zagarell's term, *narrative of community*, refers as much to an ethos as to a structural aesthetic. Thus, she explains that literary works of this kind "take as their subject the life of a community" and "ignore linear development or chronological sequence and remain in one geographic place" (499, 503). Clearly, Zagarell's work embraces cultural as well as literary criticism, and it is not surprising, therefore, that in a related but much more recent essay entitled "'America' as Community in Three Antebellum Village Sketches" in *The (Other) American Traditions: Nineteenth-Century Women Writers*, ed. Joyce W. Warren (New Brunswick, N.J.: Rutgers University Press, 1993), 143–63, Zagarell mentions "genre" not at all.

Beginning sometime in the 1960s (early, middle, or late—depending on whether one lived in France, Germany, Italy, the United States, or wherever), literary experimentation reigned (or rampaged, depending on one's perspective). Terms such as "anti-novel," the French *"nouveau roman,"* "anti-realist novel," "metafiction," "surfiction," and others became part of the common coinage. The difficulty here, terminologically, was that these terms and others carried vaguely defined genre specifications, if they carried any at all. In addition, "experimental" itself was a term that had many connotations, some good but others not so good.

Leon S. Roudiez's *French Fiction Revisited* (Elmwood Park, Ill.: Dalkey Archive Press, 1991), a revised and updated version of Roudiez's *French Fiction Today* (Rutgers University Press, 1972), provides a highly accessible overview of twentieth-century French fiction, especially in regard to such composite novels (although Roudiez does not use the term) as Nathalie Sarraute's *Tropisms* (1939) and Robert Pinget's *Between Fantoine and Agapa* (1951), whose stories, says Roudiez, are "semi-independent units" (126). Roudiez also discusses works not available in English translation: Maurice Roche's 1987 *Je ne vais pas bien mais il faut que j'y aille,* which Roche himself called a "short stories novel" (quoted in Roudiez, 274); Jean Ricardou's 1971 *Revolutions minuscules* and 1982 *Le Théâtre des metamorphoses,* whose "back-cover statement" insists that the book is a "composite-*mixte*" rather than a "mixture-*melange*" (284); and others. Further, throughout his book Roudiez makes it clear that traditional notions of "fiction" and "the novel" are outdated, and he asserts (in relation to Roche) that "linearity" is not the only way of "welding fragments together" (275).

Attempting to "rescue" many deserving works from the obscurity they suffered because they had been called "experimental" and then ignored, Sharon Spencer in *Space, Time and*

Structure in the Modern Novel (New York: New York University Press, 1971) proposed the term *architectonic novel* for those works that abandon "the principle of narration" and adopt in its place "the procedure of construction by means of juxtaposition" (xxi). Spencer credits Joseph Frank's 1945 essay "Spatial Form in the Modern Novel" as a "germinal idea" (xv) for her own work. Spencer's book is well worth studying for its exploration of the time-space aspects of linearity versus contiguity in literary works (especially regarding the disjunctive works of the early modernist period and those of the French *nouveau roman*), but it is only tangentially relative to the composite novel.

Like Spencer's book, Robert Scholes's *Fabulation and Metafiction* (Urbana: University of Illinois Press, 1979) is limited in its application to the composite novel as a genre. In one particularly intriguing chapter, however, Scholes discusses four metafictional works that are "collections of short pieces" and asserts that this composite form is necessary because "the ideas that govern fiction assert themselves more powerfully in direct proportion to the length of a fictional work" (114). Then Scholes goes on to demonstrate, even though it is not his major point, that the four "collections" are indeed coherent whole texts.

In the 1970s and 1980s, "collage" and related or similar terms ("montage," "melange," "pastiche," "assemblage") began sprouting everywhere, it seemed, in critical books and articles. John Gardner, for example, sang the praises of "collage technique," the art of "bringing disparate materials together in new ways, transforming the whole into a seamless fabric, a vision, a story" (Gardner's comments regarding "collage technique" were first made in a 1980 letter to the *Chicago Tribune,* but they are quoted and easily accessible in *John Gardner: Critical Perspectives,* ed. Robert A. Morace and Kathryn VanSpanckeren [Carbondale: Southern Illinois University Press, 1982], 29ff.). Several similar mentions occur in *Surfiction: Fiction Now and Tomorrow* (Chicago: Swallow Press), a collection of critical articles (some new and others previously published) edited by Raymond Federman (the 1975 edition was enlarged and reissued in 1981). In one essay Richard Kostelanetz, for example, asserts that "the poetic-painterly technique of collage-composition" is a "contemporary milestone" in literature (87). Robert Pynsent in another essay describes a work by Ror Wolf as a "photoverbal montage" (148).

Jerome Klinkowitz describes "the novel-like synthesis of stories in [Barthelme's] latest collection" (171). And so on.

One characteristic of Federman's book and of much criticism about "experimental" fiction is a near-exclusive focus on the work of male writers. Ellen G. Friedman and Miriam Fuchs address this by focusing exclusively on women writers in *Breaking the Sequence: Women's Experimental Fiction* (Princeton: Princeton University Press, 1989), a collection of critical essays. Once again the "collage" terminology is evident. Friedman and Fuchs, for example, refer to a work by Kathy Acker as "a self-reflexive collage" (15) and to one by Gertrude Stein as "a linguistic collage" (16). In addition, the essays in this book contain a plenitude of clothwork metaphors, such as Germaine Bree's references to the "verbal tissue" and "rich tapestries" exemplified in the fictions of Nathalie Sarraute (271, 276).

It is beside the point (and probably impossible) to determine who used what term first, or to painstakingly define differences between *collage, montage,* and so on, as they are applied to literary works. The point, rather, is that broadly and cumulatively, all these mentions indicate a critical awareness that composite-texts like *Dubliners* and *Winesburg* have proliferated.

One final work, Elizabeth Ammons's *Conflicting Stories: American Women Writers at the Turn into the Twentieth Century* (New York: Oxford University Press, 1992), is, at least in part, theoretically more closely related to the genre of the composite novel than any other critical study since Ingram's and Mann's. Ammons does not attempt to "name" a genre. But in examining the works produced by seventeen American women writers in the period encompassed by the years 1890–1930, she does make highly relevant statements about the "radical experimentation with narrative form" (5) epitomized by Sarah Orne Jewett's *The Country of the Pointed Firs,* Gertrude Stein's *Three Lives* and *Tender Buttons,* and Willa Cather's *My Ántonia* and *Death Comes for the Archbishop,* among others. Further, Ammons demonstrates the whole-text coherence in these works as convincingly as if she were arguing for their designation as "composite novels." As Ammons explains in one chapter about a work published in 1912 by Sui Sin Far (otherwise known as Edith Eaton), "*Mrs. Spring Fragrance,* as a collection of stories, focuses on many individuals' lives. Occupying its center is not, as in standard western long narratives, the all-important individual, but rather the configuration of figures who make up a group" (118). Were she using *our* terminology, Ammons would be describing *Mrs. Spring Fragrance* as a "composite novel" that develops whole-text coherence through a "collective protagonist."

An Annotated List of Selected Composite Novels

Abrahams, Lionel. *The Celibacy of Felix Greenspan: A Novel in Seventeen Stories*. Chicago: Academy Chicago Publishers, 1993. The protagonist, Felix Greenspan (like his creator, Abrahams), is Jewish and a poet, lives in Johannesburg, and has cerebral palsy. This beautifully crafted story of his life is told in 17 stories that, said *New York Times* reviewer Donna Seaman, "work best as a sequence, gliding into place like cut-glass beads strung carefully on a wire."

Adler, Renata. *Speedboat*. 1976. Reprint. New York: Vintage-Random, 1984. Seven stories set in Manhattan, told in the voice of narrator/protagonist Jen Fain—a journalist, academic, and child of the 1950s. Winner of the Ernest Hemingway Award for Best First "Novel" of 1976.

Alegría, Claribel. *Luisa in Realityland: A Novel*. Translated by Darwin J. Flakoll. Willimantic, Conn.: Curbstone Press, 1987. Described on its dust jacket as "an autobiographical prose/verse novel," it contains 89 titled passages, 52 in prose and 37 in verse.

Alvarez, Julia. *How the Garcia Girls Lost Their Accents*. 1991. Reprint. New York: Plume-Penguin, 1992. Fifteen interconnected stories about four sisters caught between the cultures of New York City and the Dominican Republic.

Anderson, Poul, et al. *Murasaki: A Novel in Six Parts*. Edited by Robert Silverberg. New York: Bantam, 1992. A "shared-world anthology" consisting of six stories, sequenced chronologically, concerning the colonization of the star-world Murasaki. (See chapter 1.)

Anderson, Sherwood. *Winesburg, Ohio*. 1919. Reprint. New York: Viking-Compass, 1958. Stories are linked by the recurring character

George Willard as he interacts with the townspeople of Winesburg and grows to manhood. (See chapter 4.)

Anzaldua, Gloria. *Borderlands/La Frontera: The New Mestiza.* San Francisco: Spinsters/Aunt Lute Book Company, 1987. Composed of many short texts, including poems and historical sketches. Spanish and English alternate (mostly English). (See chapter 8.)

Asimov, Isaac. *I, Robot.* 1950. Reprint Ballantine-Del Rey, 1983. Nine stories and a two-page introduction about the development of robots as narrated by a scientist who decides they are "a cleaner better breed" than humans. Asimov's well-known "Three Laws of Robotics" were first elucidated here.

Astley, Thea. *It's Raining in Mango: Pictures from a Family Album.* Victoria, Australia: Penguin, 1987. Astley, one of Australia's best-loved writers, creates a series of stories about several generations of the Laffey family and how they survived in the harsh Australian outback. One narrative voice throughout (Connie Laffey).

Atxaga, Bernardo [Joseba Irazu Garmendia]. *Obabakoak.* Trans. Margaret Jull Costa. New York: Pantheon, 1993. (1989 in Spanish.) Won Spain's 1989 National Prize for Literature. Stories and essay pieces share the common reference point of Obaba—a Basque village. Atxaga writes in Basque, then translates his work into Spanish. (See chapter 7.)

Auchincloss, Louis. *The Romantic Egoists: A Reflection in Eight Mirrors.* Boston: Houghton, 1954. Peter Westcott, narrator of these eight stories, tells about eight of his friends, all of whom are dissenters who refuse to conform to society's rules. Chronologically sequenced in terms of Peter's life: from a school chum he had at 13 to a friend he had in midlife.

———. *Tales of Manhattan.* Boston: Houghton, 1967. In three titled sections, the first-person narrator describes three different lives he has lived in upper-class Manhattan.

———. *The Winthrop Covenant.* Boston: Houghton, 1976. Nine stories showing the effect of the Puritan ethic on the Winthrop family from 1630 to 1976.

Austin, Mary. *The Land of Little Rain.* Boston: Houghton, 1903. Reprinted in *Stories from the Country of Lost Borders.* Edited by Marjorie Pryse, 3–149. New Brunswick: Rutgers University Press, 1987. Stories set in the dry desert areas of the far West.

Babel, Isaac. *Red Cavalry.* Reprinted in *The Complete Stories.* Edited and translated by Walter Morison, 39–200. New York: Criterion, 1955. (1926 in Russian.) Thirty-five stories and sketches, set in a border area of the Polish front in 1920. Central character named Ljutov seeks out diverse people and tells their stories.

Baldwin, James. *Going to Meet the Man.* New York: Dial, 1965. Describing the social changes in the 1950s and 1960s, the eight stories are arranged in chronological order. The various protagonists, mostly black males, are progressively older.

Banks, Russell. *Trailerpark.* Boston: Houghton, 1981. Thirteen stories about residents of Granite State Trailerpark in rural New Hampshire. Characters recur intermittently, with only one narrator. Numerous reviewers compared this book to Sherwood Anderson's *Winesburg, Ohio.*

Barnes, Djuna. *Ladies Almanack.* 1928. Reprint. New York: Harper & Row, 1972. Twelve sketches (one for each month), an introduction frame, and a foreword—satirizing the 1920s Left Bank literati in Paris.

———. *Nightwood.* 1936. Reprint. New York: New Directions, 1946. Eight titled pieces, sequentially arranged, tell the stories of Robin Vote and the people she destroys. As described in T. S. Eliot's introduction, "The book is not simply a collection of individual portraits; the characters are all knotted together, as people are in real life. . . ; it is the whole pattern that they form, rather than any individual constituent, that is the focus of interest" (xiv–xv).

———. *Spillway.* 1962. Reprint. New York: Harper, 1972. Nine stories, published three times under different whole-text titles: *A Book* (1923), *A Night among the Horses* (1929), and *Spillway* (1962).

Barnes, Julian. *Flaubert's Parrot.* 1984. Reprint. New York: Vintage-Random, 1990. Self-described as an "anti-novel." Chronicles a professor's research into Flaubertian minutiae.

———. *A History of the World in 10 1/2 Chapters.* New York: Knopf, 1989. A history of the world from Noah's Ark to a twentieth-century man's dream of Heaven. Contains letters, pictures of a shipwreck, a record of courtroom proceedings, and a dream of Heaven.

Barth, John. *Chimera.* New York: Random, 1972. Three titled stories about storytelling. Linked by recurring characters and recurrent mythic plot patterns. All sections contain framing devices.

———. *Lost in the Funhouse: Fiction for Print, Tape, Live Voice.* Garden City, N.Y.: Doubleday, 1968. Fourteen stories that focus on the joys and difficulties of writing fiction—a process suggested by the metaphor of being "lost in the funhouse" of an amusement park. (See chapter 7.)

Beam, Lura. *A Maine Hamlet.* 1957. Reprint. New York: Wilfred Funk, 1986. A series of short texts whose cumulative effect, according to May Sarton, is a cross between "a novel and journalism," between "sociology and poetry." In a prefatory note, the author says "all names are imaginary" and "I have disguised the appearance and characteristics of people I knew."

Beauvoir, Simone de. *The Woman Destroyed.* Translated by Patrick O'Brian. New York: Putnam's, 1969. (1967 in French.) Three novellas linked through a recurrent narrative pattern of development. Set in Paris. Each section features a middle-aged female protagonist. (See chapter 6.)

Birdsell, Sandra. *Agassiz: A Novel in Stories.* Minneapolis: Milkweed Editions, 1991. Twenty-three sequenced, titled stories set in the fictional Manitoba town of Agassiz. Chronicles three generations of the Lafreniere family, of mixed Metis Indian and Russian Mennonite blood.

Blaise, Clark. *Resident Alien.* Ontario: Penguin, 1986. Blaise calls this "an autobiography in tales and essays" (2). Blaise's two autobiographical stories frame four fictional stories about the Porter family, told in the first person by Philip Porter.

Boyle, Kay. *The Smoking Mountain: Stories of Postwar Germany.* New York: McGraw, 1951. Eleven stories and 77-page introduction describe Boyle's perceptions of postwar Germany in 1948. The title alludes to German military organization, a "monstrous, smoking mountain" for which all—people, culture, art—becomes fuel.

Bradbury, Ray. *The Martian Chronicles.* 1950. Reprint. New York: Bantam, 1970. Independent, sequenced stories covering 30 years of travels to Mars. (See chapter 3.)

Brody, Jean. *A Coven of Women.* New York: Atheneum, 1987. Ten stories told by a narrator named Megan—one story each about eight dead women who are haunting her, followed by Megan's own story and a "final haunting and good-bye" story.

Broner, E. M. *Her Mothers.* 1975. Reprint. Bloomington: Indiana University Press, 1985. Called on the back cover a "serial montage." Communal history about a group of girls, mainly Jewish, who attend high school together and return years later for a reunion. Examines the intergenerational influences of their mothers—real and fictional—on them, and them on their own daughters.

———. *A Weave of Women.* 1978. Reprint. Bloomington: Indiana University Press, 1985. Twenty-four titled stories (some include shorter titled pieces) about a post-1960s community (15 women and their men) in the old city of Jerusalem.

Burroughs, William S. *Naked Lunch.* New York: Grove, 1959. A nonsequential collage of 22 pieces; all but the first have titles. Considered by many a savage satire on American culture. Burroughs says (in "Atrophied Preface"), "This book spills off the page in all directions" and "is divided into units which be all in one piece and should be so taken, but the pieces can be had in any order" (229).

Busch, Frederick. *Domestic Particulars: A Family Chronicle.* New York: New Directions, 1976. Thirteen linked, sequenced stories focusing on the long life of protagonist Harry Miller, but told in part by other family members whose lives encompass three generations.

———. *Rounds.* New York: Farrar, Straus & Giroux, 1979. Protagonist is a pediatrician named Eli Silver who has accidentally let his only child die. Two narrative story lines alternate, then merge.

Butler, Robert Olen. *A Good Scent from a Strange Mountain.* 1992. Reprint. New York: Penguin, 1993. Winner of the 1993 Pulitzer Prize for Fiction. Fifteen stories of Vietnamese immigrants in the Gulf Coast region of Louisiana, all told from the Vietnamese point of view.

Caldwell, Erskine. *Georgia Boy.* 1943. Reprint. New York: Duell, Sloan, and Pearce, 1950. Fourteen stories about the Stroups family and their black servant Handsome Brown. The narrator is the Stroupses' son; set in rural Georgia.

Calvino, Italo. *Cosmicomics.* Translated by William Weaver. New York: Harcourt, 1968. (1965 in Italian.) Twelve stories about the evolution of the universe, featuring a narrator-protagonist named "Qfwfq," who in each story is some element in the process (a cell, a dinosaur, a mollusk). (See chapter 4.)

———. *The Castle of Crossed Destinies.* Translated by William Weaver. New York: Harcourt, 1976. (1973 in Italian.) Two parts, "The Castle" and "The Tavern"—each a framed collection. In each, a narrator tells (and interprets) tarot players' card stories.

———. *Marcovaldo or The Seasons in the City.* Translated by William Weaver. New York: Harcourt, 1983. (1963 in Italian.) Twenty stories connected by setting (bleak industrial town in northern Italy) and a character named Marcovaldo who seeks beauty. Each story is connected to a season.

———. *Mr. Palomar.* Translated by William Weaver. London: Picador, 1986. (1983 in Italian.) Series of brief stories about Palomar's world, arranged in three sections, entitled "Palomar's Vacation," "Palomar in the City," and "The Silences of Palomar."

———. *Our Ancestors.* Translated by Archibald Colquhoun. London: Secker & Warburg, 1980. (1951 in Italian.) Three novellas, previously published individually, about a "cloven viscount" (split from crotch to cranium by a cannonball), a baron who lives in trees, and an invisible knight.

Cameron, Anne. *Daughters of Copper Woman.* Vancouver, B.C.: Press Gang, 1991. A Canadian best-seller, assumed by reviewers to be "fiction" but described by Cameron as an ethnographic record "based on interviews." Linked stories describe a woman-centered, prehistoric secret society.

Camus, Albert. *Exile and the Kingdom.* Translated by Justin O'Brien. New York: Knopf, 1958. (1957 in French.) Six stories that explore the dynamic tension between isolation ("exile") and community ("kingdom"). Includes the well-known "The Guest." (See chapter 6.)

Carter, Angela. *The Bloody Chamber and Other Stories.* 1979. Reprint. New York: Penguin, 1981. Ten adaptations of well-known fairy tales, all exploring traditional symbologies. (See chapter 6.)

Cather, Willa. *My Ántonia*. 1918. Reprint. Boston: Sentry-Houghton, 1954. Five stories about Ántonia Shimerda at different stages of her life. Linked by a first-person narrator, the Nebraska frontier setting, and the protagonist, Ántonia—the immigrant farmgirl. (See chapter 4.)

―――. *O, Pioneers!* 1913. Reprint. Boston: Houghton Mifflin, 1937. Five long stories, arranged chronologically, about Swedish immigrant pioneers in the Midwest. Numerous interconnections, including the central figure of Alexandra Bergson and the overwhelming importance of the land itself.

―――. *The Professor's House*. 1925. Reprint. New York: Vintage, 1973. Cather herself described this unique book as a "nouvelle" inserted into the body of a novel. The "nouvelle," *Tom Outland's Story*, tells of discovering cliff dwellings—whose enduring value is in stark contrast to the ugliness of the professor's houses (old and new) and the society in which he lives.

―――. *The Troll Garden*. 1905. Reprint. Variorum Edition. Edited by James Woodress. Lincoln: University of Nebraska Press, 1983. Woodress in his introduction says this "is not simply a collection of stories. . . . There is overall design and meaning and a careful arrangement of the tales to support the themes woven into the fabric of the text" (xvi).

Chavez, Denise. *The Last of the Menu Girls*. Houston: Arte Publico, 1986. Set in southern New Mexico. Seven interrelated stories, told through shifting narrative voices, describe the passage into womanhood of Rocio—who decides by the end of book to write the stories of her people, the Chicanos she knows best.

Chopin, Kate. *Bayou Folk*. 1894. Reprint. New York: Houghton-Mifflin, 1968. Collection of stories linked by the Louisiana bayou setting.

Cisneros, Sandra. *The House on Mango Street*. New York: Vintage, 1989. Forty-four vignettes about Esperanza Cordero, a young girl growing up in a run-down Chicago tenement but creating in her stories and poems "a house all my own," "a space for myself." (See chapter 4.)

Cliff, Michelle. *Claiming an Identity They Taught Me to Despise*. Watertown, Mass.: Persephone Press, 1980. Ten titled pieces that include fragments of poems, along with quotations from literary and historical works. Linked through setting (primarily Jamaica) and the voice of a narrator-protagonist who grows to "claim" her mixed-race identity.

Cofer, Judith Ortiz. *Silent Dancing: A Partial Remembrance of a Puerto Rican Childhood*. Houston: Arte Publico Press, 1990. Winner of numerous awards, including PEN citation and Pushcart Prize. Thirteen *"ensayos"* ("essays of a life") that reflect, explains the dust jacket, "the fragmentation of the protagonist [who is] seeking wholeness and connection."

Connell, Evan S., Jr. *Mr. Bridge.* New York, Knopf, 1969. Stories and
vignettes about Mr. Bridge, arranged somewhat chronologically,
with recurring characters (family, friends, minister).

————. *Mrs. Bridge.* New York: Viking, 1959. Sequentially arranged stories and vignettes about Mrs. Bridge that also reveal her narrow,
superficial world.

Conrad, Joseph. *The Mirror of the Sea.* 1906. Reprint. Marlboro, Vt.:
Marlboro Press, 1988. This lays bare, wrote Conrad, "the terms of
my relationship with the sea." Fifteen independently titled sections (stories and sketches), told in the first person by the author-
narrator.

Coover, Robert. *A Night at the Movies: Or, You Must Remember This.* New
York: Linden/Simon, 1987. One night's "program" at an old-fashioned movie palace. The projectionist sets up the entertainment
and provides the narrator-voice; there is no audience. The narrative style shows the influence of cinematic conventions and
approximates film style.

————. *Pricksongs & Descants: Fictions.* 1969. Reprint. New York: Plume-
NAL, 1970. Short pieces that explore the possibilities of fiction.
(See chapter 7.)

Cortázar, Julio. *A Certain Lucas.* Translated by Gregory Rabassa. New
York: Knopf, 1984. (1979 in Spanish.) Fifty-one titled pieces in
three groupings: the first and third about Lucas ("Lucas, His
Disconcertedness," "Lucas, His Wandering Songs") and the middle a miscellany of ideas and narrative forms. (See chapter 8.)

Coyle, Beverly. *The Kneeling Bus.* New York: Ticknor and Fields, 1990.
Eight interconnected stories about a protagonist (named Carrie)
who comes of age in the 1950s in Florida.

Day, Richard Cortez. *When in Florence: A Cycle of Stories.* Garden City,
N.Y.: Doubleday, 1986. These fifteen stories are linked, initially, by
an event-setting: the death of a priest by heart attack at midday
on a street in Florence. Reviewer Cheryl Hiers says the stories
"spiral out to include wider and wider circles of connections."

DeVeaux, Alexis. *Spirits in the Street.* New York: Anchor-Doubleday,
1973. Six titled short texts plus surrealistic drawings by the author;
set in New York City. One *Choice* reviewer called this a novel. A
Bookman reviewer listed it under the heading of "poetry" and
described it as "a melange of narrative, lyrics, and dialogue, with
an overall poetic quality and a juxtapositional progression."

Dixon, Stephen. *Time to Go.* Baltimore: Johns Hopkins University Press,
1984. Eighteen stories focusing on Will Taub, a writer. The ten stories in part 2 describe Will's courtship, marriage, and so on; the
eight stories in part 1 are stories that the fictional Will might himself have written. One reviewer described this book as "eighteen
interlocking pieces [that are] part short story collection, part
novel."

Doctorow, E. L. *Lives of the Poets: Six Stories and a Novella*. New York: Random House, 1984. The six stories of the title seem disjunctive until pulled together by the final novella, in which the imagined writer of the stories tells the story of the stories (his life) and how they came to be.

Doolittle, Hilda [H. D.] *Palimpsest.* 1926. Reprint. Carbondale: Southern Illinois University Press, 1968. Three novellas set in ancient Rome, 1920s London, and 1920s Egypt, respectively, each featuring a female protagonist, who suffers rejection, then recovers and resumes a creative life. (See chapter 6.)

Dorris, Michael. *A Yellow Raft in Blue Water.* New York: Warner, 1987. Three novellas, each focused on a different Native American woman: Rayona; her mother, Christine; and her grandmother, Ida. (See chapter 8.)

Dos Passos, John. *Manhattan Transfer.* 1925. Reprint. Boston: Houghton Mifflin, 1953. Eighteen stories (grouped in three sections) that chronicle life in New York City in the early 1920s.

DuBois, W. E. B. *The Souls of Black Folk.* 1903. Reprint. New York: NAL-Penguin, 1982. Robert Stepto describes this early work, a precursor of Jean Toomer's *Cane,* as "an eclectic narrative of fourteen major texts, raised to the level of an integrated narrative."

Duncan, Sara Jeannette. *The Pool in the Desert.* 1903. Reprint. New York: Penguin, 1984. Four stories by the prolific nineteenth-century Canadian writer are linked through setting (India) and theme—the difficulty of achieving "the full potential of one's talents and emotional needs" (x).

Dunn, Nell. *Up the Junction.* 1963. Reprint. New York: Viking-Penguin, 1988. Sixteen stories set in working-class Battersea (South London). In the introduction, Adrian Henri writes, "There is no linear narrative; each episode is semi-independent, linked by continuity of characters and places" (x).

Eiseley, Loren. *The Night Country.* New York: Scribner's, 1971. Fourteen individually titled pieces drawn, says Eiseley, "from many times and places in the wilderness of a single life" (xi). The narrator-protagonist is autobiographical (in adulthood a professor of anthropology and human paleontology), but tells stories through a "nighttime" perspective.

Ehrlich, Gretel. *Drinking Dry Clouds: Stories from Wyoming.* Santa Barbara: Capra Press, 1991. In the four stories comprising part 1 ("During the War"), a narrator introduces ten characters; in the ten stories comprising part 2 ("After the War"), the ten characters tell their own stories in the first person.

Elkin, Stanley. *The Living End.* New York: Dutton, 1979. Three linked, sequenced stories that take a satiric poke at the idea of a benevolent Creator.

Epstein, Leslie. *Goldkorn Tales.* New York: Dutton, 1985. Three novellas about Leib Goldkorn, flautist in the orchestra at the Steinway Restaurant, last outpost of *mittel* European culture on New York's lower East side.

Erdrich, Louise. *Love Medicine.* New York: Holt, Rinehart, 1984. Fourteen interlocked stories about four native American families. After the opening story, set in 1981, the others move chronologically from 1934 to 1984. (See chapter 5.)

Esquivel, Laura. *Like Water for Chocolate: A Novel in Monthly Installments, with Recipes, Romances, and Home Remedies.* New York: Doubleday, 1992. (1989 in Spanish.) Twelve stories, one for each month of the year, tell the story of Maria Elena and her three daughters in turn-of-the-century Mexico. Best-seller in Mexico in 1990. (See chapter 8.)

Evanier, David. *The One-Star Jew.* San Francisco: North Point Press, 1983. Fourteen stories, each representing an incident in the life of Bruce, the narrator-protagonist, from adolescence through middle age. Set in New York City.

Faulkner, William. *Go Down, Moses.* 1942. Reprint. New York: Vintage-Random, 1973. Epitomizes the cultural legacy of the Old South in the descendents of Lucius Quintus Carothers McCaslin. Seven stories. (See chapter 5.)

———. *The Hamlet.* 1940. Reprint. New York: Vintage-Random, 1956. Four long stories that chronicle the misadventures and rise to power of the Snopes family in Yoknapatawpha County.

———. *Knight's Gambit.* New York: Random House, 1949. Six stories featuring lawyer Gavin Stevens, who solves mysteries (one per story) in Yoknapatawpha County. Stories are sequenced to show Stevens's development; in the last, "Knight's Gambit," he marries.

———. *The Unvanquished.* New York: Random House, 1938. Seven linked, sequenced stories with the same narrator-protagonist, Bayard Sartoris. Focus is on events during the last half of the Civil War and the early days of Reconstruction.

———. *The Wild Palms.* New York: Random, 1939. Two novellas, "Wild Palms" and "Old Man," are interleaved in this one text.

Fernández, Roberta. *Intaglio: A Novel in Six Stories.* Houston: Arte Publico Press, 1990. The author describes this as "a novel made up of six portraits of six enchanting women of the Southwest who serve as role models for the maturing narrator." Winner of the 1991 Multicultural Publishers Exchange Award for Best Book of Fiction.

Fisher, Carrie. *Postcards from the Edge.* New York: Simon and Schuster, 1987. Five stories plus prologue and epilogue, described on the dust jacket as "more of a fiction montage than a novel in the conventional sense." Centers on Suzanne Vale and her survival in Hollywood, a "fantasyland of drug users and deal makers."

Fisher, M. F. K. *Sister Age.* 1983. Reprint. New York: Vintage-Random, 1984. Fifteen titled stories about "the art of aging." The author, in foreword and afterword, explains the portrait that provoked the volume, which was planned as a whole text. (See chapter 5.)

Fowles, John. *The Ebony Tower*. New York: Signet-NAL, 1974. A novella and four stories that explore the tension between courtly and carnal love.

Frank, Waldo. *City Block*. 1922. Reprint. New York: AMS Press, 1970. Fourteen titled stories set in an immigrant working-class block of New York City. Over 50 characters, a few recurring. Author's prefatory note: "The author assures the reader that *City Block* is a single organism and that its parts should be read in order."

Freeman, Mary E. Wilkins. *The People of Our Neighborhood*. Philadelphia: Curtis, 1898. Nine stories and a short preface. Set in a very small New England town, the stories are sequenced, roughly, to follow the cycle of four seasons, ending with a "Christmas Sing." First-person narrator and recurring characters. (See chapter 3.)

Fuentes, Carlos. *Constancia and Other Stories for Virgins*. Translated by Thomas Christensen. New York: Farrar Straus Giroux, 1990. (1989 in Spanish.) Five novella-length stories, intricately interwoven through motif and plot parallels even though they range worldwide in setting: from Savannah to Cadiz, to Glasgow, to Seville and Madrid.

Gaines, Ernest J. *Bloodline*. 1968. Reprint. New York: Norton, 1976. Five stories, mythical locale (Bayonne, Louisiana). Depicts the effects of racism and matriarchy upon African-Americans. Sequenced development, each story featuring an older male protagonist. (See chapter 5.)

———. *A Gathering of Old Men*. New York: Knopf, 1983. Twenty stories, most of them portraits of African-American men in a community where a murder has been committed. The first and last stories constitute a frame.

Gale, Zona. *Friendship Village*. New York: MacMillan, 1908. A village sketch composite that was a best-seller in its time. Twenty sequenced stories about the people of Friendship Village, Wisconsin, are told by the first-person narrator, a citizen of the town.

Garcia, Christina. *Dreaming in Cuban*. New York: Knopf, 1992. Seventeen sequenced, titled shorter texts, grouped into three titled sections. Set in Havana and Brooklyn, focusing on four women of the del Pino family—two in Cuba, two in New York.

Garrett, George. *Whistling in the Dark: True Stories and Other Fables*. New York: Harcourt, 1992. This prolific author's own story told through a pastiche of stories, lectures, poems, anecdotes, family histories, and reminiscences.

Gearhart, Sally Miller. *The Wanderground: Stories of the Hill Women*. Boston: Alyson, 1979. Twenty interlocked stories, sequenced chronologically, set in a fablelike feminist utopia.

Gibson, Margaret [Gilboord]. *The Butterfly Ward.* 1976. Reprint. New York: Vanguard, 1980. Reality as perceived through the lens of schizophrenia. Six stories set in Toronto, one in a mental institution, one in a neurological hospital. (See chapter 3.)

Gifford, Barry. *A Good Man to Know: A Semi-Documentary Fictional Memoir.* Livingston, Mont.: Clark City Press, 1992. An assemblage of magazine pieces, newspaper clippings, a few maps, an FBI report, and personal stories. Author's note says this is a *"shosetsu,"* a "more flexible and generous and catholic term than 'novel.'"

Goede, William. *Love in Beijing and Other Stories.* Dunvegan, Ont.: Cormorant Books, 1988. Nine stories about the difficulties of East meeting West, all set in Beijing's Youyi Binguan (Friendship Hotel), where the foreign experts are housed. Ritter, the latest arrival, wanted to tell each foreigner's story "one at a time, but they had a way of sneaking into the other stories, and so [he] let them have their way" (9).

Gold, Michael. *Jews without Money.* 1930. Reprint. New York: Avon, 1965. Stories set at the turn of the century in New York's poverty-stricken Bowery district feature a protagonist who develops into an angry young man.

Gordon, Caroline. *Aleck Maury, Sportsman.* 1934. Reprint. Carbondale: Southern Illinois University Press, 1980. The narrator-protagonist, Aleck Maury—hunter, fisherman, and teacher—holds together these eight stories about the joys of nature. Called "a novel," though the eight texts are autonomous.

Gordon, Mary. *The Rest of Life: Three Novellas.* New York: Viking, 1993. Parallel fictions, each featuring a successful middle-aged woman who, though appearing to "have it all," has been damaged by and cannot shake her dependence on men. Gordon said to a *New York Times* reviewer that the novellas are "meditations" on "the tricky navigation through daily life."

Gunesekera, Romesh. *Monkfish Moon.* New York: The New Press, 1992. Nine stories featuring characters whose lives have been shaped by Sri Lanka, once a tropical paradise but spoiled now by resurgent violence and the constant threat of civil war. Some flee to London, others to Sydney, but all remain captive to a land barren of hope.

Hemingway, Ernest. *In Our Time.* New York: Charles Scribner's Sons, 1925. Fifteen titled stories interwoven with vignettes. (See chapter 5.)

Howland, Bette. *Blue in Chicago.* New York: Harper & Row, 1978. Six stories set in Chicago and the Lake area. Focuses on one extended family's difficulties in getting along with each other.

Huddle, David. *Only the Little Bone.* Boston: Godine, 1986. Seven linked stories, told by and reflecting the growth of narrator Reed Bryant. Reviewer Meredith Sue Willis wrote that interconnections lie in "the lines of power within the family [and] the community."

Hum-Ishu-Ma [Mourning Dove]. *Coyote Stories.* Edited by Heister Dean Guie. Caldwell, Idaho: Caxton, 1933. Edited and reissued in 1976 as *Tales of the Okanogans.* Controversial in its time because Mourning Dove received editorial assistance and because the stories were based on already-existing folktales.

Hurston, Zora Neale. *Dust Tracks on a Road: An Autobiography.* 1942. 2d ed. Urbana: University of Illinois Press, 1984. Sixteen chapters/stories focusing on the protagonist, Zora. Robert Hemenway's introduction says this is "one of the most peculiar autobiographies in Afro-American literary history," in which Hurston "redramatizes her life" by "manipulating character and event" (xiii).

James, Henry. *The Finer Grain.* 1910. Edited by W. R. Martin and Warren U. Ober. Delmar, N.Y.: Scholars' Facsimiles, 1986. Five stories (none entitled "The Finer Grain"), all written *after* publication of the *New York Edition* and arranged sequentially by James. Tenuously linked through James's conception of art as moral vision.

Janowitz, Tama. *Slaves of New York.* New York: Washington Square Press, 1986. Twenty-two titled stories set among New York City's *nouveaux artistes.* Emphasis is on difficulties of "making it" in the Big Apple, how New York makes its inhabitants slaves of fashion. Reviewers describe the book's style and structure as reminiscent of MTV.

Jarrell, Randall. *Pictures from an Institution: A Comedy.* 1954. Reprint. New York: Bard-Avon, 1980. Seven stories, sequenced, set at a small progressive women's college. Described as a "lampoon" by reviewers.

Jen, Gish. *Typical American.* Boston: Houghton/Seymour Lawrence, 1991. Titled short stories divided into five titled sections but called a "novel" on the cover. Humorous, heartbreaking description of Chinese-American life.

Jewett, Sarah Orne. *The Country of the Pointed Firs.* 1896. Reprinted in *Short Fiction of Sarah Orne Jewett and Mary Wilkins Freeman.* Edited by Barbara H. Solomon, 46–151. New York: Meridian-NAL, 1979. (This edition follows Jewett's directions for her 1896 edition.) Twenty-one linked, sequenced stories in the village sketch tradition, set in Dunnet's Landing and featuring a single narrator-observer. (See chapter 3.)

Johnson, Denis, *Jesus' Son: Stories.* New York: Harper Perennial, 1993. Eleven interconnected tales narrated by a young drifter who staggers through a contemporary American landscape of addiction and pathology. Yet the reader's ultimate judgment, like the author's, is compassionate. One reviewer wrote that "the stories demand to be read like a novel structured along a kind of Cubist chronology."

Jones, Edward P. *Lost in the City: Stories.* New York: William Morrow,

1992. Winner of PEN's Ernest Hemingway Foundation Award. Explores the lives of African-American men and women in Washington, D.C. Grainy black-and-white photos by Amos Chan convey the "sense of place."

Joyce, James. *Dubliners*. 1914. Reprint. New York: Viking-Compass, 1968. Fifteen carefully sequenced stories whose progagonists gradually mature from childhood to adolescence, middle age, and public life. The aura of Dublin at the turn of the century dominates. (See chapter 3.)

Kafka, Franz. *A Hunger Artist*. Reprinted in *Franz Kafka: The Complete Stories*. Edited by Nahum N. Glatzer. New York: Schocken, 1971. (1924 in German). Four tales ("First Sorrow," "A Little Woman," "A Hunger Artist," and "Josephine the Singer"), arranged precisely in that order and published as one volume by Kafka.

Kaplan, David Michael. *Skating in the Dark*. New York: Pantheon, 1992. Twelve stories focusing on David, a developing protagonist, through 40 years of his life. Peter Cameron calls this "a novel made up of 12 stories."

Katzir, Yehudit. *Closing the Sea*. Translated by Barbara Harshav. New York: Harcourt, 1992. (1990 in Hebrew.) Four novellas that "capture an Israel never before seen in fiction." Israel's 1990 best-seller.

Keillor, Garrison. *Lake Wobegon Days*. New York: Viking-Penguin, 1985. Twelve titled stories set in Lake Wobegon, Minnesota, where the women are strong, the men are good-looking, and the children are above-average. (See chapter 3.)

Kenan, Randall. *Let the Dead Bury Their Dead and Other Stories*. New York: Harvest-Harcourt Brace, 1992. Stories and tall tales (reviewers call Kenan a "fabulist") focusing on the inhabitants of Tims Creek in eastern North Carolina. The title story, coming last in the book, is structured as an "Annotated Oral History," with epigraphs, introduction, copious footnotes, and diary extracts.

Kenney, Susan. *In Another Country*. New York: Viking, 1984. The book jacket says that "Sara is the narrator of the six interlocked stories in this novel."

Kincaid, Jamaica. *Annie John*. New York: Farrar, Straus & Giroux, 1985. Eight stories focused on the narrator-protagonist Annie John as she grows up in Antigua.

———. *At the Bottom of the River*. London: Picador-Pan Books, 1984. Ten stories featuring one narrator-protagonist, set in Antigua (childhood) and New York (later years). Stories, though not sequenced in chronological order, are linked through the growth of the narrator-protagonist.

———. *Lucy*. New York: Farrar, Straus & Giroux, 1990. Five sequenced stories told in the first person by Lucy, a teenager from the West Indies who has come to the U.S. as an au pair.

Kingston, Maxine Hong. *China Men*. New York: Knopf, 1980. Eighteen titled stories—some myth or fable, some reminiscence. Some stories are told by a first-person narrator. Characters recur, but intermittently.

———. *The Woman Warrior: Memoirs of a Childhood among Ghosts.* 1976. Reprint. New York: Vintage-Random, 1977. Five long stories about women who influence the Chinese-American narrator-protagonist as she grows up listening to "talk-stories." (See chapter 4.)

Kornblatt, Joyce Reiser. *Breaking Bread.* New York: Dutton, 1987. Five stories ("portraits") told by one narrator about people who figured prominently in the narrator's development and individuation. Early reviewers called this "a first novel" *and* "a chain of stories."

———. *White Water.* New York: Laurel-Dell, 1985. Five first-person stories, each told by a member of the Fry family. Reviewer Barbara Thompson wrote that "the form itself [a novel composed of independent short stories] is a metaphor for the author's theme: family connectedness and domestic love provide the only 'raft in white water.'"

Laurence, Margaret. *A Bird in the House.* 1970. Reprint. Toronto: Seal-McClelland and Stewart, 1978. Narrator Vanessa MacLeod tells eight stories about her children and the restrictiveness of the small Manitoba town of Manawaka, where she spent her own childhood. Margaret Laurence is one of Canada's best-loved authors.

Lee, Laurie. *Cider with Rosie.* London: Hogarth, 1959. Thirteen stories set in a remote Cotswold village in the 1910s and 1920s. All told by one narrator in the first person. From the author's prefatory note: "The book is a recollection of early boyhood, and some of the facts may be distorted by time." (Published in the United States as *The Edge of Day: A Boyhood in the West of England.*)

LeGuin, Ursula K. *Always Coming Home.* New York: Bantam, 1985. Numerous text-pieces include stories, fables, poems, essays, artwork—all focusing on the Kesh people, who, far in the future, inhabit the northern Pacific coast. Hardcover edition includes cassette tape of Kesh music and poetry. Title page gives equal credit to "composer" Todd Barton and "artist" Margaret Chodos.

———. *Searoad: Chronicles of Klatsand.* New York: HarperCollins, 1991. Nine stories bracketed by two short epilogue-prologue pieces, and a final novella. Set around Klatsand, a small Oregon town, and the sandy coastal "searoad" that runs between town and ocean.

Lem, Stanislaw. *A Perfect Vacuum.* Translated by Michael Kandel. 1971. Reprint. New York: Harcourt, 1979. Sixteen reviews of fictitious books, including a review of *A Perfect Vacuum.* In the books he invents, Lem spoofs literary trends and silliness that masquerades as intelligence.

Levi, Primo. *The Monkey's Wrench.* Translated by William Weaver. New York: Summit, 1986. (1978 in Italian.) Fourteen titled stories described on the dust jacket as "a novel about the art of storytelling." A first-person narrator (who resembles Levi) and a construction worked named Faussone (an "Italian Zorba") trade stories of their adventures.

London, Jack. *Tales of the Fish Patrol*. 1905. Reprint. Oakland: Star Rover House, 1982. Seven linked stories involving the sixteen-year-old narrator and two other deputies of the California Fish Commission. Set primarily in the San Francisco Bay area.

McCarthy, Mary. *The Company She Keeps*. New York: Harvest-Harcourt, 1942. Six stories about a bohemian intellectual in her twenties. McCarthy, who considered this book "a novel," was attacked for being too autobiographical, too "journalistic," especially in one sex-on-a-train episode.

———. *Memories of a Catholic Girlhood*. New York: Harcourt Brace, 1957. Eight stories, autobiographical but fictionalized. Italicized interchapters comment upon the "fictionalizing" done in the stories. Includes a long foreword entitled "To the Reader."

Major, Clarence. *Emergency Exit*. New York: Fiction Collective, 1979. The life of the Ingram family is told through an assemblage that includes stories, schedules, catalogs, charts, poems, episodes, paintings, and lists.

Malamud, Bernard. *Pictures of Fidelman: An Exhibition*. New York: Farrar, Straus & Giroux, 1969. Six stories, chronologically sequenced, focusing on Arthur Fidelman's development as an artist.

———. *Rembrandt's Hat*. New York: Farrar, Straus & Giroux, 1973. Eight stories, described by Robert Phillips as "not a collection of various short pieces, but a tightly-woven tapestry." The book's thematic focus is epitomized by the well-known first story, "The Silver Crown."

Manea, Norman. *October, Eight O'Clock*. Translated by Cornelia Golna et al. New York: Grove Weidenfeld, 1992. Set in eastern Europe before and after World War II. Fifteen titled stories, described by reviewer John Bayley as "a narrative loosely divided into separate tales, but seen through the eyes of a single literary persona." Autobiographical, but fictionalized.

Marshall, Paule. *Brown Girl, Brownstones*. 1959. Reprint. New York: The Feminist Press, 1981. Set in Brooklyn. Focused on Selina Boyce and her Barbadian immigrant family, the book captures, said one reviewer, "cadences of the King's and 'Bajun' English."

Maupin, Armistead, *Tales of the City*. New York: Harper, 1978. Stories focusing on the tenants of an apartment house on San Francisco's Russian Hill. The *Literary Review*, while calling the book a "novel," says nevertheless that "nothing is lost by reading [the stories] individually." Adapted for television as an "American Playhouse" production on PBS.

Menaker, Daniel. *The Old Left*. New York: Knopf, 1987. Eight sequenced stories focus on the relationship between a professor and his uncle (a member of New York's "Old Left"). Reviewer Daniel Stern says these stories have "the connections . . . of a novel."

Mehta, Gita. *A River Sutra.* New York: Nan A. Talese-Doubleday, 1993. Stories told to a retired bureaucrat who lives beside a sacred river in India force him to confront the complexity of life. Sixteen chapters, many titled, are interspersed and interwoven with the bureaucrat's story. Literally, "sutra" is "a thread or string; also a term for literary forms, usually aphoristic in nature" (290).

Metcalf, Paul. *Genoa: A Telling of Wonders.* Highlands, N.C.: Jonathan Williams, 1965. Part history (the travels of Christopher Columbus), part biography (Metcalf is Herman Melville's great-grandson and draws on family documents for a biographical section on Melville), part contemporary fiction. Described on the dust jacket as an "accumulation, juxtaposition, 'montage.'"

Michener, James A. *Tales of the South Pacific.* New York: Macmillan, 1947. Narrator, a young naval officer stationed in the South Pacific in the early days of World War II, tells stories by and about islanders and Americans he meets. (See chapter 3.)

Miller, Henry. *Black Spring.* 1936. Reprint. New York: Black Cat-Grove, 1964. Ten independently titled short texts, linked by setting (New York and Paris) and by the voice of the narrator-protagonist. (See chapter 3.)

Miller, Walter M., Jr. *A Canticle for Leibowitz.* New York: Lippincott, 1959. Apocalyptic science fiction. Three novellas, all set in the Abbey of the Albertian Order of Leibowitz, are "Fiat Lux" (600 years after a nuclear holocaust), "Fiat Homo" (600 years later), and "Fiat Voluntas Tua" (600 years after the second section). (See chapter 6.)

Millu, Liana. *Smoke over Birkenau.* Translated by Lynne Sharon Schwartz. Philadelphia: Jewish Publication Society, 1991. (1947 in Italian.) Six stories derived from the author's incarceration at Birkenau during World War II. Set in the women's camp at Auschwitz-Birkenau, where the crematoria are in the center (hence the book's title). A first-person narrator named Liana tells all the stories.

Minot, Susan. *Monkeys.* New York: Dutton-NAL, 1986. Sequenced stories about the Vincent family's seven children ("monkeys") as they grow up. Set in a small town outside of Boston, the book is called a "novel" on the front cover. One reviewer said the book is "composed of nine chapters or sections, seven of which [were] previously published as short stories."

Mohr, Nicholasa. *Rituals of Survival: A Woman's Portfolio.* Houston: Arte Publico, 1985. Five stories and a novella about unrelated indomitable women who survive the poverty, sexism, and violence of a New York Puerto Rican neighborhood.

Momaday, N. Scott. *The Way to Rainy Mountain.* Albuquerque: University of New Mexico Press, 1969. A carefully structured composite text based on the Kiowa tribe's migration and its retracing by the author/narrator, N. Scott Momaday. (See chapter 7.)

Moorhouse, Frank. *The Americans, Baby: A Discontinuous Narrative of Stories and Fragments.* 1972. Reprint. Sydney, Australia: Arkon-Angus & Robertson, 1978. Set in Sydney. A sequel to *Futility and Other Animals,* this book continues the story of Moorhouse's "urban tribe." Contains 20 titled texts, including "Letters to Twiggy" (itself composed of seven letters, one containing a story).

———. *Futility and Other Animals.* 1969. Reprint. London: Angus & Robertson, 1988. Set in Sydney, Australia. The author says these are "interlocked stories" about a "modern, urban tribe." Twenty-four stories are arranged in three sections, entitled "Confusion," "Sickness," and "Bravery."

Mukherjee, Bharati. *The Middleman and Other Stories.* Markham, Ont.: Penguin, 1988. Winner of the 1988 National Book Critics Award. Despite "and Other Stories" in its title, reviewers in India call this a "novel." Focuses on third-world immigrants to America by alternating perspectives between the newcomers and those who react to them.

Munro, Alice. *The Beggar Maid: Stories of Flo and Rose.* New York: Knopf, 1979. Published in Canada as *Who Do You Think You Are?* Ten linked stories trace the development of Rose (childhood in small Ontario town, marriage and divorce, success as a teacher and actress), who is oberved by Flo, her stepmother.

———. *Lives of Girls and Women.* 1971. Reprint. New York: Plume, 1983. Seven linked stories and an epilogue told by and about Del Jordan as she grows from childhood (in a small Ontario town) to adulthood and a career as a successful artist.

Mutis, Alvaro. *Maqroll: Three Novellas.* Translated by Edith Grossman. New York: Harper, 1992. Published simultaneously in Spanish and English. A charismatic hero called Maqroll the Gaviero ("the Lookout") cavorts through three novellas in search of meaning and purpose. Though each novella is a gem in itself, says Oscar Hijuelos, "the cumulative effect is of an epic novel."

Nabokov, Vladimir. *Pale Fire.* New York: Perigree-Putnam's, 1962. A self-parodic, autobiographical assemblage (a 999-line poem by "John Shade" with a foreword, commentary, and index by "Dr. Charles Kinbote"). Described by Frederick Karl as a "fiercely unified work" and by Mary McCarthy as a "centaur-work" that is "half poem, half prose."

———. *Pnin.* 1957. Reprint. New York: Vintage-Random, 1989. Seven untitled stories, four of which were published separately. A first-person narrator tells the life story of Timofey Pnin, a Russian exile who teaches in an American college.

Naylor, Gloria. *Bailey's Cafe.* New York: Harcourt, 1992. Linked stories (blues narrations) told in the first person by patrons of Bailey's Cafe. Many stories are revisionist: Eve, fleeing from an abusive godfather; Esther, sold to a sadistic pseudo-husband; Jesse Bell, seeking relief through drugs; and two Marys, one promiscuous, one virginal.

——. *The Women of Brewster Place: A Novel in Seven Stories.* 1982. Reprint. New York: Penguin, 1983. Seven stories plus a prologue and epilogue, all set in a decaying neighborhood called Brewster Place. Winner of the 1983 American Book Award. (See chapter 3.)

Niggli, Josefina. *Mexican Village.* Chapel Hill: 1945. Reprint. Albuquerqe: University of New Mexico Press, 1994. Set in the town of Hidalgo in northern Mexico. Ten stories, each preceded by a "title page" with pen-and-ink drawings.

Nixon, Cornelia. *Now You See It.* Boston: Little, Brown, 1991. Seven stories that chronicle a modern family as seen through the eyes of five different characters. Nixon is currently working on another "novel in stories."

O'Brien, Tim. *The Things They Carried.* New York: Houghton Mifflin, 1990. Widely heralded stories of the Vietnam conflict. Dust jacket blurbs strain to *call* the book something: "Neither a novel nor a short-story collection" but "an arc of fictional episodes"; "Each story resonates with its predecessors, yet stands alone"; "clearly a novel"; "a kind of 'faction' presented as a collection of related stories that have the cumulative effect of a unified novel."

Oates, Joyce Carol. *Crossing the Border: Fifteen Tales.* New York: Vanguard, 1976. In these stories, characters cross lines that they don't recognize at the time. Seven stories focus on the same couple, providing a narrative thread whose episodes parallel and take on resonance from episodes in unrelated stories. All are set in Canada, near the U.S. border.

——. *Heat and Other Stories.* New York: Dutton, 1991. Grouped into three sections, this compendium of 25 stories explores not only the omnipresence of violence in everyday life, but also the ways in which violence becomes tolerable, even welcome.

O'Connor, Flannery. *Everything That Rises Must Converge.* New York: Farrar, 1965. Nine stories that explore the parent-child relationship—its potential for conflict and violence, and, ultimately, self-knowledge.

Okunlola, Dayo. *Without Extremeties.* 1991. Reprint. Leeds, England: Peepal Tree, 1992. A prologue that is a beast fable precedes seventeen *gist* ("stories" or "tales") told by Babatunde and his friends in Mama T's peppersoup joint in Nigeria.

Otto, Whitney. *How to Make an American Quilt.* New York: Random, 1991. Seven stories, a prologue, and seven sets of quilt-making instructions—all linked through an eight-member quilting circle in the California town of Grasse. The narrator's voice, the interaction among characters, and the adumbrating quilting metaphor are connective elements. (See chapter 8.)

Palmen, Connie. *The Laws*. Translated by Richard Huijing. New York: George Braziller, 1993. (1990 in Dutch.) Seven stories told by Marie Deniet, a philosophy student, about the seven men through whose knowledge she seeks self-identity ("The Astrologer," "The Epileptic," "The Philosopher," "The Priest," "The Physicist," "The Artist," "The Psychiatrist"). A best-seller in Holland, now in its nineteenth printing.

Parra, Teresa de la. *Mama Blanca's Memoirs*. Translated by Harriet de Onis. Revised by Frederick H. Fornoff. Critical Edition. Pittsburgh: University of Pittsburgh Press, 1993. (1929 in Spanish.) Autobiographical sketches couched in a fictional frame. Doris Sommer describes the book's "shape" as "fanlike," with a "central fulcrum" (xxvi). Jose Balza calls it a "frieze" (151).

Phillips, Jayne Anne. *Machine Dreams*. New York: Dutton, 1984. Seventeen titled sections that chronicle the dissolution of the Hampsons, a West Virginia family. The sections cover the family's history from the 1930s to the 1970s.

Porter, Joe Ashby. *The Kentucky Stories*. Baltimore: Johns Hopkins University Press, 1983. Eight stories told by narrators so similar that they demonstrate, in Porter's words, that "Kentucky is a state of mind."

Prokosch, Frederic. *The Seven Who Fled*. New York: Harper & Brothers, 1937. Seven stories plus a prologue and epilogue. The prologue frame explains that seven Europeans, fleeing from political turmoil, join a caravan where each traveler's story is told.

Rachlin, Nahid. *Veils*. San Francisco: City Lights, 1992. Nahid Rachlin, who now lives and writes in New York, provides keen insight into the lives of present-day Iranians who face clashing cultures whether they immigrate to the United States or remain in Iran. "Teheran's ancient Ghanat Abad Avenue," says a reviewer, "loosely links the stories into a single narrative: some residents leave as soon as they can, others can live nowhere else."

Reed, Ishmael. *Mumbo Jumbo*. Garden City, N.Y.: Doubleday, 1992. Characteristically provocative in its criticism of the establishment and the status quo, Reed's book is a verbal-cum-visual collage text that includes (in addition to two title pages, an epilogue, and a "partial bibliography"), drawings, photos, posters, graphs, dictionary definitions, and anagrams.

Rivera, Tomas. *. . . and the Earth Did Not Part*. Translated by Herminio Rios. Berkeley: Quinto Sol, 1971. (A 1985 translation by Rolando Hinojosa-Smith was published as *This Migrant Earth*.) Fourteen short texts—the first and last constituting a frame, thirteen of them preceded (on separate pages) by an italicized anecdote— focus on the lives of Texas-based migrant farmworkers. A nameless central character (symbolizing the worker) appears in many stories.

Roy, Gabrielle. *The Road Past Altamont.* Translated by Joyce Marshall. Lincoln: University of Nebraska Press, 1993. (1966 in French.) In four connected stories set in the vastness of Manitoba, a French-Canadian girl named Christine moves from childhood innocence to maturity. Gabrielle Roy is known as Canada's Willa Cather.

Saint-Exupéry, Antoine de. *Wind, Sand and Stars.* Translated by Lewis Galantiere. New York: Harcourt, 1939. Nine individually titled pieces about flying and flying machines, plus a "Conclusion." Awarded the Grand Prix du Roman for "Best Novel of 1939" and the American Booksellers award as "best non-fiction book of 1939." Andre Gide suggested, and St. Exupéry decided to write, a "sheaf, a bouquet; a grouping together, irrespective of time and place, of the sensations, emotions, and reflections of the airman."

Salzman, Mark. *Iron and Silk.* 1986. Reprint. New York: Vintage-Random, 1990. An episodic series of adventures experienced by the author, a recent graduate of Yale who taught English and studied martial arts in China from 1982 to 1984. (See chapter 4.)

Sanders, Scott R. *Wilderness Plots: Tales about the Settlement of the American Land.* New York: William Morrow, 1983. Fifty titled pieces. All are set in the Ohio Valley in the period 1780–1850, but the setting could be any place where survival is a struggle. The author says that the stories "are provoked by germs of fact, rather than history" (7).

Saroyan, William. *My Name is Aram.* New York: Harcourt, 1940. Fourteen stories and a prefatory author's "note" explaining auto-biographical connections.

Shalamov, Varlam. *Kolyma Tales.* Translated by John Glad. New York: Norton, 1980. Stories and sketches based on Shalamov's 17 years in work camps in the Kolyma region of Siberia, described by John Glad as "a vivid account of individual moments in the lives of individual men, for only in the particular can we begin to comprehend the horror of the whole" (8).

Shange, Ntozake. *Sassafrass, Cypress & Indigo.* New York: St. Martin's, 1982. A literary gumbo of recipes, letters, poems, stories, and drama—focused on three sisters and their mother in Charleston, South Carolina. (See chapter 6.)

Silko, Leslie Marmon. *Storyteller.* 1981. Reprint. New York: Arcade-Little Brown, n.d. Silko's auto/biographical historical fictional retelling of the story of the Laguna Pueblo Hopi, herself among them. (See chapter 7.)

Simak, Clifford D. *City.* New York: Ace, 1952. Eight linked, sequenced tales with frame-pieces ("preface" and "notes"). Chronicles 10,000 years of evolution of sentient species (humans and future-humans, dogs, robots, ants).

Solzhenitsyn, Alexander. *The Cancer Ward*. Translated by Nicholas Bethell and David Burg. 1968. Reprint. New York: Bantam, 1969. Set in the cancer ward of a Russian hospital, these stories of 13 patients are linked by their situation (illness) and by the central question: "What do men live by?"

Sonenberg, Maya. *Cartographies*. Pittsburgh: University of Pittsburgh Press, 1989. Eight stories focusing on people who "have traced lines and lived inside them" (3). The book's essential unifying element has been described as a sense of place—but one achieved through metaphors of mapmaking. Winner of the Drue Heinz Literature Prize.

Sorrentino, Gilbert. *Under the Shadow*. Elmwood Park, Ill.: Dalkey Archive Press, 1991. Described on its dust jacket as a "novel" that "takes the form of fifty-nine brief sketches" and "exquisite vignettes."

Steadman, Mark. *McAfee County: A Chronicle*. New York: Holt, 1971. Twelve sequenced stories about poor folks living in a fictional county near Savannah, Georgia. Covers about 50 years.

Stein, Gertrude. *Tender Buttons: Objects, Food, Rooms—Studies in Description*. 1914. Reprint. New York: Haskell House, 1970. Divided into three sections: "Objects" includes 58 titled pieces; "Food" includes 51 titled pieces; and "Rooms" is a single undivided text. (See chapter 8.)

———. *Three Lives*. 1909. Reprint. New York: Vintage-Random, 1936. Three titled sections ("The Good Anna," "Melanctha," "The Gentle Lena"), each telling the story of one woman. All set in a town vaguely like Baltimore. Stein experiments with narrative style differently in each piece. (See chapter 6.)

Steinbeck, John. *The Pastures of Heaven*. 1932. Reprint. New York: Penguin, 1982. Series of numbered, untitled stories with a prologue and epilogue. Although there are recurring characters, particularly the Munro family, the most obvious unifying device is the setting—a development called *Las Pasturas del Cielo* in central California.

———. *The Red Pony*. New York: Viking, 1945. Four chronologically arranged stories centering on Jody Tiflin, who lives with his family on a ranch in California. Jody grows, developing gradually, as he learns to handle difficult tasks.

———. *Tortilla Flat*. 1935. Reprint. New York: Penguin, 1986. Seventeen stories plus a preface, set in a shabby district in the hills above Monterey, California. The gang of scruffy inhabitants of Tortilla Flat are portrayed to resemble King Arthur's knights.

Stuart, Jesse. *Save Every Lamb*. New York: McGraw, 1964. Twenty-five stories set in "W-Hollow, Greenup County, Kentucky," arranged roughly by chronology in three sections (based on Stuart's youth, teenage years, and adulthood). The author's "introduction" says, "Since readers will not believe the truth, I have had to mix some fiction with my animal, turtle, snake, and bee stories" (4).

Styron, William. *A Tidewater Morning: Three Tales From Youth.* New York: Random House, 1993. Styron says in an introductory note that these three long stories, in the order in which they appear in the book, "reflect the experiences of the author at the ages of 20, 10, and 13." As described by reviewer Richard Bausch, however, the protagonist-speaker, Paul Whitehurst, tells stories so linked that "the effect of all three tales together becomes more important than anything we might derive from each of the stories alone."

Sui Sin Far [Edith Eaton]. *Mrs. Spring Fragrance.* Chicago: A. C. McClure & Co., 1912. Set in Seattle and San Francisco, these stories and sketches describe "from the inside" the joys and struggles of Chinese-Americans. Grouped into two parts, entitled "Mrs. Spring Fragrance" and "Tales of Chinese Children."

Tan, Amy. *The Joy Luck Club.* New York: Putnam's, 1989. In 1949 four Chinese-American women living in San Francisco formed a club to play mah-jongg, eat dim sum, and talk about China. The sixteen stories focus on all four women and their daughters, in effect eight protagonists who provide a sweeping view of Chinese-American life. (See chapter 5.)

Taylor, Peter. *The Widows of Thornton.* New York: Harcourt, 1954. Eight stories and a drama dealing with characters who are from or live in Thornton, Tennessee.

Tekin, Latife. *Berji Kristin: Tales of the Garbage Hills.* Translated by Ruth Christie and Saliha Paker. New York: Marion Boyars, 1993. (1984 in Turkish.) Tekin's magical-realist stories chronicle life in the shack-cities (*"gecekondus"*) built on garbage dumps that house more than one-half of Turkey's modern urban population.

Thomas, Dorothy. *Ma Jeeter's Girls.* 1931. Reprint. Lincoln: Bison/University of Nebraska Press, 1986. Six stories about Ma Jeeter's six daughters: told by the narrator, a schoolteacher who boards with Ma Jeeter, to whom Ma has told the stories.

Thomas, Dylan. *Portrait of the Artist as a Young Dog.* 1940. Reprint. New York: New Directions, 1968. Set in Wales, 10 autobiographical stories (Thomas is the "young dog") tell about Thomas growing up and becoming a man.

Toomer, Jean. *Cane.* New York: Boni & Liveright, 1923. Twenty-nine titled short texts that include 10 stories, 18 poems, and a short play. (See chapter 8.)

Updike, John. *Bech: A Book.* 1970. Reprint. New York: Vintage-Random, 1980. Seven episodes in the life of Jewish writer Henry Bech as he travels about Europe and the United States trying to forget his sexual anxieties and writer's block.

———. *Bech Is Back.* 1982. Reprint. New York: Fawcett-Ballantine, 1983. Seven more stories about the Jewish writer featured in *Bech: A Book.*

———. *Olinger Stories: A Selection.* New York: Vintage, 1964. Eleven sequenced stories, set in the fictional town of Olinger, follow the developing protagonist from childhood through adulthood. (Updike did the "selecting.")

———. *Too Far to Go: The Maples Stories.* New York: Fawcett Crest, 1979. Seventeen stories about the marriage, separation, and divorce of Richard and Joan Maples, a typical 1960s suburban couple.

Walker, Kath [Oodgeroo Noonuccal]. *Stradbroke Dreamtime.* 1972. Reprint. London: Angus & Robertson, 1982. Twenty-seven stories—13 reminiscent of Walker's aboriginal childhood days on Stradbroke Island, near Queensland; and 14 based on traditional aboriginal folklore. One of the latter, "Oodgeroo," about an aboriginal who finds her way "back to the old Dreamtime" (56), parallels Walker's reclaiming of her aboriginal name in the mid-1980s.

Welty, Eudora. *The Golden Apples.* New York: Harcourt, 1947. Magical tales of the small-town folk who live in and around Morgana, Mississippi. (See chapter 6.)

Wescott, Glenway. *The Grandmothers: A Family Portrait.* New York: Harper & Brothers, 1927. Stories about a pioneer Wisconsin family as seen through one member's third-generation eyes.

West, Jessamyn. *The Friendly Persuasion.* 1945. Reprint. New York: Penguin, 1981. Fourteen titled stories, covering a 50-year period in the life of Indiana's Birdwells, a family of Quakers, in the mid-nineteenth century. West's sequel volume is *Except for Me and Thee: A Companion to "The Friendly Persuasion"* (New York: Harcourt, 1967).

Wilder, Thornton. *The Bridge of San Luis Rey.* New York: Brandt & Brandt, 1927. Reprint. Pocket Books–Simon & Schuster, 1972. Five stories, the first and last framing the middle three. Brother Juniper, who sees a bridge collapse with five people on it, investigates their lives. His book comprises the middle three stories, while an omniscient narrator tells the "frame" stories. (See chapter 3.)

Wilson, Edmund. *Memoirs of Hecate County.* Garden City, N.Y.: Doubleday, 1946. Six stories set in Manhattan are told by the narrator-protagonist (an intellectual). Critic David Castronovo calls this both a "novel" and a "series of very loosely connected short stories." The title refers to the witchy quality of women characters and to "demons of commercialism and capitalist decadence."

Wright, Richard. *Uncle Tom's Children.* 1938, 1940. Reprint. New York: Perennial–Harper & Row, 1965. Five stories and an autobiographical essay entitled "The Ethics of Living Jim Crow" (the 1938 version lacked both the essay and the fifth story). All stories are set in the rural South, and they feature protagonists who, though battered by racism, refuse to be passive victims.

Yezierska, Anzia. *Children of Loneliness: Stories of Immigrant Life in America.* New York: Funk & Wagnalls, 1923. Stories and essays, many aubiographical, depict and meditate on the immigrant experience, especially that of Jewish women.

———. *Hungry Hearts.* 1920. Reprint. New York: Arno, 1975. Stories of Russian and Polish Jews in the tenement boroughs of New York and New Jersey at the turn of the century and through the 1920s. After Samuel Goldwyn bought the screen rights, Yezierska moved to Hollywood, where she was known as "Queen of the Ghetto" and "The Immigrant Cinderella."

Yoshimoto, Banana. *Kitchen.* Translated by Megan Backus. New York: Grove, 1993. (1988 in Japanese.) Two coming-of-age novellas ("Kitchen" and "Moonlight Shadow"), whose narrator-protagonists embrace life and love after coming to terms with death and loneliness. A best-seller in Japan, now in its fifty-seventh printing.

Index

Belloc, Hilaire, 18–19
Bendixen, Alfred, 2
Berji Kristin: Tales of the Garbage Hills (Latife Tekin), 12, 180
Berthoff, Werner, 154
Bird in the House, A (Margaret Lawrence), 172
Black Spring (Henry Miller), 33–34, 36, 174
Blinde, Patricia Lin, 56
Bloodline (Ernest J. Gaines), 63, 168
Bloody Chamber, The (Angela Carter), 80, 163
Blue in Chicago (Bette Howland), 169
Border culture, 109–10
Borderlands/La Frontera: The New Mestiza (Gloria Anzaldua), 6, 105, 108–11, 160
Breaking Bread (Joyce Reiser Kornblatt), 172
Bridge of San Luis Rey, The (Thornton Wilder), 32–33, 181
Brooks, Cleanth, 69
Broude, Norma, 105
Brown Girl, Brownstones (Paula Marshall), 173
Burke, William, 63
Butterfly Ward, The (Margaret Gibson), 33, 35, 36, 169

Calvino, Italo, 18, 86. *See also The Castle of Crossed Destinies; Cosmicomics; Marcovaldo; Mr. Palomar; Our Ancestors*
Campbell, Joseph, 82
Cancer Ward, The (Alexander Solzhenitsyn), 179
Cane (Jean Toomer), 7, 25, 101, 102, 115, 166, 180
Canterbury Tales, The (Geoffrey Chaucer), 21
Canticle for Leibowitz, A (Walter M. Miller, Jr.), 3, 81, 86, 174
Carabi, Angeles, 56
Carabine, Keith, 152
Carlin, Deborah, 103
Carson, Barbara Harrell, 82
Cartographies (Maya Sonenberg), 179

Cary, Richard, 153
Castle of Crossed Destinies, The (Italo Calvino), 103, 163
Cather, Willa, 28, 102. *See also Death Comes for the Archbishop; My Antonia; O, Pioneers; The Professor's House; Obscure Destinies; Shadows on the Rock*
Celibacy of Felix Greenspan, The (Lionel Abrahams), 159
Cetain Lucas, A (Julio Cortázar), 8, 105, 107–8, 114–15, 165
Cervantes, Miguel de, 95
Chatman, Seymour, 95
Children of Loneliness (Anzia Yezierska), 182
Chimera (John Barth), 8, 161
China Men (Maxine Hong Kingston), 171–72
Christian, Barbara, 45
Christie, Agatha, 17
Cider with Rosie (Laurie Lee), 51, 172
City (Clifford D. Simak), 178–79
City Block (Waldo Frank), 14, 168
Claiming an Identity They Taught Me to Despise (Michelle Cliff), 164
Closing the Sea (Yehudit Katzir), 171
Collages (Anaïs Nin), 9
Collective protagonist, 15, 42, 59–73, 109, 110; archetypal, 63–66, 73; family/tribe as, 66–73
Company She Keeps, The (Mary McCarthy), 6, 173
Composite novel, 1–19, 120; authorial intention in, 11, 12; autonomy in, 8–10, 11; as collaborative work, 2, 17; French forms, 155 (*see also Letters from My Mill, Three Tales*); as genre, 1; interconnective elements in, 15–16; labels for, 4, 145–58; predecessors, 20–29; sequencing in, 13–14. *See also* Short story cycles
Conan Doyle, Sir Arthur, 16–17
Constancia and Other Stories for Virgins (Carlos Fuentes), 13, 168
Coover, Robert, 17–18, 95–96, 165

About the Authors

Maggie Dunn is the department coordinator for English and Humanities at the Brevard Campus of Rollins College in Melbourne, Florida. Her articles on a variety of writers including William Faulkner, Erza Pound, H.D., and Zora Neale Hurston have appeared in such periodicals as *American Literature* and *Frontiers: A Journal of Women Studies*. Dunn received her Ph.D. from Indiana University.

Ann Morris holds the William R. Kenan Chair in Humanities at Stetson University in DeLand, Florida. She is the author of a number of articles, her most recent work focusing on women writers, Caribbean writers, and the connections between quilting and writing. Morris, who coordinates the Women and Gender Studies Program at Stetson, was named "Florida's Handicapped Professional Woman of the Year" in 1988. Her Ph.D. is from Florida State University.